The Fourth Self

Bible & Theology in Africa

Knut Holter
General Editor

Vol. 14

PETER LANG
New York · Washington, D.C./Baltimore · Bern
Frankfurt am Main · Berlin · Brussels · Vienna · Oxford

RICHARD E. TRULL, JR.

THE FOURTH SELF

Theological Education to Facilitate Self-Theologizing for Local Church Leaders in Kenya

PETER LANG
New York · Washington, D.C./Baltimore · Bern
Frankfurt am Main · Berlin · Brussels · Vienna · Oxford

Library of Congress Cataloging-in-Publication Data

Trull, Richard E., Jr.
The fourth self: theological education to facilitate self-theologizing
for local church leaders in Kenya / Richard E. Trull, Jr.
p. cm. — (Bible and theology in Africa; v. 14)
Includes bibliographical references and index.
1. Christian leadership—Kenya. 2. Christian education—Kenya.
3. Theology—Study and teaching—Kenya. 4. Missions—Kenya.
I. Title. II. Series: Bible and theology in Africa; v. 14.
BV652.1.T78   253.096762—dc23   2013011882
ISBN 978-1-4331-1607-0 (hardcover)
ISBN 978-1-4539-1138-9 (e-book)
ISSN 1525-9846

Bibliographic information published by **Die Deutsche Nationalbibliothek**.
Die Deutsche Nationalbibliothek lists this publication in the "Deutsche
Nationalbibliografie"; detailed bibliographic data is available
on the Internet at http://dnb.d-nb.de/.

The paper in this book meets the guidelines for permanence and durability
of the Committee on Production Guidelines for Book Longevity
of the Council of Library Resources.

© 2013 Peter Lang Publishing, Inc., New York
29 Broadway, 18th floor, New York, NY 10006
www.peterlang.com

All rights reserved.
Reprint or reproduction, even partially, in all forms such as microfilm,
xerography, microfiche, microcard, and offset strictly prohibited.

Printed in Germany

Table of Contents

	Preface	vii
	List of Tables	ix
	Introduction	1
Chapter 1	Journey from Replication to Contextualization	9
Chapter 2	Contextualization and African Theology toward the Fourth Self	23
Chapter 3	Theological Education and the Search for the Fourth Self	41
Chapter 4	Search for Contextual Leadership Training: One Mission's Experience	59
Chapter 5	Evaluation of the Theological Education Process	75
Chapter 6	Struggles in the Search for the Fourth Self	111
Chapter 7	Discovering the Fourth Self: Implications for Theological Education	157

Chapter 8	"Solidarity Partnership": the Next Step in the Search for the Fourth Self?	175
	Notes	183
	Bibliography	189
	Index of Authors	205
	Index of Subjects	209

Preface

It is with sincere gratitude that I acknowledge the contributions of my fellow pilgrims in Christ in Kenya, and specifically in Meru, who have assisted my understanding of how to better communicate the gospel cross-culturally. They continue to provide me with many wonderful insights and have broadened my understanding of God's diverse world of people created in His image. To my Meru brothers and sisters in the Lord, I am thankful that we are continuing on this journey together and searching with one heart to better represent *Mwathani wetu kiri antu bonthe*.

I could not have done this research without the generous and kind assistance of a number of Kenyan leaders who arranged interviews at the various locations. Particular thanks to Dennis Okoth, previously at Nairobi Great Commission School (NGCS) and now at Livingstone International University, Mbale, Uganda whose help not only assisted me in arranging interviews but also was a source of encouragement to pursue this research in hopes of developing a greater vision for improving the theological education process. Each of the training centers' directors were very hospitable and generous with their time in arranging interviews with their graduates. I thank Daniel Chengo, Festus Kaunyangi, Michael Mutai, Moses Mwinga and David Tonui, now Principal of Nairobi Great Commission School.

I greatly appreciate the wonderful assistance of Laura Nicholas who transcribed the many hours of interviews. Having been raised in Kenya and with her ability for detailed work, she provided me with clear and accurate transcripts where the English was often times difficult to hear and follow.

I am grateful for Faulkner University's encouragement and sabbatical time to complete the research and then revise it from its dissertation form to a more readable book. My sincere thanks to Dr. Heidi Burns, Executive Editor of Peter Lang Publishing, Inc. for her encouragement to publish this work and her patience during its preparation from dissertation to what I hope is a more readable book. I appreciate the invitation to be a contributor to the "Bible and Theology in Africa" series.

Special thanks is given to the late Dr. Paul Hiebert who shared his life and home with me and my family. He encouraged this area of research, although he never saw the end results of his guidance and mentoring. He is still greatly missed. Thanks are also given to Dr. Tite Tiénou who was the head of my dissertation committee. I appreciate his encouragement and input which enhanced the value of this work.

Finally and above all, to Marinda, my wonderful wife without whom my life's journey would never have been complete or occurred in such an amazing way. Thank you for your love, patience, and encouragement not only through this process but in our lives together. I dedicate what follows to you for we embarked on our mission together, and I look forward to completing it together.

Montgomery, Alabama, January 2013

Richard E. Trull, Jr.

Tables

Table
1. Average age and ministry years by area   80
2. Age brackets of interviewees   81
3. Type of ministries and number of interviewees' involved in specific ministries   81
4. People influential on interviewees' pursuit of theological education   82
5. Reasons for pursuing further theological education   83
6. Specific areas of ministry that Christian schooling strengthened   88
7. Evaluation of theological effectiveness   92
8. Theological education's contributions to contextualizing the gospel   115
9. Most frequently identified ministry problems   122

The father and son are one thing.

African Proverb

Introduction

In the late nineteen eighties the author and his co-worker were teaching courses on biblical exegesis and interpretation to church leaders in various village churches in Kenya, East Africa using a modified Theological Education by Extension format (TEE). They started with a course on how to do biblical interpretation and then used Philemon, Colossians and Hebrews as books on which to practice the process. They wondered how well they were getting the concepts across until they got to the Book of Hebrews. They were discussing the writer and his purpose in writing the book. The writer's co-worker posed the question, "Who wrote Hebrews?" The immediate answer was "it does not say." The follow-up question was "who do you think wrote it?" The group discussed it awhile and unanimously pronounced Paul as the likely writer. Before the writer's co-worker could proceed the leaders asked him who he thought wrote Hebrews. He put forward Apollos as a possible writer. Further discussion ensued about this possibility with the leaders proclaiming, "No; it is more likely to be Paul." They considered it a small victory for those leaders as they traveled with the church leaders in the search for the "fourth self," self-theologizing.

Over twenty-five years have passed since that day, and the significant shift in the geocentric center of Christianity to the Majority World with numerous implications for all areas of mission service continues to be evident. The task of educating and training church leaders is certainly a major area that must be evaluated carefully in light of this shift. At the heart of this shift, theological education from its Western roots continues to need adaptation and implementation in light of the new multicultural situation. Because of the rapid growth of Christianity in sub-Saharan Africa and the continued dominance of Western curriculum and theology, it raises critical issues related to theological education. The teaching of the gospel has not been imparted to the hearts of African Christians as if they were a "*tabula rasa*" but, as Kwame Bediako notes,

> Well before the dismantling of the European empires, in the so-called African independent churches, and also in the mission churches, through access to the Scriptures in African mother-tongues, African Christians were discarding such Western value-setting for the faith as there may have been, and were developing indigenous responses to the Christian Gospel, claiming validity for them from the Scriptures. (1995, 206-207)

Theological education must continually take into account the ongoing impact of the gospel message on theological education as it interacts with the cultural contexts of those committed to its value for spiritual and physical living before God. The rise of African theologies is an unavoidable outcome of committed believers' application of scripture to their life contexts. There is no longer a ministry monopoly of ordained people but instead a greater number of non-ordained ministers who seek biblical training (Bosch 1991, 467). A part of the "re-education" calls for an ongoing reexamination of the theological education process. James Owino Kombo rightly raises the question when he asks,

> Do the African evangelical theological institutions prepare their students with such creativity and critical thinking skills as fluency, problem-solving and problem-finding and evaluation desperately needed in the process of engaging with other disciplines in the construction of the new Africa? (2000, 13)

Tite Tiénou continues this line of reasoning by raising a key question. Granting the demographic shift of Christianity to Africa, Asia and Latin America, "Does this also mean that the future of Christian theology and scholarship is being decided on these continents as well?" (2006, 44) Kwame Bediako has a positive outlook about the impact of African Christian scholarship on the world stage (1995, 253). However, despite the growth and impact of

Christianity in Africa, Tennent's observation on theology in the Majority World seems correct as applied to Africa. He observes that despite the geocentric shift of Christianity "the center of theological education and Christian scholarship remains in the Western world" (2007, 11).

Tiénou reinforces this by noting he does not share Bediako's "optimism" that Christian scholarship will not be marginalized because "it is clear that Christian scholarship and theology are not yet endeavors in which scholars and theologians from Africa, Asia, Latin America, and the Pacific Islands participate fully" (2006, 44-45). Tiénou suggests three "challenges" that must be addressed to overcome Western Christianity's dominance to give rise to "globalizing theology"[1] which takes into account the diverse perspectives that manifest themselves in non-Western theological reflection. First, there is the "West's 'hegemony postulate'" using Per Frostin's terminology. In other words, the Western theology sets the ground rules for dialogue. Second, the West's self-perception that it is "the center of scholarship" while viewing others as on the margins allowing their scholarship to be dismissed "without real or adequate basis." Third, the West must be willing to listen to other theological perceptions overcoming the "dialogue of the deaf." "The dialogue of the deaf between the West and the rest is not limited to matters pertaining to theology. It is real especially in scientific matters, and it prevents Westerners from listening to people from the third world" (2006, 47-49).

Theological education in Africa must address these issues by not allowing Western hegemony tendencies to block intercultural and inter-theological reflection and dialogue. Contextualized theological education for local church leaders is a primary concern for educators. Knut Holter observes that there is a need for theological discussion to go "both ways." "Africa is a major exponent of this development, as sub-Saharan Africa throughout the 20th century has more or less become a Christian continent. This has important consequences for the global distribution of institutionalized theological and biblical studies." He goes on to note the growth of institutions of theological education in sub-Saharan Africa compared to the decline of Western institutions (2000, 2).

The growth of non-institutionalized and institutionalized theological education has been an intercultural endeavor by Western missionaries, whether intentionally or not, moving toward a greater partnership as Western support continues to be highly involved at various levels of the theological education process. Despite the Western roots and dominance in doing and teaching theology, the southern shift of Christianity means greater African participation in evaluating the contextualizing process in the midst of Western influence, whether positive or negative. This intercultural pilgrimage has been in the making for many decades, and it has been a journey for both the Western participants who were both learners and teachers and for Africans as both learners and teachers. This interaction will certainly continue as most of the institutions of theological education in Africa are still highly supported and influenced by Western theological education.

Paul Hiebert perceives a "new mission paradigm emerging" that has not fully taken shape and envisions a place for missionaries as "mediators" in the global theologizing process. He identifies six areas where missionaries could contribute to the global theologizing process through their roles as mediators: (1) between "gospel and human cultures", (2) "between Christianity and non-Christian religions", (3) "in the global church-to-church relationships", (4) "in the academy between theology and humans studies", (5) "between missions as a movement and missiology as an academic discipline," and (6) to affirm "all Christians and Christian communities" right to their own "theological reflection" (2006, 295-296). Encouraging their right to do their own "theological reflection" will highly influence the other five mediator roles as the intercultural conversation and partnership continues.

Lionel Young calls for further exploration and evaluation of the policy of building institutions and ministries by Western missionaries and agencies that are expensive to maintain and then gradually phasing out funding "in order to promote autonomy." He notes that African leaders perceive this "as either shortsighted or cruel" (2012, 93). Young's observations of church leaders' perceptions at NEGST (Nairobi Evangelical Graduate School of Theology) agree with the findings in this volume that theological education is perceived as valuable and beneficial in a number of the educational dimensions but structurally shortsighted and missiologically weak. He notes three perceptions of the leaders. First, there was a failure "to train nationals" adequately, this being an "expression of colonial rule." Yet, "with equal fervor, they expressed a strong desire for some type of missionary presence, making it clear that Africa needed 'a new breed of missionary.'" Second, he notes the church leaders "insisted on the need for continued ecclesiastical partnerships with the church in the West whenever possible."

> Third, African evangelical leaders and students at NEGST considered evangelistic activity in the African church to be one of their greatest strengths, while readily admitting that

one of their greatest weaknesses was the inability of the African church to address the myriad of complex social problems such as poverty, HIV, corruption, illiteracy and unemployment. (2012, 92)

Given the influence of the Western theological heritage, it is important that the value of the theological education be evaluated from the perception of the participants in the educational process. The question is whether our theological education efforts are providing the tools for self-theologizing where trained church leaders feel free to explore their theological perceptions from their own cultural contexts. This volume attempts to listen to the voices of those participating in a theological process and who are engaging their cultural contexts with the gospel, searching for what Paul Hiebert calls the "fourth self" (1985, 193-224). The fourth self not only indicating the right to do one's own theology or theological reflections but also allowing for equal partnership in globalizing theology as more Christian communities participate in the process and apply it to their cultural contexts. Steve Strauss defines "global theologizing" as "the sharing of local theologies from around the world" that were developed through people's own interaction with scripture and expressed in their "local idiom" that "enhances the theology of the worldwide church" (2006, 152).

The research that gave rise to this book is set within the dynamic discussion of the challenges of leadership training in East Africa with its Western roots and the continued use of the English-speaking Western theological education in many parts of sub-Saharan Africa. This research is relevant because of the continuing discussion of "globalizing theology" or, to use Hiebert's terminology, the "fourth self." It is hoped that the observations that follow will contribute in a small way to exploring the levels and types of theological education particularly utilized by evangelical fellowships. Second, it will surface strengths and weaknesses in the theological educational process as it strives to improve self-theologizing in the education institutions and local church ministries. Third, it will also surface possible directions for Kenyan ministers and teachers partnering with the American mission stakeholders in improving leadership training to move toward practicing the fourth self. Fourth, because of the shared theological education heritage Churches of Christ have with other evangelical groups, the findings in this research may be applicable to other evangelical theological education endeavors.

The central question this research is attempting to answer is what factors in the theological education process and ministry experiences contributed significantly to the ministers' understanding and abilities in applying biblical principles and developing their theological understanding of scripture as it applies to their cultural and ministry contexts. Related to this question are several sub-questions. First, what has been the type and effectiveness of the theological education utilized in training local ministers among the Churches of Christ in Kenya? Second, how do the church ministers evaluate the level of contextualization and applicability of the theological education towards improving their effectiveness in their ministries in modern Kenya? Third, what areas of theological education need to be added or modified for improving ministerial training in order to move toward a fuller articulation of self-theologizing in the modern Kenya context?

African theology identifies key elements which interact to contextualize the message in searching for the fourth self: biblical context, African traditional contexts, current socio-cultural African contexts, the church and the western Christian intellectual and cultural heritage. Taking into consideration the above elements for the purpose of analysis in this research, six dimensions will be proposed by which to evaluate the level to which the theological education process is perceived by ministers to be providing the tools for facilitating self-theologizing. The six dimensions are cognitive, affective, evaluative, missiological, structural, and ministerial. This book explores the search for the fourth self not only for recipients of the mission efforts but also for the missionaries who have their own cultural baggage to overcome.

Bediako points to this "new phase of Christianity" where Christianity in the southern continents experience life "through other cultural, historical, linguistic, social, economic and political categories than those that are dominant in the West." This among other things will provide "living data with which to pursue Christian theological scholarship afresh" (2008, 108-109). Searching for the fourth self requires those of us working in cross-cultural situations to remember that our Western heritage of Christianity does not make us the sole arbiter of orthodox theology. Cross-cultural ministry and theological education call for a shared journey for everyone who embarks on it. Listening, observing and participating in the search for the fourth self calls for those of us on this journey to keep Jesus' charge in mind that the gospel was to go into *panta ta ethne*, all people groups. The gospel has always taken its followers on a journey of doing theology in a myriad of peoples and cultures.

The reflections in this volume come from almost thirty-years of interaction in mission endeavors, primarily in Kenya among Kenya Churches of Christ, starting with an evangelism and church planting emphasis to maturing young churches and then into various means of leadership training. Much of what this writer has learned on his own pilgrimage in searching for the fourth self he owes to his Kenyan brothers and sisters with whom he has shared this journey, though at times he is sure he did not see clearly where it would lead him nor how much his own understanding of theological reflection would be influenced. It is his hope that this book will assist the reader in sharing this journey.

Chapter 1 gives a historical overview of missions' progression from what Wilbert Shenk dubs the "replication model" and Lamin Sanneh refers to as the "structural model" to the concept of contextualization. Chapter 2 discusses the development of the concept of contextualization, along with various models, and notes the contributions of African theology. Chapter 3 gives a brief overview of the development of thought related to the use of theological education in Western missions as an influential component in the missions process. Chapter 4 summarizes the evangelical leadership training and theological education processes that were influential in the missions practices of missionaries among Kenya Churches of Christ. In Chapter 5 we will listen to the voices Kenyan evangelists and pastors who have participated in the formal theological studies process in an attempt to evaluate the theological education process currently in practice among Kenya Churches of Christ. Chapter 6 reviews their evaluation of the level of contextualization and applicability of the theological education towards improving their effectiveness within the cultural context of their ministries. Chapter 7 will draw a number of implications raised by this research through delineating six dimensions in measuring the level of self-theologizing to identify strengths and weaknesses in finding the fourth self. The concluding chapter will proffer a number of recommendations for consideration to improve the intercultural and contextual nature of discussing and doing theology in search of the fourth self.

> We may characterize the new interrelationship between missionaries and Africans as reciprocity. Missionaries paid huge "vernacular" compliments to Africans, enabling many peoples to acquire pride and dignity about themselves in the modern world . . . Africans returned the compliment by coupling a faith forged in the Scriptures.
>
> *Lamin Sanneh 1989*

CHAPTER 1
Journey from Replication to Contextualization

A number of mediating forces have come together to challenge the hegemony of Western theology as the sole arbitrator of orthodox theology, not the least being African theology. First, the mission-planted churches matured and produced capable theologians of their own to enter the Christian theological dialogue. Second, the rise of nationalism and the removal of colonial rule allowed for more independent thinking and reduction of Western hegemony. Third, "the rise of anthropological thought and the growing awareness among missionaries of the impact of cultural contexts on Bible translations and theology" introduced a broader understanding of scriptural interpretation and called into question the Western interpretation and its contextual presuppositions (Hiebert 1994, 46-47). Fourth, Sanneh points out that the very act of putting scripture into the vernacular of the people to whom Christians were ministering gave power to them (1989, 172).

Another force in calling into account the idea that Western theology is the final coherent statement of biblical theology is the biblical text's own witness to the theological shifts that took place with the movement of Christianity from the Jews to the Gentiles. Although the term "contextualization" would not come into use until 1972, the concept that the gospel must be relevant to the sociocultural context of the recipients has been present since the beginning of Christian missions (Hesselgrave 2000, 149; Nicholls 1979, 51-52; Sanchez 1998, 318-19). The power of the gospel itself brings people into dialogue with scripture in relationship to their context. Lamin Sanneh and Kwame Bediako are representative of African scholars who have drawn attention to early Christianity's contextualization of the gospel message (Bediako 1999, 10-12; Sanneh 1989, 7-49). Andrew Walls' historical contributions also bring attention to the early church's precedent of contextualizing the gospel (1996, 8; 2002, 75-79).

How the gospel is understood to relate to culture continued to be a struggle throughout church history as the gospel moved into and took up residence in new cultures. Sanneh contends that "the Gentile breakthrough became the paradigm for the church's missionary expansion" (1989, 46). During the first few centuries of Christianity the gospel showed itself to be culturally translatable which gave rise to new theological perspectives or theologies. However, with the advent of Christendom its contextual nature became less pliable.[1]

The Replication and Indigenization Models

Wilbert Shenk proposes three models by which to understand Protestant mission experience. He calls the first model the "replication model", the second is the "indigenization model", and the third is the "contextualization model" (1999, 50-56). As Protestant missionaries began their missionary activities their methodology was best described as the "replication model" or the "structural model" in Lamin Sanneh's words (Sanneh 1999, 66). Shenk describes the "replication model" as one that "seeks to replicate or reproduce a church in another culture patterned carefully after that of the church from which the missionary originated." The missionary retains control and responsibility for the church (1999, 51). The missionary also becomes the final authority for theological reflection, application, and defining theological and cultural constructs.

A biblical equivalent would be if the Jerusalem council in Acts 15 had decided in favor of the Jewish Christians who were lobbying for the Gentiles to submit to Jewish customs and cultural norms. The importation of "Christendom" in which Christianity and its "Christian culture" are inextricably bound is representative of the replication model. Shenk notes two premises on which the "replication model" is based. "First, it is assumed that there is such a thing as a Christian culture.... Second, since Christendom represents the 'original,' the mission task is to reproduce or replicate this original. To propagate the gospel is to invite people into the definitive culture." This meant that the two "Cs" had to be taught; civilization as a prerequisite to the second, Christianity (Shenk 1999, 52, 62).

Through this methodology Christianity failed to take significant root in Africa between 1470 and 1785. "Thus the experiment of Christianity as a sociopolitical investiture failed, and whatever achievements remained of those pioneer centuries would be absorbed and reconstituted in the new phase" (Sanneh 1999, 66-67). The indigenization concept would move mission away from a completely replication or structural model.

Indigenization Model

Rufus Anderson is considered the founder of the "indigenous church principle" (Beaver 1967, 31). At the core of the indigenous model is Anderson's concept of the "three-selfs" which is also associated with Henry Venn and later with John Nevius. Anderson points to the work of the apostle Paul as an example for supporting the "three-selfs" principles. He states, "When he had formed local churches, he did not hesitate to ordain presbyters over them, the best he could find; and then to throw upon the churches, thus officered, the responsibility of self-government, self-support, and self-propagation" (1869, 109-10). The indigenous model coincided with the rise of modernity and a greater emphasis on education. There was still a real sense of paternalism involved despite the push for more independent churches. As R. Pierce Beaver notes, "This opening for paternalism is provided by giving the missionary responsibility to decide when a church is to be organized, to determine how it shall be organized and associated with other churches, and to exercise pastoral rule if a native minister is not available" (1967, 34).

In reacting to the "Old System" where "native churches" depend on foreign funds to support and stimulate growth, John Nevius, building on Rufus Anderson's principles, places emphasis on "applying principles of independence and self-reliance" from the inception of the new churches (1958, 8). However, the reduction of dependence on the mission funds did not reflect an equal independence from the control of the missionary. "The leader constantly superintends, directs, and examines those under him; the helper directs and examines the leaders and their stations; and the missionary in charge has a general supervision and control of the whole" (Nevius 1958, 32-33).

The early indigenous principles were later incorporated into the "indigenous church" idea associated with the efforts of Sidney J. W. Clark. Clark published a pamphlet entitled "The Country Church and Indigenous Christianity," later published and given worldwide circulation through the World Dominion Press under the title of "The Indigenous Church." By 1924 a movement was founded under the name of "World Dominion" to propagate the "indigenous church" theory. Two primary principles were added to the "three-selfs," First, "the foreign missionary should devote himself to pioneer evangelism" and not take on "pastoral duties for a congregation." Second, "nothing should be instituted on the mission field by the mission which could not be taken over, maintained, and conducted by the native church" (Clark 1928, 26; Ritchie 1946, 13-18).

While recognizing the "amazing progress" in the mission field in his time, Roland Allen provides a critique of the accomplishments made even with the indigenous ideas. He argues, "Everywhere Christianity is still exotic...not yet succeeded in so planting it in any heathen land that it has become indigenous." Second, "Everywhere our missions are dependent." The churches continue to look to the missions for their leaders, instructors, and rulers. Third, "Everywhere we see the same type. Our missions are in different countries amongst people of the most diverse characteristics, but all bear a most astonishing resemblance one to another." He points to two underlying factors for this situation: racial and religious pride directed at the "poor heathen" that approaches them with a sense of superiority and a fear and distrust of giving the natives independence (1962, 141-43). William A. Smalley also critiques the indigenous church concept with the "three-selfs" as "really projections of our American value system into the idealization of the church" (1958, 51-65).

Shenk rightly summarizes the "indigenous model" in missions when he notes, "The indigenization approach was viewed by its advocates as correcting and superseding the concept of the replication model at certain points, but it was not a radical departure from it. Control of the process remained largely in the hands of the outside agency: the missionary and the missionary society" (1999, 54). He further states that "the goal of indigenization was to find the symbols and forms in the host culture by which the Christendom view of religious life might be expressed" (1999, 55). Ruy O. Costa argues, "Indigenization meant the translation into 'native' cultures of a *Missio Dei* previously adopted by the missionary" (1988, xii). However, the growing Christian population in the southern hemisphere along with the advances in social science research, particularly in anthropology, created a greater awareness of the cultural context and its impact on the communication of the gospel (Hesselgrave 1980, 208).

Contextualization

Shenk's third model for understanding Protestant missionary experience is contextualization. It is in this stage that we find ourselves within a dynamic interactive environment of contextualization, African theology and globalizing theology. The continued practice of contextualizing the gospel challenges the American missionaries' Western theological history and Western enlightenment context to be cognizant of their own contextual roots and the existence of theologies rooted in non-Western cultures. The theologies coming out of an African context reveal that Western theologies have their own contextual moorings.

> What became clear from these [non-Western] contextual theologies was that the universal theologies that had been presented to them were in fact *universalizing* theologies; that is to say, they extended the results of their reflections beyond their own context to other settings, usually without an awareness of the rootedness of their theologies within their own context. (Schreiter 1997, 2)

The Uppsala General Assembly of the World Council of Churches particularly addressed topics related to the concept of contextualization in two documents: "World Economic and Social Development" and "Toward Justice and Peace in International Affairs." At the 1971 Bossey consultation A. O. Dyson's paper entitled "Dogmatic or Contextual Theology" directed the discussion toward contextualization. In his presentation he pointed to the influence that the scientific revolution had on dogmatic theology by the "unseating" of authorities of theology through giving "a strong impulse to a sense of human autonomy, of self-management and self-existence, in which man is an important actor rather than a passive recipient of divine laws and actions" (Sanchez 1998, 322-23). In 1972 the term "contextualization" came into mission vocabulary and has had a profound influence on missional thinking and theological education. The influence of contextualization on these two areas will be discussed more fully in chapters two and three.

The mission efforts of Churches of Christ in sub-Saharan Africa reflect their own journey from following the indigenization model to wrestling with the implications of contextualizing the gospel. These mission efforts began with an emphasis on indigenous principles. A brief overview of the emphasis on theological education by Churches of Christ in sub-Saharan Africa illustrates the movement from indigenous church ideas to wrestling with contextualization of the gospel.

Historical Overview of Churches of Christ Emphasis on Theological Education in Sub-Saharan Africa

As in other evangelical fellowships there has been a strong tradition of education and evangelistic practices. The U.S. mission teams who instituted extension centers, as well as Nairobi Great Commission School (NGCS), shared a common heritage in the Churches of Christ and were trained in Christian colleges associated with that religious fellowship. As early as 1818 Alexander Campbell was running the Buffalo Seminary in his home.[2] Churches of Christ had at their inception an interest not only in theological education but theological education that included "physical, intellectual, and moral faculties" (Campbell 1838, 256). Alexander Campbell was formative in stressing the need for education which he defined as "the full development of man to himself, in his whole physical, intellectual and moral constitution, with a proper reference to his whole destiny in the universe of God" (1850, 123). He perceived humanity as physical, spiritual, and intellectual beings which meant that education was needed in all three areas. "The idea was to give a general education, and along with it teach the Bible, for it was just as necessary to a complete education as any other phases of study" (West 1964, 269-270). In part public schools and colleges were seen as excluding the use of the Bible as a "text-book" or as a "moral science" and thus Christian educational institutions were needed and preferred for both the "material nature" and the "Inspired Volume" (Campbell 1850, 125).

Schools and colleges were not perceived to have an "organic" relationship with churches, but they had an adjunct role in Churches of Christ by helping the Christian homes to carry out their responsibility of training their children (Young 1949, 33). The emphasis on education and supplementing Christian education in the home and church was carried over into the strategy of the mission works implemented in various parts of the world, including Africa.

Churches of Christ and Christian Education in Africa

Churches of Christ followed the same mission approach as most denominations of the time period. One of the first missionaries to produce a sustained work in Africa was John Sheriff, a New Zealander, who arrived in South Africa in 1896. He promptly started a night school for adults to "learn English and salvation." Most mission efforts emanating from South Africa included schools of various types which taught secular subjects as well as the Bible. Usually the schools came in conjunction with evangelistic efforts (Reese and Walker 2001, 64-73).

Churches of Christ's Educational Influence in Nigeria

In Nigeria Churches of Christ arose as a purely indigenous movement with no Western missionaries on the ground when churches were first planted. Local Churches of Christ arose through the influence of a ministry through the mail that originally targeted men and women in the military service in Europe during and after World War II. However, the correspondences offering Bible courses by mail were forwarded to Nigeria by a German woman,

Anna-Maria Braun. Churches of Christ arose through the work of a Nigerian, C. A. O. Essien. Essien reported a large number of churches had been planted and put forward a request to his Western brethren. In 1950 skeptical Western missionaries from South Africa went to investigate the claims of Essien which indicated a large number of Nigerians were becoming Christians and churches planted. Their report notes,

> Several thousand native Africans have, without the presence of a white man, fought their way out of denominationalism and have found the church of God. This is without precedent in Africa. . . . In Nigeria, the initiative was taken by the people themselves when they requested the Bible Correspondence Course from Lawrence Avenue. Their fervor is evidenced by the fact that in three and a half short years they have established more congregations than we have in the whole of South Africa after thirty years of labor by white evangelists. (Goff 1964, 10)

C. A. O. Essien's request was for education and training of leaders and members of the churches. In response to his request, the primary work in Nigeria for the first American missionaries who arrived in 1952 and 1953 was to establish and manage schools, both Bible training schools and village schools. By 1954 the Ukpom Bible College was started. Graduates from this school started three-month Bible training programs in villages as a "feeder system" for the fuller program at Ukpom.

In response to the growing educational needs the Nigeria Christian Schools Foundation was incorporated in 1959 to oversee the various educational endeavors. It was later changed to African Christian Schools Foundation (ACSF), and its scope was broadened to include medical and benevolent assistance. The outbreak of the Biafra civil war created numerous problems as many congregations of Churches of Christ were in the Biafran area. After the war ACSF no longer participated in village schools but centered its work on higher education with Ukpom Bible College, which became Nigerian Christian Bible College in 1983. In 2000, Nigerians and members of ACSF partnered in establishing the West Nigeria Christian College, upholding ACSF's mission statement "to provide, through African partnership, centers of educational excellence to equip nationals for Christian service, leadership and evangelism in Africa" (Huffard 2001, 215-226).

Kenya and Churches of Christ's Educational Emphasis

In contrast to Nigeria, Churches of Christ in Kenya had their beginnings through the work of American missionaries who began working in 1965 shortly after Kenya obtained its national freedom. The earliest missionaries located in the capital of Nairobi, established the church's registration, and planted several churches. The early seventies saw the beginning of mission teams locating in the rural areas and establishing church planting ministries. These mission teams, for the most part, held to the Church Growth philosophy. Emphasis was placed on evangelism and church maturation to establish "a church for Kenyans, governed, propagated, and supported by Kenyans" (Van Rheenen 1980, 8).

Emphasis was placed on non-formal theological education as a more "contextual" method of teaching Bible as opposed to the formal institutional means. This was seen by American missionaries of the Churches of Christ who began mission endeavors in the 1970s and early 80s among various people groups of Kenya as supporting the indigenous church ideal and the "three-selfs" strategy. Informal and non-formal theological education was used as an extension of evangelism and church maturation and perceived as a more contextual approach to theological education within the local areas of the people groups being evangelized, thus allowing Christian leaders to practice their theology within their cultural contexts. This method also avoided the problems earlier missiological research had noted concerning "westernizing" church leaders through the Western theological educational institutions.

Leadership training was considered important, but most of the American mission teams shied away from the institutional forms of theological education. Two models of cross-cultural leadership training were used as these mission teams pursued their mission efforts, "localized courses" and Leadership Training by Extension or LTE, a modified form of TEE (Van Rheenen 1983b, 33-34; Stephens 1980, 37).[3] Both of these models were utilized by the rural mission teams and were thought to contribute to establishing indigenous churches based on the "three-selfs" principles.[4] Although the "fourth self" as proffered by Paul Hiebert had not yet entered the vocabulary of the Kenya mission teams, the concept was certainly taking shape in the thinking of some missionaries.

The Meru mission team particularly followed the Leadership Training by Extension method in providing a more structured but not "institutionalized" method of theological education and in the process developed a curriculum that emphasized biblical interpretation within the cultural context (Granberg, Pritchett, and Trull 1987, 97-98).[5] Other mission teams were influenced by the LTE movement gaining momentum at that time.

The first LTE courses in Meru were designed to teach leaders methods of biblical interpretation through the study of biblical texts and finding practical application within their village contexts (Granberg *et al.* 1990, 83-84). Providing interpretive skills in the early courses was meant to allow the leaders to better understand and use the biblical text rather than merely "proof-texting" or mimicking lessons heard.

Development of NGCS and the Extension System

By 1990 various American Churches of Christ mission teams in Kenya were moving toward a new model of theological education which allowed for the non-formal and informal theological training while also providing a more formal theological education within the country, thus still providing a more contextual Kenyan base. The "formal" theological training took the form of extension centers and a central residential school, Nairobi Great Commission School (NGCS). These would offer more "advanced" theological training and would gradually add vocational training to a limited degree.

The Meru mission team first proposed the extension center idea in conjunction with discussions of the creation of what became known as the Nairobi Great Commission School (NGCS). The Meru mission team noted the need for more advanced training for the church leaders. The Kenyan church leaders themselves voiced their need to have higher education and desired a more formal mode of theological education which was already modeled by Kenya's Western-modeled school system and other religious groups' educational institutions. The use of a local extension center with a curriculum that would prepare leaders for further education at NGCS while still providing local training within the Meru people's cultural context seemed to "serve to bridge the learning gap" that existed between the regular LTE training courses and the biblical training that NGCS was beginning to provide (Granberg *et al.* 1990, 92). Although the proposal of such a training center was seen by some Western missionaries as departing from the "indigenous" model, the Meru team pointed out that the more formal model was certainly perceived and accepted by Kenyan Christians as a cultural norm for their current socio-cultural situation. The extension center model was also seen as a means to facilitate the contextualization of the biblical training by keeping church leaders within or close to their home contexts to encourage self-theologizing.

The new model being utilized in leadership training among Kenya Churches of Christ consists of not only informal and non-formal learning opportunities but also provides extension centers within local mission areas with a central institution, Nairobi Great Commission School (NGCS), in the capitol city of Nairobi. The first functioning extension centers were the Kambakia Training Center among the Meru, now known as the Meru School of Theology (1993) and the Uzima Training Center among the Mwejikenda peoples (1994). The Meru mission team developed its curriculum, of which this writer was the primary author, to coincide with the curriculum which had recently been developed at NGCS to reflect the belief that in the future the extension centers would be associated either formally or informally with the central institution. The new, more formal model was officially accepted at a meeting of Kenyan church leaders and American missionaries in Nairobi in October of 1993 (NGCS 2003, 6). Most areas of Kenya that have had Churches of Christ mission teams currently have an extension center. Contiguous areas may have one center that serves more than one mission team's area of work. Twelve extension centers were operating in 2005 in Kenya, with three in Uganda and one in Tanzania (NGCS 2003, 23-25).[6] Most of these are now overseen by a Kenyan Principal or Coordinator in the extension center's home area. The extension centers now have an overall Director who assists local principals in coordinating the extension programs with NGCS.

Mission teams involved in establishing a number of these extension centers have primarily phased out their work as Kenyan leadership has matured. Only one or two American missionaries are actively involved on an intermittent basis. The disengagement of the American missionary teams was planned from the beginning and impacted the use of the extension centers among the Kalenjin, Meru, Mwejikenja, and in Nairobi.[7] Before the disengagement of a number of mission teams, most LTE and extension centers were operated by missionaries who also were the primary teachers. However, in the first half of the decade of the 1990s Kenyan leaders were beginning to work in partnership with American missionaries and became the primary teachers at extension centers and to a lesser degree at NGCS.

As mission teams phased out of their works, the means for continuing the training of church leaders became highly tied to providing theological education and to a lesser degree vocational training through the extension centers. Although Leadership Training by Extension and informal training continues among Churches of Christ in Kenya, regional extension centers are seen as significant forces for providing a local means of theological education as well as vocational training. Of the twelve extension centers in Kenya, eleven have Kenyan directors while one lists co-directors consisting of a Kenyan and an American missionary.

Today the "Extension School Training Programs" are seen as programs that "coordinate the training of local leadership for the purpose of unifying and standardizing a solid spiritual foundation through a sound biblical and ministry-oriented curriculum." The extension centers provide a means of education at a lower cost, greater opportunities for local leaders, flexibility in educational possibilities, and allow busy church leaders to budget their time for educational seminars and courses (NGCS 2003, 6-7). Hundreds of students have matriculated through this educational system, and many continue to receive training at the extension centers and NGCS.

Providing cross-cultural leadership training in the African context is of primary concern for Christian educators as Christianity grows and becomes more deeply rooted in Africa. Contextualized theological education for local church leaders is an ongoing concern for educators. The question for Churches of Christ in Kenya and evangelicals in general is whether the current theological education efforts are providing the tools for self-theologizing where trained church leaders feel free to explore new theological perceptions and constructively apply them to their own cultural contexts. In other words, are we allowing for the fourth self?

Current Emphasis of Theological Education for Kenya Churches of Christ

In Kenya, Church of Christ theological education is the intentional teaching and equipping of people intellectually and practically to assist them in their spiritual development and Christian service, often for leadership roles in various contexts. The aim of "theological education is to develop leaders to build and strengthen the church. Leaders are developed as they interact . . .

with the Word of God . . . and the needs of the church . . . in such a way that God is glorified" (Plueddemann n.d., 12). Theological education also is not free from the cultural and ministry contexts of the instructors and students. The contexts impact the type and nature of the theological education process.

The theological education process among Churches of Christ in Kenya is striving to provide a contextually sensitive approach to "cross-cultural Christian leadership training." This provides a broader definition of the theological education process. Expanding on the definitions for "training" and "education" proffered by Edgar Elliston, the following definition is proposed for "cross-cultural leadership training." It is the process by which church leaders develop in conjunction with the work of the Holy Spirit through education, relational activities, ministry experience, and community involvement within the worldview, culture, and conceptual contexts of the learner to facilitate spiritual formation, to exercise spiritual gifts and to enhance the cognitive, affective and ministry skills for a specific socio-cultural context for the progress of the church and its purpose in the world, thus moving the student toward a self-theologizing direction dependent on God. "Relational activities" is intended to convey the idea that leaders develop in the context of their relationship with God, other leaders from various cultures, and people who impact their lives (Elliston 1988, 206).

Effective cross-cultural leadership training through theological education aims at assisting those ministers in the educational process toward discovering and practicing the fourth self. Cross-cultural education should progress beyond the contextualized message with its "etic" roots in Western theology if the process takes seriously the worldview, culture and conceptual contexts of the learners. As spiritual maturity in God's revelation progresses, the message becomes self-contextualized, giving rise to self-theologizing or the fourth self. Self-theologizing is the working out of theology within the linguistic and cultural contexts of the local church guided by the gospel message with application to life situations as equals in the theological dialogue of the church universal. Self-theologizing brings to the forefront a number of realizations in theological reflection. First, there is the fuller realization that it is God at work in them, the receiving group, and guiding them. Second is the realization that the local church must bring scripture to bear on its life situations. Third, the original heralds of the gospel message are not the message or the authorities of the authorized interpretation but fellow pilgrims in God's kingdom. Fourth, there is a need for a fuller exploration of the scripture by the church leaders and members in relation to the culture in which the church exists and works. Fifth, God uses scripture and the unique challenges of cultures and personal experiences to increase people's theological reflections.

A driving force in Christian mission in the search for the fourth self is the concept of contextualization. This concept, particularly for evangelicals, brings to the foreground the need to understand the influence of their own cultural contexts and the context of those to whom they are communicating the gospel. In the following chapter we will consider the influence of this concept and the contributions of African theologies.

> Like the African proverb which says that "the eyes of the frog do not stop the giraffe from drinking water in the pond", neither the critical, skeptical nor advice-filled admonitions of others should prevent the creative theologian from engaging in theological output.
>
> *Mbiti 1986*

CHAPTER 2
Contextualization and African Theology toward the Fourth Self

The theological discussions associated with the concept of contextualization provide the historical missiological background for the contemporary direction of Western missionaries and missiological thinking in search of the fourth self. This direction of missiological reflection did not arise in a vacuum but was influenced by various strands of theological reflection. First, missionaries moved from the indigenous concept to the more robust contextualization model in which Western missionaries had to wrestle with their own church traditions and cultural heritage while seeking a greater understanding of the gospel in the mission context. Second, African theologies provide indicators for the direction and level of self-theologizing. Third, the literature related to the use of theological education and the search for contextualized theological education through such efforts as the Theological Education Fund (TEF) and Theological Education by Extension (TEE) were influential.

With the expansion of Christianity in sub-Saharan Africa, the concept of contexualization and the influence of primarily Western theological education have interacted in providing direction in the development of indigenous church leaders, African theologies and self-theologizing. The development of ministerial training through theological education with its Western roots is striving for contextualization among African cultures in their contemporary societies. Theological education with its Western heritage continues to be a primary means of developing ministers for the growing number of churches in the changing modern environment experienced in Africa. This chapter will explore the impact of contextualization and African theologies in moving toward greater self-theologizing.

Contextualization

Present day African theology is, as Bediako contends, "the unfolding of Christian history as a whole" within present life situations (2001, 30). Theological education through its emphasis on contextualization and African theology with its focus on bringing the gospel to bear within the African context should, ideally, be a positive influence in directing ministers toward the fourth self, self-theologizing, as opposed to holding theological hegemony over them. Ministers need to have the ability and freedom to "translate the biblical message into the cognitive, affective, and evaluative dimensions of another culture" (Hiebert 1994, 97, 89). Self-thologizing is not so much a matter of "system building," to use Schreiter's words, but application of the gospel to the needs and context of the people (1985, 22).

Lamin Sanneh contends, "We may characterize the new interrelationship between missionaries and Africans as reciprocity. Missionaries paid huge "vernacular" compliments to Africans, enabling many peoples to acquire pride and dignity about themselves in the modern world, and thus opening up the whole social system to equal access" (1989, 172). In fact Bible translation "fosters a climate of choice and persuasion" (Sanneh 2003, 115). At the same time, as an American missionary to Africa, it must be said that Africans have paid a huge compliment to Western missionaries by making the gospel their own and by calling our attention to our own cultural biases and theological blindness while also improving the theological dialogue that challenges our entrenched theological systems. In a similar vein, Timothy Tennent states, "Indeed, I believe that there is a growing realization that the majority World church may play a crucial role, not only in revitalizing the life of Western Christianity, but in actually contributing positively and maturely to our own theological reflection" (2007, 13). It is in this context that the search for what Paul Hiebert calls the "fourth self," i.e. self-theologizing, has taken place and ultimately led to "globalizing theology" where theology is no longer controlled primarily by Western theologians. Hiebert defines the fourth self as the right of leaders "to study the scriptures for themselves and to develop their own theologies" in light of their cultural contexts (Hiebert 1994, 46).

The concept of contextualization moves beyond the indigenous church principle and provides the missiological backdrop for the discussion of self-theologizing and contextual theology as it emerges from the struggle of Western Christianity to be more culturally aware and relevant in bringing the gospel to bear on other cultures. The literature on "contextualization" is important to theological education as it provides a theoretical construct for understanding the direction, purpose and goals for theological education relative to the development of cross-cultural education.

The missiological import of "contextualization" originated from a non-Western church leader, Shoki Coe [C. H. Hwang], a Presbyterian church leader and principal of Tainan Theological College. Even before "contextualization" became a missiological concept, Coe was calling for reform in theological education because of the uncritical repetition of Western patterns of theological education (Coe 1962, 7-34; Shenk 2005, 206-208). Coe indicates that the term came to him in "a flash" from deliberation in the Theological Education Fund but also because of his long "personal pilgrimage as a theological educator from Asia" (1973, 240).

The terms "contextuality" and "contextualization" came upon the missiological scene during the working out of the third mandate program of the Theological Education Fund (TEF) from 1970-77 (Coe 1973, 239-241). It came to the forefront with the publication of the *Theological Education Fund 1972 Ministry in Context: The Third Mandate*. TEF observes that contextualization conveys "all that is implied in the familiar term 'indigenization' and yet seeks to press beyond for a more dynamic concept which is open to change and which is future-oriented" as opposed to indigenization which "tends to be used in the sense of responding to the gospel in terms of traditional culture" (Coe 1976, 21; 1973, 240). Contextuality is "the conscientization of the contexts in the particular, historical moment, assessing the peculiarity of the context in the light of the mission of the church as it is called to participate in the *Missio Dei* " (Coe 1973, 241). As Lienemann-Perrin would later articulate it, "Authentic contextualization is always prophetic, arising out of the genuine encounter between God's word and His world, and moves towards the purpose of challenging and changing the situation through rootedness in the commitment to a given historical moment" (1981, 1974).

Bosch points out that "contextual theologies claim that they constitute an epistemological break compared with traditional theologies" (1991, 423). Simon Kwan understands Soki Coe as perceiving the concept of contextualization as a paradigm shift in the sense that Kuhn has put forward although Coe does not address the idea of paradigm shift in this way (2005, 238). Kwan argues that the "shift from indigenization to contextualization" as a way of doing theology is not a paradigm shift. If we limited contextualization to Coe's initial definition, Kwan might possibly make the case that there is not enough difference between indigenization and contextualization to constitute a paradigm shift. However, the continuing discussion of contextualization, the growing recognition of other voices in the theological discussion and the increasing global theological conversation is changing the rules or as Kuhn says, "can replace explicit rules as a basis for the solution . . . (1962, 175).

The paradigm shift is taking place in the realm of greater global theological conversations and maybe more importantly in the thinking of Western missionaries and theologians. That shift is the realization that to contextualize is to ultimately release theologizing control from its Western heritage. It is not that the concept of indigenization did not move in that direction to a degree but that the indigenous church concept and the three-selfs construct limited the indigenous model to emphasizing the ecclesiastical structural forms in developing a church more than emphasizing indigenous theological expressions or self-theologizing. The contextualization conversation has decidedly changed the rules by which evangelicals understand theologizing through more global contributions or as Bosch rightly recognizes, the "circulation of experience with praxis" involving the third-world and the marginalized (1991, 425).

An indication of this "circulation of experience with praxis" among evangelicals may be seen in the twentieth annual Wheaton Theology Conference in 2011 and the publication of *Global Theology in Evangelical Perspective: Exploring the Contextual Nature of Theology and Mission* (2012). The conference was intended to showcase "the varied colors of the global theological tapestry" (Green 2012, 5). The publication of the *Global Dictionary of Theology* is intended to "take the form of a conversation" to share "common concerns" and share "theological issues in different parts of the world" (2008, i).

Contextualization in the TEF Third Mandate is divided into four areas that need to be addressed for "renewal and reform" of theological education: missiological, structural, pedagogical, and theological. Missiological contextualization focuses on developing training that addresses renewal and reform issues in the church particularly with human development and justice in specific contexts. Structural contextualization seeks to develop structures that are appropriate to the needs in the socio-economic and political contexts. Pedagogical contextualization is understood to be a process that encourages a type of theological training that is liberating and creative, giving rise to a "servant ministry" and not "elitism and authoritarianism" while being sensitive to the "gap between the 'academic' and the 'practical.'" Theological contextualization is concerned with finding "appropriate and authentic" ways of doing theology in its various contexts and related to the issues of ministry and service within and outside a particular context (TEF Staff 1972, 31). James Bergquist expands on these four areas by adding a fifth area of what he calls "crises" in the "structures of theological education." He points to "financial dependencies" as a contextualization issue because of the financial dependence of "Third World" theological institutions on Western support.[1] He raises the issue as to whether such dependence may block the "way that progresses toward a more authentic form of theological education" (1973, 249-250).

These areas of contextualization can be seen in the emergence of contemporary consideration of the contextualization concept for the African context in various African consultations. Daniel R. Sanchez summarizes a number of issues that were discussed at these conferences. One issue revolved around the role of the Old Testament in relationship to its use in formulating African theologies and whether traditional religions take the place of the Old Testament as the root of Christianity. Another issue was the place of traditional religions in forming African theologies. The third issue was concerned with who should be involved in contextual theology: should it be simply an African endeavor or broader? The fourth issue dealt with the influence of urbanization on developing African theologies (1998, 321).

Definitions of contextualization point to the above issues and other areas of concern. Stephen Bevans defines contextual theology as "a way of doing theology in which one takes into account: the spirit and message of the gospel; the tradition of the Christian people; the culture in which one is theologizing; and social change in that culture, whether brought about by Western technological process or the grassroots struggle for equality, justice and liberation" (1992, 1). Victor Cole defines "contextualization" as "a theological formulation from exegesis of biblical texts within a sociocultural context, and a living out of that theology within the given cultural context, utilizing the Bible as the only authority while recognizing the progress of biblical revelation" (1998, 12).

The literature on contextualization related to missiological concerns is significant. From the time of its conceptualization by TEF, a proliferation of writings has debated its nature and the extent of its application. David Hesselgrave's texts on *Communicating Christ Cross-Culturally: An Introduction to Missionary Communication*, the first and second editions, contribute to the discussion on contextualization from a communication perspective (1978; 1991). Bruce Nicholls' book *Contextualization: A Theology of Gospel and Culture* and Bruce Fleming's text *Contexualization of Theology: An Evangelical Assessment* follow a direction similar to Hesselgrave's in which the contextualization process is primarily controlled by the communicators who provide the categories by which the message is understood (1979; 1980).

Paul Hiebert's article on "Critical Contextualization" in *Missiology* and in *International Bulletin of Missionary Research* continues to be a key article pushing the bounds of the evangelical perspective in coming to terms with the contextualization process and its implications for the rise of theologies (1987). Hiebert moves the discussion beyond the conception of contextualizaion presented by David Hesselgrave and others. He argues "for the people corporately to critically evaluate their own past customs" and establish their own understandings and "response to their new-found truths" (1994, 89).

Following the line of Paul Hiebert, Scott Moreau outlines what he calls a "comprehensive contextualization" that "*is a two-way process in which all sides contribute.* It is not a one-way process in which people from one culture go to another to show the members of the second culture how they should express their faith and live their lives" (2006, 327). In *Contextualization in World Missions: Mapping and Assessing Evangelical Models*, Moreau surveys various evangelical approaches to contextualization (2012). Charles Van Engen notes the movement in evangelicals' understanding of contextualization as a way of doing theology in a particular context that is primarily "communicating the gospel meaningfully" to the receptor to a realization that "it is the receptor who ascribes meaning to any communications" (2006, 94). Daniel Shaw in his article "Beyond Contextualization: Toward a Twenty-First Century Model for Enabling Mission" sounds a similar tone.

> This point demands that we reexamine our understanding of contextualization. Instead of outsiders reconfiguring local cultural forms to fit the shape of Christianity with which they are familiar, we need—following the theological implications of the incarnation—to allow local people to contemplate the implications of God-in-their-midst. (2010, 211)

Among non-evangelicals, works by Robert Schreiter are worthy of note, such as his book *Constructing Local Theologies*, a later article entitled "Contextualization from a World Perspective" in *Theological Education*, and *The New Catholicity* (1985; 1993; 1997). In relation to contextualization, Schreiter contends, "More and more, local theology is pointing the way to a return to theology as an occasional enterprise, that is, one dictated by circumstances and immediate needs rather than the need for system-building." He defines local theologies "as the dynamic interaction among gospel, church, and culture" (1985, 22). He later notes the wider acceptance of the role of context in doing theology.

> Be context construed as culture, social structure, or social location, it always plays an important role in framing any theological articulation. . . . Theology must also have a universalizing function, by which is meant an ability to speak beyond its own context, and an openness to hear voices from beyond its own boundaries. (1997, 3-4)

Bevans's work, *An Introduction to Theology in Global Perspective*, notes that "theology is and must be 'contextual.'" He contends that this perspective of the theological endeavor is relatively new. "Formerly, theology was understood as the reflection in faith of two theological 'sources' or *loci theologici*: Scripture and Tradition. However, today. . . theology also considers *present human experience* as a theological source or *locus theologicus*." This third source Bevan's argues is not only to be considered equal to "Scripture" and "Tradition" but "in a certain sense it has priority over them" (2009, 165). Timothy Tennent warns that some forms of contextualization are "a vague synonym for cultural particularity." This places "too much emphasis on cultural particularity at the expense of some universal core element of the gospel . . ." and gives rise to syncretism (2010, 350).

Contextualization as a concept elicits a wide range of understandings about exactly what is included in it. One simplified understanding is that it is the process of "packaging" the biblical message in the appropriate language of today so that it conveys the biblical ideas and meanings to the contemporary listener (Spanje 1998, 206). On the other end of the spectrum, contextualization has been associated with liberation theology (Bosch 1991, 421). Certainly, there is a range of understanding contextualization from mere cross-cultural communication to cross-cultural communication with cultural application to defrocking the cultural clothing of the message to developing theologies (Haleblian 1983, 96).

Models of Contextualizing Theology

The complexity in specifically locating the parameters of "contextualization," or "contextual theology," is due to the fact that the parameters are involved in the whole discussion in the field of hermeneutics (Spanje 1998, 198). Since the inception of the concept of contextualization a number of models have come into use from diverse perspectives. Significant contributions on this discussion from the evangelical perspective include Charles Kraft, Paul Hiebert, Dean Gilliland and Scott Moreau. Stephen Bevans and Robert J. Schreiter enter into the discussion from the Roman Catholic perspective, while Max L. Stackhouse claims to represent an "ecumenically oriented Protestant" view (Stackhouse 1988, 3). The proposed models represent various ways of conceptualizing the process of contextual theology as a hermeneutical process.

Bevans provides a helpful delineation of six models of contextual theology. He places them on a continuum from "scripture tradition" or "experience of the past" that emphasizes the gospel message to "context" or "experience of the present" centering on social change. The "anthropological model" represents the farthest position toward emphasizing the importance of culture. On the other end of the spectrum is the "countercultural model" that represents the "scripture tradition." It emphasizes scripture's "encounter" or "engagement" with the culture. In between these two poles, moving from the anthropological model to the countercultural model are four models: the "transcendental model," the "praxis model," the "synthetic model" and the "translation model" (2009, 170-71; 1992, 27).[2] Dean Gilliland proposes seven models of contextualization, four of which are the same as Bevans'. He adds the "semiotic model," the "adaptation model," and the "critical model" (1989, 315-317).

The "anthropological model," more than the others, "focuses on the validity of the human as the place of divine revelation and as a source (locus) for theology that is equal to scripture and tradition." Or more specifically, "human nature, and therefore human culture, is good, holy, and valuable. It is within human culture that we find God's revelation—not as a separate supracultural message, but in the very complexity of culture itself. . . ." (Bevans 1992, 48- 49). Gilliland argues that it is erroneous to suppose that "culture is an adequate guide to truth." Rather "culture must be the matrix in which the theology takes root and grows; but, equally, it must be brought under the scrutiny and judgment of the Word of God" (1989, 314).

The "praxis model" focuses on the place of Christians within a culture as a force of social change, particularly as it relates to socio-political contexts. It is often identified with the theology of liberation (Bevans 1992, 63; Gilliland 1989, 314-315). This model assists the Christian faith in relating its message to the everyday life situation (Bevans 1992, 70). Gilliland notes that the "praxis model" fails to give adequate place for the biblical message but is socio-politically based with "knowledge transmitted through participation in history" (1989, 315).

The "synthetic model," sometimes referred to as the "dialogical model," brings together "four basic elements—the gospel, Christian tradition, culture and social change." As Bevans notes, this model brings together elements of the "translation model," "anthropological model," and the "praxis model." "It endeavors to keep the integrity of the traditional message, while acknowledging the importance of taking culture and social change seriously" (1992, 81-83; Gilliland 1989, 316). Bevans argues that one primary problem with this model is that this "model is always in danger of 'selling out' to the other culture or tradition, and so always needs to be appropriated with some suspicion" (1992, 88).

The "translation model" is taken from the field of linguistics in which the equivalent meanings are transferred from the source to the receptor culture, "even though the form that expresses the meaning may be something different . . . , therefore, the attempt is made to separate the absolute or 'supracultural elements' of the gospel from what is secondary" (Gilliland 1989, 314). Bevans argues that this approach is not able to "get at the deep structures of a language, which are more than simple vocabulary and grammar correspondences" (1992, 31). Charles Kraft notes that such an approach gives close attention to the source documents but is limited by only providing a surface-level understanding to the receptors and not giving attention to the "deep-level cultural context" (1979, 264). Schreiter seems to have this approach in mind when he states,

> Much literature about contextualization has focused upon the sending process, to assure that the evangelist or contextualizer is presenting an orthodox account of the biblical witness. But it is becoming increasingly apparent that the reception of that message needs more attention than we have given it in the past. (1993, 75)

In the end this model emphasizes what has been done in the church tradition rather than in the new local cultural setting (Schreiter 1985, 7).

Bevan's "countercultural model" indicates the perspective that the gospel has precedence over the context because the context is seen as a "hindrance to the gospel and the gospel message." The previous five models see cultural contexts as generally positive where the countercultural model takes a more negative view of culture which is in need of "engagement" or an "encounter" with the gospel message (2009, 185).

Not too unlike the "counter cultural model," the goal of the "adaptation model," according to Gilliland, "is to make, as much as possible, the historical foci of systematic theology fit into particular cultural situations." This model assumes that there is "one philosophical framework" from which cultures may approach theological discussion. This model does not take into consideration other forms of knowledge and philosophical frameworks by which religious truths may be expressed. "The hope in adaptation theology is to keep thirteenth-century European thinking alive!" (1989, 315).

Semiotics was popularized by Clifford Geertz as a way to analyze cultures. He contends,

> The view of man as a symbolizing, conceptualizing, meaning-seeking animal, which has become increasingly popular both in the social sciences and in philosophy over the past several years, opens up a whole new approach not only to the analysis of religion as such, but to the understanding of the relations between religion and values. (1973, 140)

Gilliland draws from this a possible model of contextualization, the "semiotic model" in which culture is seen as containing the truth in some degree revealed in its signs and symbols.[3] The limitations of this model, according to Gilliland, rest in its dependence on Western-trained people or outsiders because the contextualization process is "taken out of the hands of local Christians and becomes an exercise for the elite only" (1989, 316).

Bevans opts for what he calls the "transcendental model" for contextualizing theology. His model proposes that the task of constructing a contextualized theology is not about producing a particular body of any kind of texts; it is about attending to the affective and cognitive operations in the self-transcending subject. What is important is not so much that a particular theology or "product" is produced but the "process" that the theologian goes through who is producing it operates as an authentic, converted subject. Contextual theology in this model does not focus on the "essence of the gospel message or tradition" nor try to "thematize or analyze culture or expressions of culture in language." Rather it is centered on the person's "own religious experience" and the experience of oneself (1992, 97-98; 2009, 184).

This broad range of understanding contextualization is due to the movement of the message between cultures and the interaction of the dynamic elements: scripture from its cultural context, the missionary from his culture and Christian heritage, and the host people in their culture and religious heritage. The question is which one of these is the focal point for contextualization. These models of contextualization seem to move from primary emphasis on culture to primary emphasis on scripture. The existential form of contextualization in Bevans' "transcendental model" appears to be a modified form of the "anthropological model" with its emphasis on culture having priority in the contextualization process. The praxis model leans in this direction as well. It lends itself to relegating scripture to simple support of socio-political agendas with careful exegesis of the culture and society but with scripture being dogmatized to provide scriptural credence or a religious foundation to cultural perspectives.

On the other end of the spectrum, the "countercultural" leaves little room for a positive contribution of culture to doing theology. The "translation model," taken strictly as a simple correlation of meanings through grammar and vocabulary without regard to the deep cultural meanings and forms, is not adequate for full contextualization of the biblical message and people's responses to it. The "adaptation model" may give more credence to the importance of culture, but it gives priority to Christian tradition and interpretive frameworks from a Western perspective.

In the middle of the two extremes it seems appropriate to place the "semiotic model" and the "synthetic model." Both attempt to take seriously the need to understand culture and religious perceptions. However, the "semiotic model" is heavily influenced by Western anthropological concepts and largely dependent on insights of highly trained researchers. Bevan's "synthetic model," on the other hand, only provides a general recognition of the basic elements that need to be involved in contextualizing theology but provides little substance into how these elements are brought together into a dynamic process of contextualization (1992, 81-83).

Paul Hiebert's "critical model" integrates elements from several of the other models with careful consideration of the specific contexts (Hiebert 1987, 109; Gilliland 1989, 317). Bevans and Hiebert share some terminology that indicates that both models share some common goals with the involvement of those receiving the message playing a primary role in the contextualization process. Bevans points to the "affective" and "cognitive" operations in the "authentic, converted subject" as doing the theologizing but not producing a "particular body of any kind of text." For Bevans, the end is a "religious experience" and the experience of oneself (1992, 97-98). Hiebert carries a similar thought when he notes that critical contextualization must "translate the biblical message into the cognitive, affective, and evaluative dimensions of another culture." However, Hiebert sees critical contextualization as fostering contextualized theologies that are biblically based and not just a religious experience (1994, 89-91).[4]

In a 1988 essay that was reprinted in 1994, "Metatheology: The Step beyond Contextualization," Hiebert calls for going beyond contextualization and toward a "metatheology." He also put forward the need to add the "fourth self," self-theologizing, to the three-selfs already a part of mission practice from indigenization to contextualization. The fourth self implies that young churches exercise their abilities in relation to God to interpret scripture for themselves from their own cultural contexts (1988; 1994, 96). Hiebert again reflects on the need for a "metatheology" in his essay, "The Missionary as Mediator of Global Theologizing." He suggests that all parties in the theologizing process participate in developing a "metatheological frame" that "enables them to understand, compare, and evaluate local theologies, the questions each is seeking to answer, and the sociocultural contexts in which each must define the gospel." He contends that once the framework of understanding is formed, the "process of developing a global theology that is true for everyone can begin" (2006, 302).

Scott Moreau calls for a "contextualization paradigm" that is comprehensive rather than just concentrated on theology. He lists seven characteristics as foundational for "comprehensive contextualization." First, it is "concerned with the whole of the Christian faith." Second, it "is both propositional and existential." Third, it "is grounded in Scripture." Fourth, it "is interdisciplinary." Fifth, it "is dynamic." Sixth, it "is aware of the impact of human sinfulness on the process." Seventh, it "is a two-way process in which all sides contribute." He notes the two poles of the contextualization models from Bevans' "translation" models to the models that emphasize scripture to the "existential" models that emphasize the context. Moreau uses Ninian Smart's model for understanding world religions to articulate his "comprehensive contextualization" process that takes into count both poles of the contextualization models (2006, 325-334).

The search for the fourth self continues in the midst of the global shift of Christianity to the south. This is moving the conversation beyond contextualization. Recognizing this shift in Christianity and the effect it is having on the theological process, Mika Vähäkangas proposes a contextualization process composed of five variables in a "hermeneutical circle." After a critique of Schreiter's and Bevans's taxonomies, he opts for five variables which consist of Gospel, worldview, social context, theologian's choice of themes, and theological method by which to have "a more detailed picture of the contextual process" (2010, 288-289).

Daniel Shaw argues for a twenty-first century model that goes beyond contextualization, "a missional approach" that "reflects God's intention for people 'from every race, tribe, nation, and language.'" "It is relational, with a focus on being rather than doing." He discusses five elements to this "missional approach," i.e. "dynamic and interactive," "relevant," "global," and "transformational," each of which has a relational emphasis with God and others entering the theological discussion (2010, 212).

Literature dealing with African theologies takes many of the contextualization issues and provides categories for the on-going theological reflection from Africans' perspectives. African theologians provide perceptions on African contextualization where scripture, church history and cultural contexts interplay, integrate, and interrogate the process of doing theology. African scholars through their pursuit of African theology have and will continue to contribute to Christian theology from their varied African contexts. Hopefully, this will lead to greater interaction with Western theology in order to decrease the hegemonic tendencies of Western theology.

African Theologies' Contributions toward Self-Theologizing

A number of significant works explore the area of African theology. In his book *Toward an African Theology,* John Pobee proposes "a dialogue between the Christian faith and African tradition and custom" related to practicing contextualization. He contends that theology always begins with the "Christ event" in order to discover what it "looks like when seen from within the particular world view. Thus, to some degree, theology is always being written by those to whom the gospel is being communicated. Furthermore, it is the task of theology to keep on reconstructing and repairing a holistic Christocentric world view . . ." (1979, 10, 28).

John S. Mbiti defines African theology as "the theological reflection of African Christians" and "the attempt to couch essential Christianity into African categories and thought forms. Such an exercise is not to be confused with an exercise in couching African world view in Christian form. This means that there are certain aspects of the Christian faith which are *nonnegotiable*" (Mbiti 1976, 18). He also argues that theology must consist of mutuality and reciprocity. There is a real but false dichotomy "between Western Christianity and the Christianity of the so-called Third World." It is false because such a dichotomy should not exist. He states,

> When will you make us part of your subconscious process of theology? How can the rich theological heritage of Europe and America become the heritage of the universal church on the basis of mutuality and reciprocity? . . . There cannot be theological conversation or dialogue between North and South, East and West, until we can embrace each other's concerns and stretch to each other's horizons. . . . We feel deeply affronted and wonder whether it is more meaningful theologically to have academic fellowship with heretics long dead than with the living brethren of the Church today in the so-called Third World. (1976, 16-17)

In *Theology in Africa*, Kwesi A. Dickson points out that meaningful theology can only take place in context and identifies four main factors that come into play when doing theology in light of a particular context. These factors are the scriptures, experience, tradition, and culture (1984, 15-28).

Western theology has claimed a universal position while being narrowly focused on concerns of Western culture according to Justin S. Ukpong. He argues that we are now entering a new era of a "world-church" and a "world-theology" which is not limited to one particular culture. Theologies of different cultural perspectives are emerging which give rise to this new era. "The framework of genuine world-theology must be developed from insights derived from these theologies arising from different cultural backgrounds" (1984, 61).

Two works of Ukpong are important in the discussion of African theologies, *African Theologies Now: A Profile* and "Inculturation Hermeneutics: An African Approach to Biblical Interpretation" in *The Bible in a World Context: An Experiment in Contextual Hermeneutics* (1984; 2003). Ukpong describes the hermeneutical process for producing African theologies as consisting of "four poles that interplay: the text, the context of the text, the reading community, and the context of the reading community." He sees meaning as produced by a community within their "*sociocultural context*" through "reading the text against its *sociohistorical context*." Therefore, "both the contemporary sociocultural context and the sociohistorical context of the text are analyzed to establish a meaningful relationship between them" (2003, 27- 28). He contends,

> The distinctive characteristic of this approach is its emphasis on making the African context the subject of interpretation of the Christian message through the use of the people's conceptual frame of reference in the interpretation process. It also embodies a holistic understanding of culture whereby both secular and religious issues in society are seen as interrelated, and critical ideological questions are raised in the process of reading the Bible. (2003, 32)

Tite Tiénou's doctoral dissertation, "The Problem of Methodology in African Christian Theologies," provides a significant discussion in this area (1984). Other related writings by him are also noteworthy: "Issues in the Theological Task in Africa Today" in the *East Africa Journal of Evangelical Theology* (1982); "The Theological Task of the Church in Africa: Where Are We Now and Where Should We Be Going?" in the *East Africa Journal of Evangelical Theology* (1987); "Forming Indigenous Theologies" in *Toward the 21st Century in Christian Missions* (1993); and "The Theological Task of the Church in Africa" in *Issues in African Christian Theology* (1998). He notes that as Christianity has taken root in non-western cultures, it has become clearer that it is composed of a "mosaic of peoples" wearing its "multi-colored cultural garb." This requires that African Christians study their own culture, as well as "the cultures of the biblical world and western culture" (1982, 5). He proposes a "three dimensional method for forming 'indigenous theologies'."

This method "begins with the church, then proceeds to the investigation of the culture, and concludes with interpreting the scripture" (1993, 249-250). He notes,

> The theologian should not start with the traditional cultural and religious context because his responsibility is not primarily to society in general. His task is not to develop a theology for people of a given cultural and religious tradition. Rather he must help Christians, in a given cultural and religious tradition, develop a theology suited to their needs. In that sense, responsible theology is one which causes Scripture to speak to people in the context of their history, their culture, their religious heritage and calls them to be God's ambassadors where they are. (1984, 129)

Bediako notes the need to see the "African Christian story" in connection with the wider Christian tradition and history. "The point here is that the African Christian story is necessarily part of the unfolding of Christian history as a whole and may not be made exotic so that it appears to have no analogues anywhere else" (2001, 30). He particularly sees a strong connection between the early church fathers' understanding and implementation of the gospel's message and present day African theology. He contends that the gospel

> not only provided them with a precious interpretative key for discerning the religious meanings inherent in their heritage, so that they could decide what to accept and what to reject; in the Gospel they also found an all-encompassing reality and an overall integrating principle which enabled them to understand themselves and their past, and face the future, because the Gospel of Jesus Christ became for them the heir to all that was worthy in the past, whilst it held all the potential of the future. (1992, 439-440; 1998, 57)

Agbonkhianmeghe Orobator sees theology for Africans as well as others as "not an exercise in conceptual weightlessness. It develops within the particular culture and context of the community that attempts to utter a word or two on the reality of God and the demands of faith for daily living" (2008, 152). He states, "When we talk about African theology, we understand this to mean the ongoing attempt to make sense of the African reality in the light of Christian faith and revelation" (2010, 5). Orobator observes that "Word does not suppress flesh; it becomes flesh and dwells in our midst. Christian faith recognizes and embraces the truth of African religion, just as African religion receives and celebrates the truth of Christianity." This encounter between Christianity and African beliefs gives rise to an enculturation process that includes such realities as "faith, gospel, religion, and culture" that are themselves "not static or closed; they are dynamic and open to growth and change" (2008, 129). As with other peoples' experiences, Africans' experiences in doing theology "will stimulate a dialogue on the understanding of faith and its practice for Christians in other contexts" (2008, 154).

Stan Chu Ilo points to "an emerging third phase in African theology." This phase follows in the heels of the two previous phases, inculturation theology and liberation theology approaches. Theology in the first phase was practiced by "inculturation theologians (flourishing from 1956-1980)" who "were concerned with orthodoxy and the integrity of the gospel in the African context." The second phase of liberation theology from the late 1960 to 1980s "sought contextualization in African Christianity" by focusing on theological engagement of social issues, applying "a more critical and historical approach to Western Christianity." The third phase is what Ilo refers to as a "theology of hope that is rooted in missional cultural hermeneutic" where the goal of African theology is to take into account the "historical analysis of African social context affected by Christian consciousness." He notes, "The search for human and cultural development should be the concern of African theology using the categories, terms, and relations offered by the Christian message and African cultural and religious history, as well as the African social context" (2012, 198-199).

With the rise of the discussions related to "African theologies" in the 1960s and 1970s, Byang Kato warns against syncretism or "Christo-paganism" while still making "Christianity culturally relevant without destroying its ever-abiding message (1975, 1223). He notes, "The term African theology has come to mean different things to different people. Furthermore, it has the inherent danger of syncretism." He suggests instead that it might well be better to just talk about "Christian theology and then to define whatever context it is related to, e.g., reflections from Africa; the context of marriage in Africa; and the spirit world in Africa." He believes every effort should be made "to relate Christian theology to the changing situations in Africa", but this will only be possible by keeping the Bible as the "absolute Word of God" which does not seem to be emphasized by some uses of African theologies (2004, 148).

As the above survey indicates, African theologies integrate the biblical context, the African traditional cultural context, the church, and the Western Christian intellectual and cultural heritage of interpretation while bringing the African interpretation into the discussion from its non-Western heritage and its own grappling with their current contemporary contexts. There is also a push for "academic fellowship" and "theological dialogue" between all concerned. The Festschrift in honor of Paul Hiebert, *Globalizing Theology: Belief and Practice in an Era of World Christianity* contributes significantly to this discussion. In the concluding chapter of that book Craig Ott envisions a "global round table of theologians" where

> there would be no head of the table where Western theologians are seated making the rules and guiding the discussion. There would be no protests or complaints rising from non-Western theologians suffering under a sense of inferiority or motivated by ethnic pride. Privilege, rank, and ethnicity would fade into the background altogether. In fact, the bi-polar distinction between Western and non-Western theologians would no longer be useful or necessary. (2006, 329)

As Tite Tiénou encourages, "Today authentic Christian theologizing and provincialism are incompatible. . . . Let us move forward then, in Christian theology as if we truly belong together" (2006, 50).

The significance of contexualization and the place of African theologies are highly integrated within the discussion of providing cross-cultural theological education or leadership training. Since Western theological education has been the primary source for the educating of mission church leaders, the Western missiological heritage regarding leadership education has played a major role in the training and development of African leadership. Understanding the precedents of Western missiological currents in striving for greater contextualization in present day Africa through education are important for setting the stage in evaluating current theological education and the training of church leaders toward more self-theologizing rather than practicing theological hegemony by imposing Western methodology or epistemology biases (Frostin 1985, 140-141). Chapter 3 will discuss the impact of theological education in searching for the fourth self.

> A literate person was regarded as 'civilized', 'cultured', and even 'Christian'. This was inevitable since no one could become literate except through a mission school. . . . hence a Christian was synonymous with a 'scholar' (muthomi)."
>
> Nthamburi 1982

CHAPTER 3
Theological Education and the Search for the Fourth Self

"Missionaries established and pioneered schools everywhere, and these schools became the nurseries for change: they sowed the Gospel, they sowed Christianity and perhaps unawares and unintentionally they sowed the new revolution" (Mbiti 1969, 283). Historically, the training and development of Christian ministers on mission fields is highly connected to the enlightenment emphasis on education, societal betterment, and missiological thinking related to the means and methods of "civilizing" and providing "qualified" church ministers. Developing church ministers in the mission fields is tied to the historical development of educational endeavors in modern missions and has had profound affects for Christianity as well as in socio-economic and socio-political arenas.

The use of education in missions is intertwined with the enlightenment environment in evangelical Christianity. In the eighteenth century two strands of thinking combined that pushed education forward as a methodology for missions, the unity of humanity and the need to be civilized by the measurement of Western cultures and Western Christianity. Education was seen as the means to "raise even the most degraded specimen of humanity" (Stanley 2001, 11). William Carey drew the two strands, the unity of humanity and civilization, together in his *Enquiry*. He asks, "Can we hear they are without the gospel, without government, without laws, and without art, and sciences; and not exert ourselves to introduce among them the sentiments of men, and of Christians?" (1792, 69-70)

Alexander Duff, following on the heels of Carey's work in Christian education in India, became a key figure in pushing Christian education in English for training church ministers for the future leadership of the church. Duff notes the existence of many reasons for teaching in English but lists above all that the lack of "European works" translated into Sanskrit was an obstacle and that Sanskrit terms were inseparably linked to Hinduism so as to continue to indoctrinate them more and cause the people to "become tenfold more a child of Pantheism, idolatry, and superstition" (1840, 543-544). Duff would become a leading figure in championing this model (Day 1879, 15). Rufus Anderson argues for the necessity of education because "the savage has few ideas, sees only the objects just about him, perceives nothing on the relations of things, and occupies his thoughts only about his physical experiences and wants." Without the power of miraculous gifts, "missionaries are constrained to resort to education in order to procure pastors for their churches" (1845, 4-13).

Modern Missions and Theological Education to WW II

African Christian leadership developed in a context of what Lamin Sanneh calls "world Christianity," which he defines as "the movement of Christianity as it takes form and shape in societies that previously were not Christian, societies that had no bureaucratic traditions with which to domesticate the gospel." "World Christianity" is contrasted with "Global Christianity" which he defines as "the faithful replication of Christian forms and patterns developed in Europe" (2003, 22). Though one may speak of the lack of "bureaucratic traditions with which to domesticate the gospel," there still remain forces and influences from sources within and from without Africa that shaped and continue to influence Christian leadership development in Africa. Influences such as the translated scripture in the multiple languages of Africa, modernity and globalization, Western

Christian missions and education, and African traditional elements have certainly been central in shaping African Christian leadership.

"Leadership poses a central issue for mission because a primary focus of the *Missio Dei* is influencing people to submit to the lordship of Christ" (Elliston 2000, 567). Jesus Christ was the culmination of God's redemptive work and the beginning of the lordship of Christ as an incarnate example of leadership. Like Jesus, Christian leadership takes place in a cultural and sociological context with theological underpinnings that impinge on its practice. A significant role of Christian leadership is not only in the role of "influencing people to submit to the lordship of Christ" but to use their leadership skills to engage the socio-economic challenges of the people. In Africa, improved leadership for the political and socio-economic well-being of the nations is important to the church. As John Mukumu Mbaku notes,

> Available evidence now indicates the quality of life for the majority of Africans has either not improved since the 1960s when the African countries began to gain independence or has done so only marginally. Many researchers believe that only drastic measures and radical changes in leadership can arrest the deteriorating economic and social conditions in the continent and allow for significant improvements in the living standards of the people. (Assensoh 1998, vii)

The discussion of leadership in missions has a long tradition in the modern Protestant mission movement, particularly as Christian missions grew dramatically in the 19th and 20th centuries. The importance of the need and role of Christian leaders in the new mission fields was a major topic of the missionary conferences as the modern mission movement progressed into the 20th century. Christian and Western education was seen as the key means in Africa by which leaders were developed for the church and the social, economic, and political arenas. As Dyrness notes, "Whatever their own educational backgrounds, missionaries made education one of their central activities" (2008, 375).

As the progress of "world Christianity" expanded in the 19th and 20th centuries, Christian missions were struggling with the need for more trained church leaders to keep up with the growing church population. The predominant method for training ordained leaders was through the western-style theological education system imported into the mission field or through sending potential leaders to institutions of higher education in Western countries. The literature of the World Missions Conferences provides primary resources on the modern missions movement as it progressed into the twentieth century. Education as a missions method would take center stage in the twentieth century. The presentations related to the place of and use of education in the mission enterprise particularly reveal the overriding direction of missions based on education for the "civilizing" of the "heathen" and meeting the need for trained leaders who are both "civilized" and educated in classical Western theology. An appraisal of the literature of the World Missions Conferences provides insights into the Western mission's dialogue concerning the place of education in the modern missions movement as it progressed into the twentieth century.

At the 1860 Liverpool Missionary Conference, J. H. Titcomb's comments summarize the direction of the discussion on the use of Christian education. He describes three stages through which education progressed in mission efforts: introductory, permanent, and reproductive. The "Introductory Stage" is the period of "pioneering and civilising processes" where English is used because the missionaries are most familiar with it, there are few books in the vernacular, and English attracts "the natives" and "opens to them all our own store of sacred literature." The "Permanent Stage" foresees education as the means by which a qualified "native agency" is created to evangelize the large masses of society through the vernacular. The "Reproductive Stage of Missionary Education" foresees the need for further training the "native teachers and pastors" so as not to be dependent on a constant supply of missionaries but to provide "native training-masters" to fill the need for teachers in the rising number of "vernacular village schools" (*Conference* [1860], 124-126).

Andrew Walls notes of this conference that Alexander Duff's successor Thomas Smith argues that teaching should be understood as another mode of evangelism on par with preaching (1996, 203). He also advocates for teaching topics other than the gospel as long as the goal is to provide Christian teaching for the people. As Smith states, "I maintain that cultivating all its faculties and powers is a legitimate method of fulfilling the great obligation of Christian missionaries" (1996, 203; *Conference* [1860], 118-120).

The 1888 Centenary Missionary Conference devoted three sessions to "The Place of Education in Missionary Work" and three sessions to "The Missionary in Relation to Literature." Five broad categories of strategies for using education were discussed in the presentations given: strategy for growth in biblical knowledge, strategy for conversion, strategy for individual and church maturation which is "self-supporting and self-propagating", strategy for training "agents" of the church, and a strategy for social reform and national improvement (Johnston 1888, 185-86, 234). The training of Christian leaders is seen as the key to the future for the success of missions' longevity. "Education is not fostered and provided for mere purposes of culture.... We train those men to be teachers; we educate those men to be pastors...." Christian education is the means for training leaders that will take the place of missionaries in the ministries and bring social reform (Johnston 1888, 190, 214, 226).

The introductory chapter to the volume on the Ecumenical Missionary Conference of 1900 states, "Human progress is inseparably bound up with Christian missions" (*Ecumenical* 2 [1900], 10). A reoccurring theme for the potential of education in missions was the raising up of the future generations of "native agents." Only through these trained leaders would the various lands be converted. It was the training-school "that is the heart from which the blood goes out for the whole body of the church. If it is weak, the whole church will be weak." With the training came the need for quality institutions and cooperation in building those facilities. These institutions were perceived as being "similar" to institutions in Europe or America, though starting at a "lower stage" (*Ecumenical* 2 [1900], 126-27, 144).

The missionary conference at Edinburgh marked a high point of the missionary enterprise. The systematic nature of studying missionary efforts in the area of education can be seen in the *Report of Commission III, Education in Relation to the Christianisation of National Life*. The goal for developing competent national leadership is summed up when the Commission states, "If the races dwelling in these lands are to be developed to the full, it must be through their fellow-countrymen" (*Report* [1910], 303). The commission looked at the training of teachers and leaders for the broad needs of the various societies in industry, education, government service, politics, and religion. Some emphasis was laid on the need for pursuing non-western methods of training where the foreign teacher "will guard carefully against moulding his students after his own methods and ideas" (*Report* [1910], 320). Calls were heard for indigenous churches, but it was still argued by many that English was the best medium of educating students because of the available literature. However, others were warning that the use of English would bring the students under "the bondage of Western usage" (*Report* [1910], 41, 91, 320-322). The use of the Western model of education was not seriously challenged although sensitivity and accommodation to cultural issues were encouraged. The chapter devoted to the "relating of Christian truth to indigenous thought and feeling" concludes with a number of recommendations for Christian education to be more indigenous and to promote an indigenous Christian church. The recommendations made in this report continue to be a part of mission theory and practice today.

First, truth from whatever source should be recognized and the Christian elements extracted from it. Second, the missionaries should not "transplant to the country in which they labour that form or type of Christianity which is prevalent in the lands from which they have come, but to lodge in the hearts of the people the fundamental truths of Christianity, in the confidence that these are fitted for all nations and classes, in a type of Christian life and institution consonant with the genius of each of the several nations". Third, the missionary spirit should be "constructive, not destructive" in dealing with societies by commending what is "good in their thought or practice." Fourth, the missionary should be well-versed "with the ethical and religious systems which prevail among the people to whom he brings the Christian message, both as they are taught in the books and as they are commonly held among the people." This allows the missionary to "enforce his presentation of Christian ideals of conduct by appeal to neglected elements of the prevalent non-Christian systems." Fifth, existing "native literature" should be utilized if it is suitable for the purpose of Christian education. Sixth, Christian education should assist in the development of "native literature permeated with Christian ideas." Seventh, religious worship and instruction should be done in the vernacular of the people. Eighth, the work of "acclimatising" the Christian message must move beyond the missionary to the "native teachers" (*Report* [1910], 263-266).

The above concerns indicate the important role given to education as a missiolocial means of developing Christian leaders. There was an increased sense of awareness of paying attention to the culture of the people and working toward making educational goals assist in the growth of indigenous churches with well-trained leaders. However, despite the greater emphasis on creating indigenous churches, Western education became a primary means of training leaders.

An example of the position of education in the mission endeavor may be seen in the example of the work of the Methodist Church in Meru, Kenya, which began shortly after the Edinburgh Conference. It was the first Protestant church to establish a mission station there. It was established in September of 1912 with a school established shortly thereafter in 1913 "to teach both academic and technical subjects" (Nthamburi 1982, 60). The Western missionary compound combined the missionaries' housing with a school to separate the students from the African community's influence. As Nthamburi notes, "It was generally envisaged that to know Christian principles one had to have access to Christian literature. . . . The school and the Church which began at the same time in 1913 had complementary roles to play, and they slowly but surely claimed the allegiance of the Meru." Reaching the Meru was accomplished "with the introduction of education and medical work, curiosity coupled with the need to acquire white man's magic [which] led the Meru to the pursuit of knowledge and power" (1982, 67). In the twenty-first century the educational influence of the Methodist church through such educational institutions is seen through the prevalence of many religious, political, economic, and educational leaders taking on important functions in various aspect of Kenya's socio-cultural and socio-economic activities.

Mission theory such as the "three-selfs" and the "indigenous church" concepts were seen as compatible with the goals of education. In fact education became the quintessential means by which the indigenous, self-governing, self-supporting, and self-propagating churches could be established. This was particularly true as education was seen as providing the means to raise up both men and women in leadership, taking on the roles of the Western missionaries, teachers and preachers. Institutionally-educated Christians were seen as the answer to the leadership needs and the future strength of the church. By the 1938 Tambaram, Madras International Missionary conference the call for a renewal of theological education went out, the fulfillment of which would have to wait until after World War II. Robert W. Ferris summarizes a number of reports that were produced between the Second World War and the institution of the Theological Education Fund (TEF) that drew attention to "the vast need for ministry training in the developing world" (1990, 10).

Education and Post Colonial Vision

The need for improved education, as well as theological education, in the developing world would be a continual theme for the coming post-World War II decades with a growing nationalism present in the new nation-states. Education itself would be seen as the key to the success of the emerging new independent nation-states in the religious, socio-political and economic spheres as they looked toward the future. Better theological education would be pursued using a Western model.

Western education was instrumental in educating the elite who would provide the core leaders in the independent nations. These leaders generally worked to maintain the socio-economic systems inherited from the West. Education played an important role in the new independent states in "promoting economic and social development after the achievement of independence" (Sifuna 1990, 76-77). "To be precise, new nations in Africa see education in relation to economic development. Education stands at the very centre of nation-building, in its economic development, in the business of social planning and development of political institutions" (Makulu 1971, 31). President Julius K. Nyerere from the socialist perspective notes, "In order to train Tanzanians for the middle and senior posts in the administration and the economy of the country, it was necessary immediately after independence to emphasize the creation of secondary and postsecondary educational facilities" (1977, 11). Political leaders of the emerging nations and the populations as a whole "saw education as an instrument of power, either a tool for transforming Africans into black Europeans, or a tool to gain power and wealth through 'modernization'" (Curtin *et al.* 1995, 484). African political leadership was forced to wrestle with the tension between cultural traditions and modernity (Assensoh 1998, 149).

Organizations and institutions from the West played pivotal roles in the expansion of education in the early years of the newly independent African nations. A series of conferences, beginning at Addis Ababa in 1961, were sponsored by UNESCO which provided forums to discuss educational concerns and set priorities for the educational goals of the various developing nations. Attention at these conferences focused primarily on using education to provide more manpower for modern productivity. Makulu delineates four educational concerns that the Addis Ababa Conference identified. First, there is a need for the "development of education in relation to African cultural and socio-cultural factors." Second, leaders should develop "an inventory of educational needs for economic and social developments." Third, there needs to be a realization that education is "a basic factor in economic and social development" of African countries. Fourth, "patterns of international co-operation for the promotion and implementation of programmes of educational development" should be developed (1971, 32-33). As Sifuna observes, "The orientation of education shifted towards training Africans to fill hi-level positions in the public and private sectors . . ." (1990, 80).

There was a sense of optimism with the emergence of the new independent nation-states. In essence, continuing Western education was seen as foundational to moving Africa toward greater "development." Greater financial expenditures, curriculum changes, and improvements in the quality of education became apparent. However, that optimism has been tarnished by the economic and political realities of many countries in Africa (Blakemore and Cooksey 1981, 215). Theological education was also influenced by viewing the Western educational enterprise as the answer to missional concerns and to the advancement of the rising independent states.

Searching for Contextual Theological Education in Modern Africa

Christian leadership in Africa was developing within the context of the new nationalism, modernization and the modern "knowledge sector," all of which were bringing forces to bear on the traditional values. Christian leaders also were often influenced by the Western education with its modern enlightenment biases. Between the modern industrial forces, the "bureaucratic form of social organization," and Western education system as it was being passed down, a reevaluation of theological education was initiated.

Shortly before the 1961 UNESCO sponsored conferences on educational concerns and setting priorities for the educational goals of the various developing nations, the Theological Education Fund (TEF) was initiated which called for the improvement of theological education in developing nations. The First Mandate (1958-64) centered on improving ministerial training through raising the theological education standards by "duplicating, as best they could within their own cultural settings, the patterns of the Western theological seminaries" (Bergquist 1973, 244). Shoki Coe points out that the First Mandate did not totally ignore the indigenous emphasis and included the statement that TEF should seek "to develop and strengthen indigenous theological education" (1973, 235).

The Second Mandate of the TEF (1965-69) was a call to "rethink" the ministry training in the theological institutions. Coe's 1962 paper, "A Rethinking of Theological Training for the Ministry in the Younger Churches Today," indicates the direction TEF would follow.[1] Coe states,

> The excellence to be sought should be defined in terms of the kind of theological training which leads to a real encounter between the student and the Gospel in terms of his own forms of thought and culture, and to a living dialogue between the church and its environment. The aim should be to use resources so as to help teachers and students to a deeper understanding of the Gospel in the context of the particular cultural and religious setting of the Church, so that the Church may come to a deeper understanding of itself as a missionary community sent into the world and to a more effectual encounter with the life of the society. (1973, 236)

With the Third Mandate of the TEF from 1970 to 1977, there was the "call for reform in theological education." The central question being asked was what was theological education in the "Third World" to look like given the drastic changes and cries for justice and liberation that were being sounded. Coe points to theological education as responding to three areas: "the wide spread crisis of faith, and search for meaning in life"; "the urgent issues of human development and social justice"; and the "dialectic between a universal technological civilization and local cultural and religious situations" (1973, 237).

As noted in chapter 2, it is in the Third Mandate that Coe verbalized the concepts of "contextuality" and "contextualization." Coe's introduction of the term "contextualization" would have far-reaching effects in missiological thinking and practice, but for Coe it had its genesis in his struggle to contextualize theological education. As he states, "In these years of search and renewal I had become more and more convinced that theological education, for better or for worse, occurs invariably as interaction between text and context, and out of this interaction the form is shaped" (1973, 237).

Lois McKinney adds to the call for reform when she succinctly notes three of the major areas in need of reform. First is the "overreliance on a professional clergy." Second is the "overreliance on residence seminaries." Third is the "myopia that looks upon modes of theological education practiced in the United States, England, or Germany as being equally appropriate in Brazil, Kenya, or Indonesia" (1980, 182-183). Other calls for the "renewal" of theological education would continue to be articulated. Robert W. Ferris' book *Renewal in Theological Education* provides an overview of these (1990).

The predominant method for training ordained leaders was through the western-style theological education system imported into the mission field or through sending potential ministers to institutions of higher education in Western countries. The limitations of this method were coming under increasing review. The difficulties posed by a western-style education system led to missionaries looking for alternative training methods by which to meet the needs of the rising number of Christians, churches, and ministry obligations. Also, missiological concerns for indigenous churches, contextualizing the message and the search for better-trained indigenous ministers within their cultural context gave rise to calls to reform institutional theological education. Theological Education by Extension (TEE) became a major "alternative" by which to provide theological education more contextually in mission areas.

Before Coe's development of the concept of "contextualization," Theological Education by Extension (TEE) was developed to integrate theological teaching to the indigenous leaders "within their social, economic, cultural, educational, family and ecclesial realities" (Kinsler 1999, 12).[2] Emery notes a number of contextual factors that precipitated the call for change in the institutional style education program so that it would respond to the larger cultural context. First, education needs to be available to the leaders already integrated in the local community. Second, students would not be required to leave their community, family, and livelihood. Third, the courses could be adjusted to fit the different academic levels and learning paces of the students. Fourth, financial support would be reduced. Fifth, the program could be carried on when foreign personnel were not present. Sixth, the educational training and ministerial development could be carried out at more than "one cultural level" (1963, 126-129).

By 1980 Africa was seeing the greatest growth in the number of TEE students, even surpassing Latin America where it began. TEE was seen as a possible answer to the lack of trained church ministers for the growing number of churches while providing more contextual training.[3] As Hogarth, Gatimu, and Barrett note in their study, *Theological Education in Context: 100 Extension Programmes in Contemporary Africa,*

> The church in Africa today as in other parts of the world is facing possibly the most massive serious crisis in its entire history. It is primarily a crisis of numbers, where too many Christians have far too few pastors to guide and shepherd them. But it is not only a crisis of numbers. Pressures from both within and outside the church are calling it to an examination of its relevance to the life context in which it finds itself, and within this overall framework and context to examine more particularly the educational system. (1983, 6)

The "relevance" of TEE to the "life and context" of the growing church, particularly in Africa, was constantly under scrutiny during this time period. Throughout this "period of rapid expansion" a significant amount of literature was produced in discussion of the need to train the pastors within their actual ministerial and community contexts, using an extension rather than an extraction model (Hogarth *et al.* 1983, 28). Contextual considerations were seen to include the historical, sociological, economic, and educational realities of those being trained (Kinsler 1981, 177-178).

However, by the mid-1980s there was increasing criticism of TEE. Kinsler observes that TEE had "come of age" and that its shortcomings could no longer be overlooked. "TEE must submit to the same rigorous critique that has been applied to other forms of theological education" (1983, 16).

With the publication of *Cyprus: TEE Comes of Age* in 1986, a period of evaluation was well on its way with its critical reflection on TEE. Lois McKinney argues in this volume that TEE failed to keep its "promise of transformation and renewal in theological education." Focusing on the lack of separation between "a schooling approach to education" and a "developmental and church based" approach, she further notes,

> TEE programs take theological education to the students, but for the most part they have done so in a schooling mode. And because of this, my opinion is that most of these programs have stopped short of the radical renewal of churches and church leadership that seemed to be promised by the TEE movement. (1986, 28)

McKinney defines TEE as "the contextual experiential development of servant leaders for the church." By contextual, she means that actual ministers are trained in their community life and work situations where the major focus of their education relates to their church and community context "so their learning becomes experiential" (1986, 29-30). She seems to be indicating that contextualization of theological education has only taken place in changing location rather than substance.

From a non-evangelical perspective, the book *Theological Education in Africa: Quo Vadimus?* examines theological education and TEE's influence and usefulness for greater contextuality (1990). Basil Manning identifies two crucial sociological factors for an effective TEE program. First, there is a need "to avoid the mistakes of the past and begin to train people who have the tools to relate theology to living situations . . . in order that the message can speak to real people in real situations. . . ." Second, there is a need to provide courses that deal with pressing societal, economic, and ethical issues confronting the African context (1990, 81).

Stewart G. Snook notes in his volume *Developing Leaders through Theological Education by Extension: Case Studies from Africa* that seventy percent of the TEE administrators surveyed indicated that TEE was "conducive to contextualization." Other marks of success for TEE were identified, such as "expanded programs," "church growth," "developing leaders," "growth of individuals," "acceptance by the church" and "evangelism" (1992, 45-50).

Theological Education by Extension remains a significant influence in Africa as many such programs continue along with the more traditional residential schools. Kiranga Gatimu observes that 342 "church based TEE programmes" in Africa are listed in the "Christian Learning Materials Centre at Karen in Nairobi" (1999, 11).

TEE is one attempt to emphasize the "bottom up" direction and life-situation centered position. Others have noted the need for both TEE style schooling, i.e. decentralized, as well as centralized institutions to accomplish the educational goals in contemporary Africa (Pobee 1990, 62; Manning 1990, 73; Makhulu 1990, 2-3). Kinsler argues that both models should work together to construct diversified and integrated models of theological education. He identifies five "key issues" in setting the missiological atmosphere for fostering improved contextualization: the nature of the ministry; the model of theological education; the relationship between theological education and the agents of ministry; "personal, ecclesial, and social transformation; and structurally rooted in the realities where participants live, work, and carry out their ministries" (1999, 11-15).

In the All Africa TEE Conference held in Livingston, Zambia in 2006 the All Africa Theological Education by Extension Association (AATEEA) was formed and collaboration between the TEE programs, and residential school programs were explored and encouraged (Gaikwad 2007, 25-27). From that conference, a number of initiatives related to TEE are identified in some sectors of theological education in the twenty-first century. Colin Smith discussed moving urban mission courses out of the college context and into "Kibera," a Nairobi slum area, to make theological education more contextual (2007, 16). Kinsler notes, "We believe that there has been a significant shift away from the polarization between TEE and residential programs and concepts of theological education toward an increasingly diverse use of methods, models, and concepts of theological education." This has given rise to the concept "Diversified

Theological Education" (2007, 10). He believes "the key to TEE's success is weekly or bi-monthly or even monthly gatherings to debate and deepen and apply what has already been studied individually." Such gatherings, he stresses, are useful at regional and national levels "to share more widely critical issues and challenges of ministry and mission." He advocates for partnering with "ecclesial and educational institutions" which are made more convenient through computer access. "Each of the components of the learning system should add to the essential processes of action/reflection, to the hermeneutical circle of social analysis/biblical foundation/concrete action, to personal/ecclesial/social transformation, to growth in knowledge/abilities/ attitudes" (2007, 13).

Kinsler continues this discussion in his book *Diversified Theological Education: Equipping All of God's People*. He advocates for "diversified theological education," i.e. DTE. "As the top-down solutions, locally and globally, are most likely to fail" because of the continued disparity between poor and the wealthy in economic and healthcare areas, he sees the value of a bottom-up movement. He contends, "So we must turn, sooner or later, to grassroots, community-based movements. . . . And we must ask our theological formation programs, especially TEE and DTE, what resources and models and curricula they can offer in response to these vital and urgent challenges of our time" (2008, 20).

The emphasis among evangelicals on a more contextual form of theological education on the mission field was very influential on mission theory and practice in Churches of Christ. This emphasis, particularly on TEE, influenced missionaries who developed church planting ministries in Kenya.

Non-Institutional Approach and TEE in Church of Christ Mission Literature

The effects of this re-envisioning theological education can be seen with its influence on the mission work of Church of Christ missionaries in Africa in the 1970s and 80s. They were influenced by their own missiologists and other evangelical missiologists in their church planting ministries and leadership training. They utilized informal, non-formal, and formal forms of theological education. A modified form of TEE was particularly influential with a number of the mission teams engaged in various locations in Kenya. In planning the disengagement of most of the American missionaries from the mission work in Kenya a system of theological education utilizing extension centers and a central institution had come into existence through the initial impetus of these missionaries. These centers are now primarily administered by Kenyan leaders. Literature from Churches of Christ missiologists provide a background to the goals and methodology of theological education as practiced in Kenya.

George Gurganus who was a missionary to Japan became the father of missiological training in Churches of Christ colleges. The book entitled *Guidelines for World Evangelism* which he edited deals with areas of "vital concern" in missions and mission strategy (1976). It reflects the missiological thinking of a number of missiologists from among the Churches of Christ and their application of missiological research for Churches of Christ. Ed Mathews' chapter on "Leadership Training in Missions" calls attention to "one of the most important innovations" in missions, Leadership Training by Extension (LTE). Mathews notes that LTE is commonly called TEE. He prefers LTE to TEE because he feels TEE refers primarily to the training of preachers where as he uses LTE to refer to the training of leaders who may or may not preach (1976, 123). As a professor of Missions and Director of the Missions Department at Abilene Christian University in the 1980s, he was influential in bringing concepts of leadership training to prospective American missionaries who would later work in Kenya, of which the author was one. He critiques both the institutional model of theological education and the TEE model. He notes problems with the institutional model which LTE addresses: the failure to train enough leaders, the high cost, the type of students it draws, and the cultural dislocation of students (1976, 127-129). He continues by listing "three problems" that the "resident Bible schools" have regarding type of students: age, aptitude, and education. The age problem related to older family men not being able to attend resident institutions because of family considerations. The aptitude problem arises from people attending that have not shown any "prior evidence" of aptitude in leadership. The education problem is related to not training the proven church leaders because they do not meet the education requirements of institutions that primarily teach in English (1976, 128-129). He views the institutional and extension models as not contradictory but complementary. He concludes that LTE is "a promising aid to world evangelism" and moving in the "proper direction" but warns against it being seen as the final solution (1976, 137).

Daniel Hardin in his book *Mission: A Practical Approach to Church Sponsored Mission Work* draws from his experience as a missionary and director of Korea Christian College (1978). He notes a number of problems associated with the institutional approach to biblical training patterned after the U.S. college and university systems. His critique, among others, of the institutional model set the tone for many of the American missionary teams in Kenya. Emphasis on the indigenous church model and a non-institutional approach to leadership training greatly influenced the mission teams which instituted and set patterns for theological education in Churches of Christ in Kenya.

By the late 1970s a number of American missionary teams in Kenya were utilizing concepts of LTE in their leadership training programs (Kenya Mission Team 1980, 37, 41). The general direction of leadership training among Churches of Christ in Kenya may best be seen from Gailyn Van Rheenen's early book *Biblically Anchored Missions*. He notes the problems of the institutional model and proposes two other models, localized courses and LTE, which he argues overcome a number of the institutional drawbacks (1983, 33-34). Gailyn Van Rheenen influenced a number of mission teams' perspectives in church planting and leadership training. His book, *Missions: Biblical Foundations & Contemporary Strategies*, reflects his perception of leadership training after his mission team's disengagement from the field in Kenya. Van Rheenen points to the applicability of all three modes of leadership training, formal, non-formal, and informal, in the mission context. He notes that "four general guidelines" are fundamental in every context. First, the training should be appropriate to the leaders' ministries and time schedules. Second, "effective training integrates various modes of training." Third, the modes and methods of training should vary with the "maturity level of the Christian movement." Fourth, leadership training should be integrated with a "comprehensive strategy for phasing out missionary personnel" (1996, 170-174).

The influence of this literature can be seen in the Meru, Kenya mission team's writings related to leadership training. LTE was the primary means of non-formal theological education used in Meru. Two church growth studies have chapters devoted to leadership training describing the goals, strategies, and modes of theological education used by the Meru mission team (Granberg *et al.* 1987; Granberg *et al.* 1990). By 1990, in discussion with other American missionaries who had well-established works, the Meru team began plans for developing a training center for theological training to move beyond the LTEE (Leadership Training by Extension and Evangelism) training that was currently being used.[4] The Meru team was responding to the Meru

Christians' desire for more formal education opportunities. Meru Christians perceived formal education as experienced in Kenya's educational system as equally important in theological education. LTEE was seen as useful but not leading to higher educational goals. The training center was seen as a means of providing higher education that would "serve to bridge the learning gap which exists between regular LTEE training courses and formal biblical training such as that provided by the Great Commission School in Nairobi" (Granberg *et al.* 1990, 93). This later developed into the extension system for Churches of Christ that is currently in use in Kenya.

Despite the increasing use of training centers and the establishment of the Nairobi Great Commission School (NGCS), there is limited literature on training leaders by Kenyan leaders of Churches of Christ. There is only brief mention of theological education in the Africans Claiming Africa Conference in 1992, and most of that was associated with support and financial concerns. However, currently Kenyan leaders are at the forefront of directing the training centers and providing the majority of the teaching.

Conclusion

The reality in Kenya today is that both the institutional and extension models are accepted and are being used by Kenya Churches of Christ as well as others. The present system of extension centers and a central institution developed during the height of American missionary activity in Kenya. It evolved from informal and non-formal TEE styles, moving toward a more formal education model while trying to maintain a contextual environment. The mission teams that instituted significant church planting ministries and established the majority of the centers were highly influenced by indigenous church principles and the concept of contextualization.

Before evaluating the current theological education process of Kenya Churches of Christ, an overview of its search for contextual leadership training will give one a sense of the historical development of this mission. Chapter 4 will trace the missionaries' vision and ministries as they moved from a simply indigenous church model to taking seriously the need for developing an environment that fosters self-theologizing in search of Hiebert's fourth self.

"How is it possible to train servants of God for Africa without taking into consideration African life styles and ways of thinking?"

Isaac Zokoué 1990

CHAPTER 4
Search for Contextual Leadership Training: One Mission's Experience

Churches of Christ in Kenya have developed a theological training system since the 1990s that can best be described as a decentralized extension system. This system was not initially envisioned by the mission teams who later would facilitate the development and construction of the majority of the training centers. The extension system arose after mission teams had wrestled in various ways with training church ministers in their local areas, usually among specific linguistic people groups. The American missionary teams developed their areas of ministry independently of each other and as a result the various extension centers developed semi-independently of one another with the Nairobi Great Commission School (NGCS) acting as a central training center by which curriculums and graduation requirements could be coordinated.

One unanimous perception of the training centers by those interviewed in this research was that these centers are important to the local areas and that there needs to be more of them offering broader levels of training. However, no research has been done analyzing the system currently in use or evaluating the perspectives of those that matriculated through the system as to its perceived value to their ministries, limitations, potential for the future, and the level of self-theologizing it fosters.

To understand the development of the current system, one needs to explore the earlier vision of the American missionary teams' ministries and leadership training views and visions. They were not monolithic but shared some commonalities and desires for providing mature leadership in the local churches which gave rise to the present system of theological education.

Background of the Established Mission Areas

The mission efforts of Churches of Christ in Kenya may be divided roughly into three periods: first, the ground breaking period; second, the vernacular period; third, the phase-out period. This author participated in the last two periods in conjunction with ministry among the Meru.

The first period began shortly after Kenya won its independence in 1963 and covers the years to 1972. The first American missionaries began their work in urban Nairobi and Central Kenya, but they also would make some of the first contacts in other areas of Kenya that later teams would select as the people groups with which they would concentrate their mission efforts. By 1969, work was initiated in Western Kenya starting in Kakamega and later in Kisumu. The missionaries in this group were advised by the missionaries in Central Kenya to focus on Western Kenya. Both of these mission efforts used Swahili and English in their ministries, particularly because of the mixture of various tribes in both areas (Merritt 1980, 40).

The year 1973 saw the beginning of the second wave of American missionaries into Kenya. The second period was initiated with missionaries stressing the need for teaching in the vernacular. The Sotik mission team that began the work among the Kipsigis was influential on most of the subsequent mission efforts, including the Eldoret team which located near the Sotik team among the North Kalenjin in the west, the Meru team in north-central Kenya, and the Malindi team among the Mwijikenda tribes along the coast. It is from this period the mission strategy of the Churches of Christ's missionaries is articulated and generally agreed upon. By 1980 the "Kenya Mission Team" articulated its mission perspective as a "philosophy of Church Growth." The characteristics of this philosophy were listed as "body oriented," "harvest oriented," "identificational," and "autonomous" congregations (Van Rheenen 1980, 6-8). The "philosophy of Church Growth" was particularly influential in the areas that were chosen for the purpose of this study although three of the areas, North Kalenjin, Meru, and the Mwijikenja, would not see mission teams working in them until later in the 1980s.

Mission teams were concerned with establishing self-sustainable, indigenous churches with strong leaderships which would be able to carry on the work initiated by the missionaries. In contemplating the future, the mission teams envisioned the American missionaries phasing out of their mission efforts and turning the work over to "mature" ministers and leaders in the local churches. However, leadership training took several forms.

The Development of Contextual Leadership Training among Churches of Christ in Kenya

The Sotik mission team set the foundation for the vernacular period of Churches of Christ in Kenya. Their work provided a foundational model which future teams adapted for their particular mission contexts. Their first church growth study covering the years 1973 to 1977 does not directly address leadership training. Leaders are seen as arising out of planted churches. They note the future need for written material for training leaders when they state, "The solution to the whole problem is teaching a few 'faithful' men who in turn will teach others, (II Tim. 2:2), men who can deal with cultural problems and who know the language as their mother tongue" (Allison 1977, 28). Leadership training was informal at this point with local church evangelists accompanying the American missionaries on evangelistic trips to new areas (Allison 1977, 38).

The 1980 church growth report from the Sotik mission team which included mission teams' reports from other western Kenya mission teams and from central Kenya provides a few insights into their perspective on contextual training of leaders.[1] The Sotik mission team focused primarily on evangelism with "one of the premier aims" being "to involve as many nationals as possible in evangelism" (Allison 1980, 78). This reflects what Van Rheenen calls "personalized training" where leaders are "trained in action" much like Jesus' training of the twelve. This is in contrast to the "institutional classroom setting" where the teacher cannot demonstrate or model the concepts being taught and the students are so "busy studying the message that they have little opportunity to apply the message." The cross-cultural use of the "institutional mode" was seen as having several major limitations.

First, the institution is foreign created and usually foreign controlled. Second, there is a "dislocation of students" where they are placed "in a Western environment; distinct Western solutions to problems are learned that may not fit the local situation." Third, students learn in a *lingua franca* rather than their heart language (1983a, 30-33). Van Rheenen summarizes their perspective,

> Our emphasis was first church initiation and maturation and secondarily leadership training. We believed that leaders develop naturally in a growing, vibrant fellowship. If leaders are trained before a church develops cohesiveness, a distinction typically is made between the clergy and the laity. If . . . many men are simultaneously matured in the context of a vibrant body of believers, many more men evolve into evangelists, elders, and deacons. Thus we initially matured churches and only at a later time trained leaders who grew out of these fellowships. (1985, 83)

Evangelism was the priority for the Sotik team and their use of a nonformal mode of theological education fit well with training leaders with what they called an "identificational" and "on-the-job" approach. This approach emphasized that learning takes place best within the context of life situations within the cultural context, cognitive knowledge is more effectively internalized and applied, and evangelists rely on the support of the congregation, thus encouraging self-supporting leadership (Van Rheenen 1983b, 42-44). By 1981 the Sotik team was using special three-day leadership seminars beyond the previous evangelists' meetings. These too were directed toward practical church planting goals (1983b, 38).

The vernacular period of team missions in Kenya saw the rise of two prevalent forms of leadership training. Each of these forms was used in an attempt to avoid the problems of the "Western institutional model." These were the non-formal "localized courses" and Leadership Training by Extension (LTE). By 1981 "localized courses" and LTE were being used by the Sotik team (Van Rheenen 1981, 52-53). Van Rheenen defines "localized courses" as "programs of Bible study organized and overseen by local churches" with the possible assistance of missionaries and evangelists. The sponsoring church or churches invite other congregations to participate and may ask them to provide speakers for various lessons (1983a, 33-34). LTE was also being implemented by the mission team working among the Abaluyia (Stephens 1980, 37, 41).

Four mission teams would enter the field in the first half of the 80s. The Eldoret team which was initially recruited by Van Rheenen located on the northern border of the Kipsigis region among the North Kalenjin arriving in 1982 (North Kalenjin Team 1987, 41). The Kitale team located in a multi-tribal region north of the Eldoret team beginning in 1981. The Meru team which located in north central Kenya began arriving in December of 1982. The Meru team had used the Sotik team as a resource before starting their work in Kenya. The Malindi team which located on the coast at Malindi arrived in 1985 and 1986 (Malindi Team 1987, 6).

A "bible school" format for training leaders was used by the Kitale mission team within a year of arriving on the field in 1981. By 1985 they had "decentralized" their training and were taking the courses to the students in their church areas (Kitale Team 1987, 22).

Monte Cox outlines the Eldoret team's direction and development of theological education. They first "emphasized informal, oral biblical training through evangelism patterned after the approach of the Sotik team and informed by the 'discipling' method of Jesus as outlined by Robert Coleman (1963)" (Cox 1999, 149-158). Recognizing some of the limitations of the informal approach, particularly the slow growth of "raw Bible knowledge" and its "tendency to be haphazard," they began adding additional training venues. Cox states,

> The team responded with special programs such as annual preachers' meetings in which the volunteer evangelists gathered for several days of in-depth study of a biblical text, (usually a biblical book related to evangelism). They conducted "mini-preachers' meetings" throughout the year in clusters of churches with a similar format. On occasions, they organized "marathons" in which a group of leaders in a given area would study an entire book of the Bible in a single setting. (1999, 153)

The Eldoret team was moved to consider more formal forms of theological education as they sensed a "growing frustration among volunteer evangelists" who felt they were receiving inadequate biblical preparation (Cox 1999, 156). By 1992 after the Nairobi Great Commission School was opened, they began to hear calls by some leaders for further training. Cox notes two reservations the Eldoret team had in supporting further education of this sort.

> First, they feared that evangelists who went to Nairobi for two years of formal schooling would have neither the desire nor the necessary skills to return to rural ministry in the future. Second, they suspected that those who earned a degree at the school would expect to enter full-time ministry with financial support from their rural churches, support

that the missionaries believed the churches could not yet provide. In that case, the missionaries feared that the graduates would expect support from them. (1999, 157)

An LTE program was put in place in 1995 as "a compromise between the formal schooling" and the "discipling approach." This program ran until 1997 when it was put on hold as "the missionaries contemplated what to do next in the way of theological education." The one remaining missionary "felt a lot of pressure" to "upgrade the LTE program to the Extension Program of the Nairobi Great Commission School" (Cox 1999, 158).

Meru Mission Team: A Case Study in Leadership Training Development in Kenya

The work of the Kenya Church of Christ in Meru had its beginning in 1979 with contacts through correspondence courses which were offered. Four churches were planted with the help of visiting American missionaries from Nairobi. Three of the churches were on the verge of collapse by 1982, primarily due to poor leadership and lack of missionary presence for teaching. Two of those three would later totally collapse (Granberg *et al.* 1984, 18-21).

The Meru Mission team began arriving on the field in December of 1982 with the final two families arriving in February of 1984. Within six months the first two families that had come to the field had returned to the U.S. and less than a year later a third family returned to the U.S. This left two families who primarily developed the direction of the long-term ministry in Meru.

The two families of the Meru mission team had graduated from Harding University and Harding Graduate School of Religion where the team originally developed it mission strategy. The Meru team was also influenced by the Sotik team. They assisted the Meru team in doing a survey trip with one of their team members accompanying them in 1982. They also met with Gailyn Van Rheenen who was Missionary in Residence at Harding University before going to the field. The following quote indicates the similarities in the approach of the Meru team with both the Sotik and Eldoret teams.

If we are to fulfill our mission task, we must be able to communicate the gospel in ways which readily allow the people to understand, accept, and practice the will of God. The implications of this are demonstrated in: 1) going to the people, 2) identifying with the people, 3) speaking the language of the people, 4) knowing the culture of the people, and 5) preaching to the needs of the people. (Granberg *et al.* 1984, 7)

The Meru team specifically oriented its work within a village context "rather than bringing them to a central location or institution." This approach was seen to have four contextual advantages. First, "the church receives credibility as a functioning part of the community as it matures within the local setting." Second, "the influence of the gospel can work more directly among groups and families rather than individuals." Third, "individuals can maintain their ties and functions in the community with less disruption, which in turn gives them greater influence among their families and neighbors." Fourth, "local patterns of communication and leadership can be seen more easily and tapped for spreading the gospel" (Granberg *et al.* 1984, 8). The Meru team adopted the stages of church growth established by the Sotik team and saw leadership training as beginning at the established church stage after the initial evangelization of the community and a viable church was established.[2] Leaders that emerged from these new congregations would serve as resource people for evangelizing in other communities and were encouraged and taught to evangelize through informal teaching and on-the-job experience with and without a missionary involved. One of the goals of the last three stages of the church, that is, established, independent, and mature, was to "produce other fellowships" (Granberg *et al.* 1984, appendix 2).

In 1985, the Meru team made a visit to Sotik to observe their work and receive some input for the mission effort in Meru. One observation that came out of that trip and influenced the direction of the Meru team was what appeared to be the lack of a coherent leadership training program. The Meru team agreed with the informal method employed by the Sotik team but failed to see an organized direction in the leadership training.

By 1987 the church planting ministry in Meru saw the establishment of fifteen churches that comprised over four hundred members. Working with fifteen relatively new congregations with emerging leaderships raised an awareness of the need to focus on some type of contextual leadership training. The chosen focus was reported in the 1987 church growth study in chapters five and seven entitled "Leadership" and "Leadership Training by Extension and Evangelism" where the preliminary leadership training ideas began to be implemented (Granberg *et al.* 1987, 67, 96).[3] The impetus for initiating a strong leadership training program early on in the work was the limited number of missionaries working among the Meru as well as the local need for mature Christian leaders for the new churches and their communities.

The 1990 church growth study found the work in Meru with a decadal growth rate of 900% with twenty congregations with a combined membership of 900 members. By 1990 leadership training had become the primary focus of the work for the two original team members (Granberg *et al.* 1990, 29-30). New team members were encouraged to focus on evangelism, church planting and maturation before moving into leadership training to increase their understanding of the contextual situation and to develop relationships with communities, churches, and the emerging leaders.

In the middle of 1994, this author and his family returned to the U.S. There were thirty-two churches with 1800 to 1900 active Christians. At that time, the leadership program known as LTEE was being carried out by the remaining American missionaries and local Meru leaders.

The Influence of TEE

The influence of the TEE concept went back to this author's and his co-worker's missions training in graduate school where TEE was taught as a contextual method of leadership training. The early writings of Lois McKinney, George Patterson, and Ted Ward were particularly influential in developing what became known as "LTEE" (Leadership Training by Extension and Evangelism).[4] The 1987 church growth study notes that

> the program in Meru is significantly different from most TEE programs. The men we train have an average educational level of 4th to 5th grade. Our program is not designed to produce university level students. We are taking emerging leaders from the churches and training them—using the education they already possess. It focuses on biblical knowledge and practical church work. It is available to both the semi-literate and literate. (Granberg *et al.* 1987, 96)

The focus of the LTEE program in Meru may be surmised from the headings of various sections of the two chapters written by this author. The sections entitled "The Servant Church Leaders," "Training Leaders within the Congregational Setting," "Biblical Instruction," "Evangelistic Experiences," "Church Maturation Experiences," "Growth in Abilities," "The Maturing Process of Leaders," "Leadership Levels," "Extension," and "Evangelism" fit very much under McKinney's definition of TEE as "the contextual experiential development of servant leaders for the church" (Granberg *et al.* 1987, 67-102).

Meru Mission Team's Search for Contextual Theological Education

"The first trial leadership training course was held at the Mukuuni church in April 1986." Eight men attended the first course held at the community coffee factory. The meetings were held every week for six weeks. The first course was used to test material written in Kimeru developed by the missionaries to Meru. Topics studied in the initial course were "What is a Teacher?" "How a Teacher of the Church Should Live," "How to Study the Bible," and "How to Prepare a Lesson." Weekly assignments were to be done by the students during the intervening week in their local churches (Granberg *et al.* 1987, 96).

The LTEE program underwent a number of changes after this author and his co-worker attended a seminar by Fred Holland in 1987. Two major results came out of that seminar. Leadership training seminars were added and programmed course material began to be written and used. From the first LTEE course came the first course book on *How to Be a Teacher* followed by a second course book on *Colossians*. These two books were designed to teach students to interpret scripture through study of the biblical text. The first course provided the guidelines for biblical interpretation and application as a teacher. The programmed instruction course book on Colossians written by this author was designed to have them use the exegetical and application skills from the first course on the text of Colossians.

One of the earliest challenges faced by the Meru team in teaching leaders to preach and teach was their tendency to proof text. We felt they lacked a grasp of the context of the scriptures they were using to make a valid point so we developed our first courses to address this issue. We found that those going through the courses improved their exegetical skills and made their application on a sounder understanding of scripture. The 1987 church growth study notes that LTEE "is a type of leadership training developed to meet the needs of training church leaders within their rural environment (extension). At the same time, it allows them to gain practical experience in preaching and teaching within their home areas (evangelism)" (Granberg *et al.* 1987, 96).

By 1989 courses were regularly being taught in church cluster areas. One church among a group of churches would act as host for the LTEE course. This allowed ministers from various congregations to interact, support, share experiences, and encourage one another in their studies and ministries. Nominal fees were charged to offset a portion of the cost of the course materials.

Two major improvements in the LTEE courses occurred in 1990. First, Meru church ministers began to co-teach with the American missionaries in the program to gain more experience in preparation for being teachers and seminar leaders. Second, women were incorporated into the LTEE program. Along with these two improvements, grading was changed from a pass/fail system to a percentage grade for the more advanced courses.

A general quantitative and qualitative evaluation of the status of the LTEE program was completed in 1990. The quantitative evaluation showed that 153 students had taken courses which represented 17% of 880 active members of the congregations. "Sixty-one percent of these students completed their courses satisfactorily. Eleven students participated under a special status. This category indicates students who are non-readers who attended the classes. A healthy 23% of the students were women. . . ." At this time there were seven church cluster groups where courses were being held in Meru. However, only nineteen courses had been taught which was well below the target of the thirty-five courses originally planned (Granberg *et al.* 1990, 86-88).

The qualitative evaluation attempted to gauge the students' responses to the level of usefulness they found the courses to be in their ministries. Feedback was collected from the students, but this was not done in any systematic way. The quantitative and qualitative evaluations surfaced a number of strengths and weakness of the LTEE program.

The strengths identified in the 1990 study, less than four years after the initiation of the program, included an improved ability of students to study material more in-depth. Second, the structured nature of the LTEE "courses with required activities and a level of standardization" helped "the students to gain confidence in their abilities and knowledge." Third, the programmed material developed by this author and his co-worker proved to improve the reading skills of those involved in the program. Fourth, the written materials allowed the students to collect resource materials for reference and review. Fifth, because students met together from various villages and congregations, they were "able to share their ministry problems and their victories with one another" which helped to develop a ministerial support system.

Sixth, the churches were "gaining greater confidence in their leaders as a trained, competent corps of leaders."

Three major weaknesses were also identified through the same study. First, it was "difficult for one course teacher (the missionary author) to teach a new course at every center within the targeted time frame of one year." This problem was compounded because of the difficulty in reaching all the areas with new courses while teaching older courses in areas where new churches had been planted. Second, the time to develop a course, write it, test it, print it, and introduce it was a major time consuming task. On average it was taking six months from development until the first course was taught. Third, there was "a loss of focus" which had developed because of the time required not only for the LTEE program but also for the Leaders' Meeting program. Both programs were beneficial and met different needs but raised issues of prioritization and the need for more Meru church leaders to take greater leadership responsibilities in training ministers (Granberg *et al.* 1990, 89-91). Looking toward the future of LTEE from the 1990 vantage point it was observed,

> the Meru work has changed considerably since the LTEE program began in 1986. The church is larger now. Congregations are looking for higher levels of leadership. There is a definite group of leaders who have reached the latter stages of leadership maturity which has not been present before in the Meru Churches of Christ. (Granberg *et al.* 1990, 89-91)

From 1991 to the middle of 1994, the priorities for the LTEE and other forms of leadership development shifted to writing materials and training leaders as course leaders. The two missionaries that initiated the program were scheduled to return to the U.S., one family in 1993 and this author and his family in the middle of 1994. During those years two significant transitions were implemented. The first was an increase in the number of church leaders teaching and co-teaching LTEE courses. Second was the building of a regional training center for all of Meru, Kambakia Training Center (KTC). Kenyans at this time were voicing a desire for a more formal type of theological education similar to the formal Kenya-wide educational system. The vision for the use of the training center was presented in the 1990 church growth study which states,

> The training center will allow us to conduct intensive training to those who are in the recognized, experienced, and mature stages of leadership. . . . We anticipate that the

> training materials used for these courses will be written on a higher academic level. This will serve to bridge the learning gap which exists between our regular LTEE training courses and formal biblical training such as that provided by the Great Commission School in Nairobi. (Granberg *et al.* 1990, 92)

The Meru team had planned to have the team members who joined the ministry later to continue the work into 2002. However, this did not come to pass leaving only one American missionary as late as 2000. Between the end of 1995 and when the last missionary phased-out, missionaries kept KTC operating and taught many of the courses. Based on the author's four visits between 1995 and 2001 to follow-up on the work in Meru, preliminary observations indicated that the proposed infrastructure and support system that were instituted in 1994 and intended to be functioning without American missionaries on site by 2002 had only been partially successful. When the last missionary family phased-out in 2000, the training center failed to operate at its potential because of the lack of qualified leadership and the missionaries' failures to prepare people adequately to administer KTC.[5]

In a meeting at KTC in the summer of 2001 with a cross-section of most of the church leaders, they expressed to this author a number of problems that were impacting the training of leaders.[6] Their observations ranged from funding concerns, transportation problems, lack of course offerings, problems with the off-site American missionary liaison, the absence of a person given responsibility for the daily running of KTC to problems with the integration of the whole program into the church communities.

Meru Leadership Training Program: Current Status

The LTEE that was begun at the local "cluster" church level was expanded by incorporating a regional training center with a curriculum compatible with the country-wide central institution, Nairobi Great Commission School (NGCS), which offers an Advanced Certificate, Advanced Diploma, and a BA degree in conjunction with Daystar University. Currently, LTEE courses continue to be held at the church clusters as church leaders see the need. Courses are held at the training center nine times a year. To date, twelve people from the Meru area have completed an Advanced Certificate level or BA degree from NGCS. Fourteen men have completed the Advanced Certificate at Kambakia Training Center (KTC) in Meru. In 2010 the Advisory Board changed the name of KTC to the Meru School of Theology (MST). Fifteen men have completed the Basic Certificate. Course attendance for current students is about twenty per course with one-third on the Advanced Certificate track and two-thirds on the Basic Certificate track. Most of the courses taught at MST are taught by Kenyans with a Kenyan leader from another area of the country teaching the Advanced Certificate course while a Meru leader teaches the Basic Certificate course.

Conclusion

This summary of leadership training development as seen through the Sotik, Eldoret, and Meru mission teams indicates the direction most of the mission teams took in training leaders resulting in a mixture of informal, non-formal and formal theological education. The directions these teams pursued were intended to provide leadership training that was as contextually connected as possible so leaders could effectively minister to people in culturally appropriate ways.

Although American missionaries were not using the terminology of "self-theologizing," their struggles with contextualizing leadership training point toward their desire for leaders to contextualize the biblical message for their cultural contexts. In Meru, specific training in the area of biblical interpretation methods was developed to assist leaders in making relevant application of scripture.

Curriculum plays a role in the theological education process in facilitating self-theologizing, though it is not the primary focus of this research. Curriculums were instrumental in the education process of the Kenya Churches of Christ and impacted the ministers who matriculated through the educational system. This research is not an evaluation of those curriculums but of the contextual applicability of the cross-cultural educational process to the cultural heritage of church ministers in providing and facilitating self-theologizing. However, the results of the study may be used to facilitate the evaluation of current cross-culturally centered curriculums in theological education. Therefore, curriculum will be discussed in relation to what educational outcomes facilitate self-theologizing.

Educational evaluation, notes Elliot Eisner, "is a process that can be directed toward three important subject matters: the curriculum itself, the teaching that is provided, and the outcomes that are realized" (1985, 200). The research process for this study will in some respects touch on all three;

however, the primary concern is with the educational process and "outcomes" as they relate to the extent to which self-theologizing is being practiced by local ministers. Elliot Eisner notes that one source for evaluating educational practices for the purpose of illuminating a situation or event in order to appreciate its significance is to interview the "students about their work and asking their views about what is transpiring. . . ." He states, "The interview is a powerful resource for learning how people perceive the situation in which they work" (1991, 81- 82). Robert Stake notes a distinction between "informal" and "formal" evaluation of education. Informal evaluation which is dependent on "casual observations, implicit goals, intuitive norms, and subjective judgment" enters into the current research process as students give their perceptions of the validity of their theological education. In such an evaluation, the evaluator seeks out and records "the opinions of the persons of special qualification. These opinions, though subjective, can be very useful and can be gathered objectively, independent of the solicitor's opinions" (1967, 523-527). Particular attention is given to "transactions" and "outcomes" which are two of the three data areas in an evaluation report as distinguished by Stake. "Transactions are the countless ways by which encounters of students with teacher, student with student, author with reader, parent with counselor" provide a "succession of engagements which comprise the process of education." "Outcomes" include such things as

> abilities, achievements, attitudes, and aspirations of students resulting from an educational experience. . . . Outcomes to be considered in evaluation include not only those that are evident, or even existent, as learning sessions end, but include application, transfer, and relearning effects which may not be available for measurement until long after. (1967, 528)

Therefore, curriculum, "transactions," and outcomes are important areas of discussion with the Kenyan ministers in order to understand the extent to which their theological education facilitated the self-theologizing they practice in their local contexts. These "transactions" and outcomes will be explored in the following chapters.

The landscape of leadership training has continued to develop in Kenya Churches of Christ with an increase in the number of extension centers as well as an increase in the number of people desiring to attend NGCS. The question is what in theological education makes it conducive to fostering self-theologizing and how do those trained in the current system evaluate how their theological education facilitated their ability to self-theologize? Is it intellectual formation focused on biblical and theological content with application to ministry which is only marginally related to the social, cultural, and historic context? Or "is it structurally rooted in those realities where the participants live and work and carry out their ministries?" (Gatimu 1999, 15)

An evaluation of the current theological education process which takes place through a combination of local training centers and a central in-country residential school is needed in light of maturing church ministers, the declining American missionary population, and the challenges facing the church ministers in Africa and Kenya specifically. Do the church ministers participating in the theological education process of Churches of Christ in Kenya perceive their education as lending itself to self-theologizing in order to meet the current needs of the church? Alternatively, is the training perpetuating Western theological education patterns that do not facilitate students' progress in self-theologizing nor bring the gospel to bear on the shared problems and culturally distinct challenges facing the current Kenyan context? The following chapter is designed to summarize the Kenyan ministers' evaluations of the theological education process to shed light on whether it is facilitating or hindering their contextualization of the Gospel and whether it is enhancing the search for the fourth self.

A person can see the sun from many different places.
African Proverb

CHAPTER 5
Evaluation of the Theological Education Process

As chapter 4 describes, over the years missionaries and Kenyan church leaders developed a decentralized theological education model that began being implemented in 1994 in hopes of providing a more contextualized education process. Since the mid 90s to the present this decentralized model has grown and continues to graduate a large number of students. However, no study has been done to evaluate how well this theological education process is meeting ministers' needs, ministry challenges, and, particularly, how well it is assisting ministers in self-theologizing. The following pages and chapter 6 attempt to listen to the voices of ministers as they evaluate their theological education in light of their contexts.

This chapter is divided into six main sections. The first section provides an overview of the ethnographic process utilized for this research. The second section reports on the ministers' overall perceptions of their informal theological education before embarking on their more formal education. Section three provides a profile of the interviewees noting their geographical locations, ages, years in ministry, and other relevant data. Section four discusses the interviewees' perceptions of the local church's view of trained leaders. The fifth section will review how the interviewees' rate their theological education. The last section summarizes how the local ministers evaluate the effectiveness of their theological education.

Ethnographic Methodology Overview

Ethnographic interviews conducted in 2005 are the primary methodology for obtaining this data. In the interview process the researcher assured the interviewees of confidentiality and the protection of identity to allow them the freedom to be open and honest. Therefore quotes and references of respondents are coded. The researcher explained to the ministers that the purpose of the interviews is to discuss the theological education they received and ways it has and continues to impact their ministries in the church and their communities in order to improve the educational process and their ministry capabilities.

The author had contact with a number of these ministers prior to these interviews, particularly in the Central province around Meru over the ten years of 1984 to 1994 when he worked in Kenya. He has also made yearly visits since that time to work with leaders. Rapport had already been established with a number of the ministers in some of the areas and in Meru especially. The author was previously known by a number of the ministers in the western and eastern areas. He built on the existing rapport and developed greater trust as the interviews were conducted and data gathered for this research. He was also involved with the development of the Kambakia Training Center (KTC) in Meru and designed the initial curriculum for it in conjunction with the Nairobi Great Commission School's curriculum.[1]

The author functioned as a participant-observer during the ten years of work in Meru with the primary focus of the last five years being involved significantly with the training of church ministers. In the seventeen years since leaving the field as a permanent resident, he has been involved in the ongoing training of ministers through visiting many local churches and teaching courses while working with church leaders in Meru to improve the curriculum and ministry goals of the Kambakia Training Center. The participant observation done over the years serves to help "elicit from people their definitions of reality and the organizing constructs of their world," in this case, their experience related to the usefulness of their theological education in facilitating self-theologizing (Goetz and LeCompte 1984, 110). The author has kept ethnographic records, recordings, fieldnotes, photographs, and collected relevant documents and records. Relevant historical information contained in documents and reports related to educational levels, as well as methods and goals of theological education and ministerial training in Churches of Christ in Kenya, were collected and analyzed as they related to research objectives.

The qualitative interviewing model "interpretive approach" proposed by Rubin and Rubin is used in this research project. This approach is designed to see "how people understand their worlds, their work, and the events they have experienced or observed." This type of research is "not about categorizing and classifying, but figuring out what events mean, how people adapt, and how they view what has happened to them and around them" within the various aspects of the complexity of life (1995, 34-35; 2005, 28).

This research utilized "responsive interviewing" where the interviewer and interviewee influence each other. Though the interviewer initially established the general direction of the interview, the conversational partner was encouraged to open more specific directions (Rubin and Rubin 2005, 31-35). The interview format was a semi-structured or focused interview approach that used a written interview guide to facilitate the acquisition of reliable and comparable data (Bernard 2002, 204-205). This approach permitted the interviewer to note patterns and themes discovered with the initial questions which allowed for preparing more specific questions (Rubin and Rubin 2005, 4). This involved an outline of "a set of topics to be explored with each respondent." The semi-structured approach allowed respondents to "express their view of a phenomenon in their own terms" (Gall, Borg, and Gall 1996, 309). Data gained in this interview process was susceptible to bias so a pilot test was conducted to ensure the integrity of the interview guide and procedure in soliciting unbiased data (Gall, Borg, and Gall 1996, 316). In order to facilitate collection of data, the interviews were digitally tape recorded and notes taken.

English is the language of higher education in Kenya and students in the Advanced Certificate and Diploma Programs must be "proficient" in it. Because the sample population is from the Advanced Programs, the interviews were conducted in English, though over ten language groups were represented. The level of proficiency varied and occasionally the grammar and syntax of the responses to questions are difficult to follow for those uninitiated in hearing English spoken as a second or third language. To make for smoother reading of this research smoother, the author has not always quoted the respondents verbatim, i.e. with grammatical mistakes. The author has removed "ah," pauses, and confusing grammatical errors. The removal of these items did not alter the meaning of the interviewees' responses.

Overall Perception of the Informal Theological Education Process

Despite the greater availability of a formal style of theological education through the extension centers, the interviewees maintain that the informal and non-formal education was helpful and still has its place in the overall training of church ministers.

> The informal training grounded me. I have to accept. I was rough, because I did not know so much about the church doctrine . . . but I do believe that the informal trained me on who is a Christian, how a Christian should stay and worship pattern now biblical and all those kind of things. I mean they grounded me in the faith so much that I went out to speak. I would speak what is doctrinally sound from the scriptures. So I do accept that, again, informal training was useful to me because at that particular time I was not able to leave my station of work and be fully in the formal school for training. (N01 2005)

The continued uses of both formal and informal biblical training are seen as needed, even with the availability of extension centers because "not every leader is able to go for the formal training" (N02 2005).

The interviewees did not disparage the use of informal training and saw it as valuable although not as organized or as in-depth, at least in comparison to more formal training. A leader from the coast notes the higher degree of organization in the formal education when he states,

> But it was not all that organized. Yeah, it was some kind of a seminar where we could come for two or three days, maybe on a specific lesson that they are teaching, that has something to do with the work that we are doing. Yeah, but I, when I came to join the training center, that is when we had now the formal teaching, which is more organized and they were following some kind of a syllabus. (C04 2005)

A leader from Nairobi observes that more indepth learning is possible in the formal setting while immediate practical application is possible with the informal mode (N01 2005). Other leaders note that the use of seminars in informal and LTE non-formal settings was useful "for basic training" in areas of ministry and how to manage the church (N07 2005; N08 2005).

A leader who heard the gospel from the original Sotik team summarizes well the consensus of the interviewees' perceptions of their training from the informal setting until the opening of NGCS. He states,

> And immediately [after] we were converted and baptized, he [the missionary] started lessons and he used to come every week to our village to teach us the Bible and once in a while he [would] take us to a seminar whereby we might spend three consecutive days studying the Bible and writing notes. And along with that, this missionary would take us to [leaders'] meetings whereby preachers, lots of preachers from all over Kipsigis, and there would be several missionaries and experienced preachers, and they would teach us the Bible. . . . The old [former] missionaries, those who planted the churches in Kipsigis continued teaching us and training us. And when they left, another group of missionaries came . . . and they continued in the work that the other missionaries left . . . and all the training from the early missionaries to last missionaries to leave Kipsigis and Nairobi Great Commission School have been very useful in ministry. (C03 2005)

Profile of the Interviewees

Since the late 1990s to the present Churches of Christ in Kenya have seen an increasing rise in the use of extension centers in conjunction with the Nairobi Great Commission School (NGCS) for training church leaders who are primarily evangelists, preachers, church planters, and youth ministers. The church leaders interviewed for this research received their training at either NGCS, one of the extension centers, or both. These interviews were conducted at four extension centers and NGCS. Thirty-seven interviews were conducted at five different locations: NGCS in Nairobi; Siriat Bible School near Sotik; Mombasa Extension Center and Uzima Training Center in Malindi, both along the coast; and Kambakia Training Center in Meru.

Of these, twenty have received an Advanced Diploma from NGCS and fourteen had received an Advanced Certificate from one of the extension centers or NGCS.[2] Three have degrees above the Advanced Diploma, two Bachelors and one Masters. One interviewee did not complete an Advanced Certificate but was interviewed because of his years of involvement in ministry and his leadership in the church.[3]

The locations represent the geographical locations of major mission efforts established by American missionaries but are now primarily ministry efforts of Kenyans. These training centers also represent the most active training centers in Kenya. At the time of the interviews, each center has a Kenyan acting as the Principal or Director. Occasionally, one of two or three resident missionaries still present in Kenya or a visiting American missionary teaches a course along with the African teachers. Currently, there is a Kenyan Coordinator for all the extension centers in East Africa (2003, 5).

The table below gives a breakdown of the average ages and years of ministry experience of the interviewees at the time of the research. The table indicates that generally "older men" were interviewed given the average Kenyan life expectancy of 56. Also the average years of ministry, 11.8, indicate that about half of those interviewed were involved in ministry when American missionaries were very active in the locations of the training centers and the other fifty percent came into ministry as American mission teams were phasing out with direct missionary influence decreasing. The mean age is 39 while the median age is 41.5 years. Table 1 below gives a breakdown of the average age and years in ministry by location.

Table 1.--Average age and ministry years by area

Training Center	Location	Average Age	Average Years of Ministry
Kambakia Training Center	Meru	44.6	12.6
NGCS	Nairobi	37.6	12.1
Siriat Bible School	Sotik	35	11.7
Uzima Christian Training Center & Mombasa Extension Center	Malindi Mombasa	39.6	10.9
Total Aggregate		39.2	11.8

Table 2 below divides the ages of the interviewees into four age brackets. The largest age bracket of leaders interviewed fell into the 41 to 50 years old age group. This, combined with the 51 to 60 years old age bracket, indicates that almost fifty percent were 41 years old or older, indicating a number of years of experience. Only one fourth of those interviewed were in the youngest age bracket of 20 to 30 years old.

Table 2.--Age brackets of interviewees

Age Brackets	Number in Age Bracket
20 – 30 Years of Age	9
31 – 40 Years of Age	10
41 – 50 Years of Age	12
51 – 60 Years of Age	6

The majority of interviewees were active ministers, preachers or evangelists in local congregations. Table 3 gives an overall view of the primary ministries listed by the interviewees with local ministries and church planting dominating the types of ministry activities in each of the five locations. The category of "teacher" includes teaching at local congregations, localized or LTE courses and at training centers. Almost as many listed church planter as they did teacher. Youth ministry as a separate area of ministry is a rising phenomenon in Churches of Christ in Kenya. The more rural areas, Meru and Kalenjin (Sotik), did not list a single youth minister.

Table 3.--Type of ministries and number of interviewees involved in specific ministries

Type of Ministry Involvement	Number of Interviewees Listing this Ministry
Evangelist/Preacher/Minister	33
Teacher	18
Church Planter	17
Youth Minister	6
Principal	5
Elder	1
Deacon	1

What is noticeable is the lack of church leaders who listed elders and deacons as ministry activities. Given the ecclesiastical importance historically of elders and deacons in Churches of Christ, it is noteworthy that these leadership functions are not emphasized by the interviewees in this research. However, given the emphasis of the informal and formal training toward evangelism and church planting, the importance of elders and deacons in church leadership may have been eclipsed.

Those persons who influenced the interviewees the most in pursuing their theological education were almost evenly split between Kenyans and American missionaries with missionaries being listed slightly more often than Kenyans. Three main categories of responses regarding who influenced the interviewees the most to pursue their theological education were delineated: American missionaries, African leaders or their church, and family. There was some overlap between family and African leaders as some of the family members functioned as church leaders as well. If family is combined with African leaders the breakdown is as follows in Table 4. Generally those that listed more than one influence listed both American missionaries and African leaders. When missionaries were mentioned, it was usually the names of missionaries who worked in the interviewee's home area. When African leaders were mentioned, it was a mix of local church leaders, family members, and Kenyan teachers from other locations who taught courses in other areas.

Table 4.--People influential on interviewees' pursuit of theological education

People Influential in Pursuing Theological Education	Number of Times Mentioned
American Missionaries	22
African Leaders and Church	19

When interviewees were asked to give reasons for pursuing the more formal theological education beyond the informal, the desire for more biblical knowledge was noted above others. The second most listed area was the need for improved ministry skills followed by evangelism and church planting skills which might be placed under ministry skills in general. Table 5 below summarizes the interviewees' main reasons for pursuing more formal theological education at NGCS or a local training center.

Knowledge was not seen as an end within itself. Greater biblical knowledge was seen as essential for the majority of interviewees, particularly in the context of being able to minister in their churches and being more effective in evangelism and church planting. Those who had a vision for their future ministries saw the need for more knowledge to improve their ministry abilities. As one older evangelist notes, he could not adequately explain biblical teachings in the World Bible School material and the scriptures used for people who were being evangelized and new Christians. This led him to say, "I was not really helpful and as time went [on], I found that it was important for me to, if I was going to help these people to be strong and to make their decisions, I needed to, to get some bit of training or guidance, in Bible" (C01 2005). Or as another notes, "The more you read the word of God, the more you understand Him, and the more you get good knowledge of how to, to train others. Yes, and to evangelize to people" (M07, 2005).

Table 5.--Reasons for pursuing further theological education

Reasons for Pursuing Further Theological Education	Number of Times Mentioned
Biblical Knowledge	24
Ministry Skills	10
Evangelism & Church Planting	7
Improved Educational Level	5
Vision for the Future	4
Leadership	3
Cultural Change	1
Missionary Influence	1

A second connection can be seen in some interviewees' association of greater knowledge with being able to teach people with higher education levels in a culture that is producing more people with higher education. This particularly comes across in those who listed improved educational level, leadership, and cultural change as reasons for more formal training. As one thirty-three year old evangelist and church planter notes, "The reason why I joined the school is, is that, I realized these, the world now is changing, and we need also preachers who are educated" (W04 2005). Another minister and church planter notes the rise of educated youth who are trained as high as the university level and how "they want leaders that have gone to school also; they want leaders that can dialogue together" (N09 2005). One interviewee notes that uneducated preachers may be seen as "bush preachers" who have little knowledge except maybe John 3:16 and are not seen as legitimate preachers today (N07 2005). The changing culture with greater education is seen as calling for higher theological education.

> Well, we are living in modern, advanced world. . . . So, in the modern world, one should have training. Training is mandatory, training is compulsory, for any minister. This one will make you to know how to reach people with the message, because we have

groups of people. We have those who are illiterate. . . . We have those who are learned. And also in between we have the youths. So with the training, it will help you [know] how to reach these three categories. . . . And then, in the present world, whoever is preaching, people want to know, "Is that person having a theological knowledge? Did he went to any school?" (N11 2005)

Ministers note their desire to learn to improve their effectiveness in ministry and to reach their changing society. However, does this coincide with the desires or needs of the local churches? The section below explores the leaders' perceptions of the local church and leadership.

The Local Church and Trained Leaders

In assessing the relationship between the local churches and their leaders and the local churches' desire for trained ministers, the interviewees were also asked, "What training do you think churches want their ministers to have these days?" Since the average number of years of ministry among those interviewed is almost twelve years, their perception of the type of training churches desire in their leaders may be instructive. Their perceptions probably reflect the general attitude of local churches toward formal theological education since local churches must recommend leaders for training and provide a portion of the support for their leaders to attend.

Four primary areas emerged from the interviews that elucidate the interviewees' perceptions of what they think churches want in church leaders. First is a higher level of education for church leaders. Second, churches are looking for better leadership skills. Third, greater spiritual maturity is desired. Fourth, better biblical knowledge is sought.

Higher Education Level

Almost all respondents perceived the local churches as placing a high value on their leaders having a higher level of education. "I think the idea of someone going to a theological school is the ideal training to most of our churches" (C01 2005). Theological training is seen as moving the leaders beyond preaching that is mere pandering to the people, or "what people are telling them to do" but instead making the scriptures applicable to what the people need (M02 2005). Theological education is necessary in order to have leaders at the same educational level as other religious groups. This allows them to better enter into theological discussions without an "inferiority complex" or to confront Islam (M05 2005; N07 2005; C09 2005). Also, a church with a better educated leadership has recognition in the community (N01 2005). One minister notes, "They [the community] expect to see a trained minister and one who commands their respect" (N04 2005). The perception is that "the more training you have, the more effectiveness you have in the ministry" (W03 2005; W04 2005). As one leader states,

> It will be the training that will equip the leader in all areas that pertains to the Christian work, whereby he can be able to reach out and be of service in every Christian life that could be either, reaching out in evangelistic work, reaching out in mentoring and maturing, and also be in a position to kind of, do other things like conflicts to solutions. (W02 2005)

Three significant areas of training that interviewees note repeatedly that churches desire in order to meet church challenges are increased knowledge, leadership skills, and spiritual maturity. A desire for leaders to have greater biblical knowledge and be able to apply it was mentioned most frequently.

A Higher Level of Biblical Knowledge

Being "well equipped in knowing what the Bible says . . . so that if any questions arise he should be able to answer, because they expect him to know everything" is the church's perception of leaders (N08 2005). Knowledge alone is not the goal but rather making application of the message for the people and not misusing scripture (M02 2005; N05 2005). Others note problems with doctrinal confusion or in defending the gospel in discussions with Muslims (N01 2005; C09 2005). Churches are looking for greater leadership skills in the application of Bible knowledge.

Improved Leadership Skills

Leadership skills to enhance ministers' abilities in handling problems and "resolving issues" within the local congregations are identified as important "because even in the church you find families giving up because of problems" (W02 2005; C01 2005; C05 2005). Others mention "administration" or "management" of the church as a congregational concern. They note that churches are looking for leaders with better administrative skills in the areas of finance and community development (N11 2005; N03 2005). A leader from Nairobi notes, "I think they need to have training in handling church properties, maybe finance, something like finance" (N09 2005).

Spiritual Maturity

Although not mentioned as frequently as the leadership qualities above, congregations are perceived to want leaders with greater spiritual maturity. They expect trained leaders to have "godly hearts" who work effectively in the church and community (N08 2005). The leader's maturity is seen in his ability to "mature" the flock and in his personal and family life reflecting a similar maturity (W02 2005; W04 2005). His spiritual maturity is reflected in his behavior (W06 2005).

Given this perception of congregational desires for their trained leaders, the following sections will discuss the church leaders' perceptions of the effectiveness of their theological education in improving their ministry abilities.

Local Ministers' Rating of Their Theological Education

In discussing the present theological education experience with the interviewees, they identify a number of areas in which they feel the educational experience was positive and contributed to their effectiveness in ministering in their local contexts. They also identify areas of weakness in their training which will be discussed more fully in a later section that addresses evaluating the effectiveness of their theological education. This first section discusses the satisfaction levels and how the interviewees rate their theological education experiences. The second section explores the interviewees' perceptions of the effectiveness of their theological education process. It discusses what the ministers deem positive and what contributes to their effectiveness in ministry and personal growth, and secondly, those areas that they perceive are lacking or in need of modification.

When asked, "How satisfied are you with the present theological education process?" the responses were overwhelmingly toward the positive with comments ranging from very satisfied or very helpful to satisfied. Typical of such statements is "we are getting quality training, which is making us be very, very effective in the field" (N11 2005). Most respondents emphasize satisfaction with their theological training, particularly in improving their ministry skills in evangelism, church planting and leadership within their cultural contexts. Others note improvements in personal development and knowledge.

In elaborating on their satisfaction level with their education, they indicate that the nature of the theological education they received is rooted in the realities of where they pursue their ministries and see "the fruit of the training that people have received" (N04 2005). As one minister notes,

> I see myself before coming here to have been blind. I was not seeing very many things. But this school opened my eyes. Because after training I got from here, is when we started to involve ourselves deeply in ministry, planting churches, maturing them, taking some of our leaders to school, and I see that this school has really helped me, as a leader. (N02 2005)

Another gives credit to his training as opening him up to his own culture when he states, "It has been very helpful. Especially when I joined NGCS, I came to know that my culture was very important, yes" (M01 2005). Others saw their theological education as being applicable from one location to the next from an urban area like Nairobi to the rural areas (N04 2005). "I'm satisfied in that it does not focus [on] the Kenyans alone, but it also considers some people from different countries, like Sudan and many other countries" (C06 2005).

A number judge the effectiveness of their training by looking at the results of their ministries and their ability to cope with various problems (W06 2005). One interviewee from the coast notes, "This Bible training I've received here has been very much helpful to me personally, to my family, and to the ministry that I have back in my home area" (C04 2005). A minister in western Kenya notes,

> It has been helpful on my part, and it has also been effective, as far as the results are concerned. Because, yes, we have been able to venture into unconquered territories, and not knowing what will come out but effectively or success, good enough, we have had some good results. (W03 2005)

When asked, "What things helped you the most to apply your Christian schooling experience to be a better minister in your culture?" these active ministers identified specific areas of ministry for which they feel their theological training effectively prepared them. The table below gives the breakdown of replies in order of frequency from the most frequent to least frequent. The area of culture and contextualization is mentioned more significantly than the other areas. The next two areas were mentioned almost half as often as the first area. The last two areas are mentioned only a few times.

Table 6.--Specific areas of ministry that Christian schooling strengthened

Studies from Christian Schooling that Helped the Most in Ministry
Culture and Contextualization
Evangelism, Missions and Church Planting
Ministry Skills, Leadership and Administration
Spiritual Formation
Knowledge

Culture and Contextualization

Cultural understanding and application of scripture to the interviewees' contexts are mentioned above all other areas as being the "most helpful" in improving their ministry. A later section of this study will explore fully how church ministers evaluate the level of contextualization and applicability of the theological education towards improving their effectiveness in their ministries. The intent here is to note that the church ministers rate highly their theological education as being beneficial in contextualizing the gospel and in making better application of scripture to their cultural contexts.

Given the mission experience of most of the teachers among the American mission teams who initially taught the bulk of the courses, the emphasis on application of scripture to culture identified by those interviewed is not surprising. Also, most of the Kenyan teachers received their training from the missionaries with only a few attending Western institutions in the U.S. This fits very well with the core philosophy of the American mission teams which focused on contextualized evangelism and church planting.

Evangelism, Missions, and Church Planting

Training in evangelism, missions and church planting ranks second among the interviewees as to what training they find most helpful to their ministries. Since most of the American mission teams had this activity at the foreground of their ministry emphasis with the training centers developed to foster evangelism and church planting, it would appear that this emphasis is still present and appreciated by those receiving their training at the institutions.

As one interviewee says, "Let me say from the bottom of my heart, evangelism, how to reach souls" has been most helpful (N04 2005). A minister from the coast saw his training as particularly helpful in reaching non-Christians. He comments, "It really helped me a lot, because I know how I can face those people who are not Christians and love them. . . . Not to see the difference, to see God in those people" (C05 2005). Another minister notes that his theological education prepared him to plant a church "some place" and currently the church that came out of that training has a membership of eighty (C01 2005). An urban minister points to his training in helping him to realize the importance of community involvement for reaching people. "So, we try to interact with the entire community and in that process we win people to ourselves. . . . And then they recognize us as part of the family, that has helped us" (N01 2005).

Ministry Skills, Leadership and Administration

Mentioned almost as frequently as evangelism and church planting is training related to ministry skills including leadership and "administration." Although these will be explored individually more fully later, they are placed together here to note the interviewees comments on more practical ministry matters.

A number of interviewees see their theological education as providing them with the tools beyond just intellectual understanding. As one minister notes, "Okay, most of the things that we learned in the college we're not just learning things that were just going to be in our heads. But there were things . . . that were to be used" (C01 2005). Such practical matters as how one presents himself in his preaching, or how to teach various groups in the church from youth to women to non-Christians are mentioned (N07 2005; N08 2005). Within this broad category of practical skills, "leadership" and the leader's role and responsibilities are mentioned as having been helpful in their ministries.

Ministers note the development of the types of attitudes a leader should have: a servant heart rather than wanting to be served (C09 2005), and a cooperative attitude (N09 2005). Others stressed the improved abilities that their training provided: an ability to train other leaders (N08 2005); being able to have a vision for oneself and one's ministry (N04 2005); and working more effectively with "lay-leaders" (N09 2005).

The term "administration" is used frequently enough by the interviewees that it suggests it is a separate category worth exploring. For the present purpose it is placed among ministry skills that the interviewees identify as a benefit from their theological training. "Administration" as used by a number of respondents generally relates to those activities the minister does to organize and keep the church functioning well. Some saw their training as helping them to be organized as a minister and having a vision for where one is going as a minister of a church (N04 2005). One interviewee identifies it with the ability to "administer" the message more effectively in his "African context" (N05 2005).

The last two areas identified by those interviewed as being most helpful are spiritual formation and knowledge. However, these two are mentioned less frequently than the others.

Spiritual Formation

"I would say that [courses] have been encouraging since the, what you call, what I would term as Christian spiritual formation, whereby it causes the individual to grow as a person in the Christian way" (W02 2005). One leader identifies his improved prayer life and its positive effects on his ministry to families he visits (W03 2005). Other ministers focus on their own "personal development" as what was most helpful in allowing them to better "imitate what Jesus was doing" (N05 2005; N04 2005).

Knowledge

Better knowledge is identified three times as being most helpful, and it is tied to improving the minister's ability to apply that knowledge to his cultural context. One minister ties it to understanding the church as "an inclusive, integrated part of the community" and the "thousands-and-one ways" that a church can be useful in a community (N01 2005). Another sees his improved understanding of the "biblical background" of the Bible as better helping him "contextualize the message" (N07 2005). A third interviewee points to a fuller understanding of salvation history and how the "current generation of Christians" is involved in that activity (W02 2005).

Local Ministers' Evaluations and Perceptions of the Effectiveness of Their Theological Education

The church ministers who matriculated through NGCS and the various Extension Centers shared their perceptions as to the effectiveness of their theological education. Their observations were elicited through a number of questions designed to encourage a critical evaluation of both positive and negative elements. The general question, "How helpful has the theological education been in training ministers for an effective ministry?" allowed them to pursue their first thoughts on the matter. More detailed questions would ask about specific areas of effectiveness, particularly in contextualizing their training and improving or modifying their education experience. These additional areas will be discussed in subsequent sections.

To a person, the interviewees hold their theological education experience to be worthwhile and instrumental in improving their ministry abilities. They also identified areas of training that were either lacking or with which they raised theological questions. Their responses identified ten areas. These are listed in the table below and will be explored individually.

The first six areas overlap with the aspects of their theological educations that are identified by the ministers as "most helpful" to their ministry. Each of these areas will be explored more fully to give the ministers' evaluations of each, including criticisms noted. The last four are areas the ministers identify as either needed, substantially lacking, or in need of improvement.

The majority of respondents note an improved effectiveness in ministry among those receiving training either at NGCS or one of the extension centers. As one forty-one year old preacher states,

> I am happy because today we have got ministers, good ministers in the Church of Christ who have come through the Nairobi Great Commission School or any other extension center. Yeah, because most of them are effective in the ministry, and

most of them work well with whatever churches they minister to, which is very different from some other days when I was looking at the church. There were no trained leaders and many things they were doing could not be accepted by the community around. (N06 2005)

Table 7.—Evaluation of theological effectiveness

Evaluation of Theological Effectiveness
Leadership and Ministry
Knowledge and Application
Evangelism and Church Planting
Church Organization and Administration
Spiritual Growth
Culture and Contextualization
Education Level
Financial Support of Ministers
Vocational Training
Socio-Cultural Concerns

Another leader draws attention to the significance of the theological education as being helpful after the American missionaries had mostly phased out in his area. He notes,

After the missionaries left, the last missionaries left in 1997. Most churches cooled off. And then after I graduated, I gave them strength. Even now we have the missionary schools . . . [but before] there was no meeting, there is no preachers' meetings, [and] women's meetings. So now every morning when I'm meeting preachers, we are having women seminars, youth seminars, one meeting. So, after graduation, came a lot of strength to my area. . . . There is a lot of things that we are now doing. (W04 2005)

Both of these comments point toward what other ministers identify in various ways as improved leadership and ministerial skills provided by their theological education. The ways summarized below surfaced most frequently in the interview process.

Leadership and Ministry

Reflections on interviewees' theological education and its impact on their leadership within their ministry contexts were significant. "Servant leadership" was a commonly used phrase or concept within various discussions on leadership in the local church. "The teaching I received has taught me on the aspect of servanthood and, okay, serving people has been what I've been doing all through" (C03 2005). A twenty-six year old youth minister observes,

> The training has really helped me, especially, as I said . . . about servant leadership, and focus on Jesus himself, who was Son of God. He was supposed to be a big man. But when we look at him, he was able to associate with people of the lowest class. . . . So before I came to the training center, I thought, "No, there is a certain class I cannot mix up with. . . ." But when I came to the training center, you see, it has helped me to know that I as a minister am not supposed to minister unto the righteous. But I am supposed to minister unto the sinners. And not unless I am with them . . . they'll not be able to receive the gospel. (C09 2005)

A church leader of sixteen years notes the tendency of church leaders among some denominations to produce preachers who are *"Bwana Kubwa"* (Big Chief) but the Churches of Christ tend to "disregard" this understanding of preachers (M01 2005). Another emphasized patterning his ministry in "the way Jesus did it" (M05 2005). The church leaders highlight "servant-leadership" as a foundational biblical teaching and as providing the underlying attitude of many leaders. Local ministers also identify various ministry skills that their theological education improved.

Aspects of leadership qualities and skills, as related to the interviewees' ministries, are mentioned in a wide variety of ministry contexts. Specific ministry skills are identified as helpful in leadership and ministry, such as teaching and preaching, nurturing and counseling. However, the latter, counseling, is seen as less effective due to some limitations identified by the leaders.

Teaching or Preaching. Skills that assist in developing the ministers' preaching and teaching abilities are seen as effective aspects of their theological training. Teaching skills are seen as improving the local minister's ability to prepare lessons (N03 2005; N11 2005), communicate the gospel more effectively (C06 2005), and are able to be done successfully without missionaries because of the "ministers that have been trained" (C04 2005). As one minister observes, "You may not know the way to deliver that message [but] now I feel better that . . . I know how to plan the work that I have in a way that it will be easy for the people to understand the message" (C06 2005). A forty-one year old evangelist and preacher from the coast states that his training has helped him in the church to be a better "preacher" and "teacher." "It has helped me in that now I'm teaching the word of God in a better way and interpret the word of God in a good way. And it helped me to evangelize in a better way" (C02 2005). An evangelist and preacher of fifteen years points out the ministry skills he feels the theological education has improved or brought to the point of being "well-rooted."

> I realized that growth for mission work, or even standing in front of a congregation unprepared, means that you are going to present a message that is not well-cooked to the people. But when I went for training at Nairobi Great Commission School, I came to learn of how to make lessons, to prepare lessons, how to organize myself physically for the mission work, how to approach people, different classes of people with the gospel. And, also, how to conduct church services in a satisfactory way or in an effective manner. (W03 2005)

Integration of biblical teaching to the ministry context is seen as an effective element of the theological training. An evangelist and church planter states concerning the ministerial skills,

> They've really helped me a great deal, to apply the gospel, I mean, to reach the lost in my community. That is why I was able to plant that new church, and let me speak of hermeneutics. It is really helped me to apply it in my situation, what it meant over there, in that, in those times and what does it mean today. It has really helped me a lot. (N04 2005)

A number of the local ministers see their training as assisting them in better interpersonal relationships within and outside the church (W04 2005). The ability to have better relationships with other church leaders is seen as another positive aspect (N09 2005). Related to these are two areas of ministry skills specifically identified from the interviews as positive aspects of the leaders' ministerial training: nurturing and counseling.

Nurturing. A greater ability to nurture their churches is identified by the ministers as a positive contribution of their theological education. There is a sense of being better able to strengthen the churches (M06 2005), teach (C06 2005), train leaders (N02 2005), deal with problems that occur (C07 2005), and promote greater cooperation. One minister reflects that his theological education "helped me to strengthen the church here, in the sense of . . . being able to sympathize the idea of sharing the work together [with] members of the church" (C01 2005). A young minister speaks of the value of his training by noting how it provides him a greater means of not only reaching people but increasing retention in the church. He says, "I realized so many things that I learned in the books. And, it was very helpful because it teaches us how to approach the people, and also how to keep those who have come to the church . . ." (M04 2005).

The church leaders observe another aspect of nurturing to which their theological education contributed positively. They see it assisting them with skills to "revive" churches that have declined or died. "But now, once these people have gone through training, they know what they should do. . . . Even some of the churches have been revived through this kind of training" (N10 2005).

A number of interviewees see their increased abilities to deal with problems and issues in the churches as a benefit from their educational experience and applicable to their ability to nurture their churches (C03 2005; M08 2005; W02 2005). As one forty-six year old preacher notes of his theological education, "Because in the first I have had no stamina and I was not strong enough to face some of the challenges within the community. But now . . . I even feel proud when I'm tackling some of the problems or challenges because I know the way to do it" (M05 2005). Or as a thirty-four year old minister of thirteen years among the Maasai observes,

> So people in our area are very local. Some of them don't know how to take care of children, how to take care of their husbands and wives. So this Christian life, according to me, I've been teaching them on how to behave in a Godly way in their families [and] in their work. And teach them how to do something else, instead of just looking after only cows, [and] only sheep. (N08 2005)

Related to the area of nurturing, leaders often point to their training in counseling as very helpful. This is particularly the case in assisting them with dealing with the individual church member's problems.

Counseling. Preparation for counseling church members is identified as helpful, but it is also mentioned in the context of areas that are lacking in theological education. The one counseling course provided in the curriculum was deemed helpful, but others called for more training in this area. A leader on the coast states that "the counseling has helped me a lot. She further states,

> But at the kiosk, I can never finish one day without having women who have come for counseling. Even some other churches, women from other churches, who have got broken homes, I mean broken marriages. Like last month even I told Daniel I don't know what God has for me, because I had so many women coming to the kiosk. (C05 2005)

Others also point to their use of counseling skills in their daily ministries (C09 2005; M01 2005). "Because the church is almost a hospital, most of them come there with different needs, a need to counsel. Yeah, when you apply Bible and the little you have for counseling you do it best" (M02 2005). An evangelist and church planter in western Kenya notes that his counseling training was "very, very effective when it comes to talking face-to-face with a person, especially a person who is suffering, who is in problems" (W03 2005).

Others note the lack of training in counseling available because of only one course being offered and the lack of counseling courses readily available at the training centers (C01 2005; C10 2005). Continuing education for church leaders is mentioned frequently and more counseling is one of the areas suggested as being a part of that education process (C05 2005). Closely associated with leadership and ministry skills, interviewees identify Bible knowledge and its application in ministry as an area in which their theological education is particularly effective.

Knowledge and Application

Most of the interviewees mention the value of gaining more biblical knowledge through the theological education they received. Mentioned with the increased knowledge are observations that their increased knowledge also allows them to make better application of the biblical message in their ministry contexts. In a subsequent section, the level of contextualization as perceived by the interviewees will be fully explored. This section will explore the general perceptions of the ministers on their growth in biblical knowledge and their abilities to make application. A young local preacher and church planter represents others when he says that his theological education gives him a knowledge "just to bring people from culture to the word of God" (W05 2005; C08 2005). Or as another notes from the coast, "It makes me to have the knowledge of Bible. . . . And now, I can apply the Bible and it's also helped me to know people, how I can communicate with people in a way which they can understand the word of God properly" (C02 2005). One interviewee states,

> I find this school very important because those who come from here, they create an impact outside there. Because they take them the knowledge and they transplant that knowledge into practice, and when we do that, it is very helpful. And the work they do is a bit different from what they were doing before they came to school. (N02 2005)

Having a strong and comprehensive biblical knowledge is important to the church leaders because it is seen as allowing them to carry out their ministry more effectively in a variety of contexts. There is no criticism related to the level of Bible knowledge provided by their educational experience. Their ability to make appropriate and valid applications is also assessed positively. Positive assessments are also given for the training received in areas of evangelism and church planting.

Evangelism and Church Planting

Interviewees from all areas are unanimous in stressing that their training in evangelism and church planting prepares them well in those areas of ministry. No one points to any lack of training related to evangelism. Considering the historical emphasis of American missionaries on evangelism and church planting and the emphasis at all the schools, one would expect that they would experience a significant level of training in these areas. As one leader notes, "Surely, I cannot imagine today the way I am because I cannot imagine me planting a church. But when I joined Kambakia Training Center, after brothers, missionaries, who helping me so much to be equipped, I have gained a lot" (M01 2005). One of the oldest evangelists and church planters interviewed points to the changes from the time of the American missionaries to the current situation and the effects of their theological training.

> Here, in this area, most of those who have gone through the program and have been trained in the theological teaching are very active and very effective in ministering in the churches, and have promoted evangelism in their areas. As opposed to the earlier times when missionaries came here and they were doing almost everything, they were planting churches, teaching men, helping churches grow and that work now is being done by ministers that have been trained, . . . especially in evangelism and church growth. (C04 2005)

Others indicate that their theological education provides them with the tools to evangelize and plant churches successfully. One interviewee points to his education as what helped him plant "more than seven churches" while others point to similar successes and a greater vision for evangelism (M07 2005; C08 2005; W01 2005; W02 2005). Others point to their training as helping them reach other cultures and social levels (N06 2005; N04 2005). As one leader notes, "So, theological training in Africa, or rather Kenya, is very helpful because our evangelists have gone out to open churches." He further states,

> The skills I learned from Great Commission School, or rather the theological training, one to one evangelism. . . . I rely on evangelism, one on one, which I learned in this class, and discipleship skills, in small groups, which I learned from the theological training here. They've really helped me a great deal, to apply the gospel, I mean, to reach the lost in my community. (N04 2005)

Although all the leaders are pleased with their training in evangelism and church planting, the issue of support for evangelists and ministers is a recurring issue and seen as a negative element that has not been fully addressed in their training. The lack of support of evangelists is seen by those interviewed as detracting from the evangelism and church planting efforts. The issue of support will be addressed in a subsequent section.

Church Organization and Administration

Two terms surface in the interviews that draw attention to church organization and structure. The terms administration and autonomy are mentioned frequently. A number of interviewees mention that their theological education helps them in the "administration" and "organizing" of the church. However, the term "autonomy" is mentioned as a concept that causes problems in the church, particularly, in clusters of local congregations.

As mentioned earlier, "administration" as used by a number of respondents generally relates to those activities the minister does to organize and keep the church functioning well. As one respondent says, "I learned a lot about administration when I was here [NGCS] which is very important how to administer to all, to a congregation. That is the leadership and also division of labor" (N06 2005). Most feel positive about their training in church administration (C01 2005; C02 2005; N01 2005; W02 2005). A minister of twelve years states, "My Christian education, it has helped me to strengthen them in the way that we handle them, on day to day activities of the church" (N07 2005). However, this was not a unanimous view as one person notes, "I've seen that we are not getting in our church is the administrative part" (W06 2005). One leader notes,

> I think they need to have training in handling church properties, maybe, finance, something like finance. That is a problem in the church because even it's a sadaka [contribution], the small sadaka that the church can remove. . . . There is no trust to the leaders because when the leaders handle those sadakas maybe there is misuse of funds, such things. (N09 2005)

The term "autonomy" is brought up by interviewees as a concept that causes problems in the church.[4] Interviewees unanimously identify the concept as being used divisively by church leaders to avoid accountability and have dictatorial control. One evangelist notes,

> Some of us don't really understand what autonomy is. Maybe they look at autonomy as "You stand on your own. You do your own things. Nobody questions what you do. You are the one to be on top of everything." Something like that. Or you become a dictator. Anyone who is not following your kind of vision, you throw them away, or you send them out of the church. . . . Autonomy is something which I think they don't understand it very well. That's why we have some problems, even right now in Kenya. (N02 2005)

The term "autonomy" is a part of the ecclesiastical heritage of the Churches of Christ. It is used to describe the congregational structure of Churches of Christ where no hierarchy outside the local body exists. "The independence by the local church is often called 'congregational autonomy,' that is, self-governing congregations." Each congregation is "autonomous" in the sense that leadership of each local body of believers, "a church," is responsible to that church and not to some greater or broader group of churches or presbytery. Cooperation between local churches is considered expedient and biblical. "Each Eucharistic community was in full unity with the rest by virtue not of external superimposed structure but of the whole Christ represented in each of them" (Ferguson 1996, 344-45).

Others reflect on the "African" group-oriented nature and how the doctrinal assertion of "autonomy" is used to avoid cooperation between churches and avoid leadership accountability or does not provide an apparatus for dealing with leaders causing problems across local church lines. "This self-autonomy has been misunderstood to the point that some church leaders don't want to have anything to do with other churches, because they think 'Oh, we're self-autonomy, so . . . nobody's going to tell us what to do here'" (N10 2005). In the ensuing discussion, one leader suggests the need for a group of elders that can oversee the churches and deal with problems as they arise and, "if anything goes wrong, this head has to put all of us together, to square out the problem in the society" (N05 2005).

Concerns over the concept of "autonomy" were expressed by ministers in Kenya as early as the Africans Claiming Africa Conference in 1992 held at Thuchi River Lodge in Embu, Kenya. Though the issue was addressed at the conference, it continues to be perceived as an ongoing problem in the structural issues of congregations' relationships to each other. The issues surrounding the autonomy concept will be addressed more fully in chapter 6.

Spiritual Growth

The interviewees see their theological education as contributing to their broader spiritual growth. They note that their personal lives have been "changed" to a "Godly way of living" and in "family affairs" (C07 2005; C09 2005; M01 2005). Spiritual growth is perceived as having been facilitated by their training and providing guidance for continued growth (N08 2005; W02 2005; W07 2005). "In fact, I've, through the training, I've learned that my only lifestyle, my lifestyle is also important and the way I live" (C10 2005). As one older evangelist notes, "What I would term spiritual formation, whereby it gives to the individual to grow as a person in the Christian way. . . . Whereby this way you have a person working, relating to God in a good way and also relating to others" (W02 2005).

Culture and Contextualization

Ministers feel that the theological training related to applying the gospel to their cultural situations is helpful and gives them confidence in dealing with various cultural issues. "Yeah, because before I used to be afraid. Maybe sometimes they would make noise and I felt that I should not teach. But now I think I'm strong through the training" (C05 2005). Others note their increased ability to "look critically" at their own culture and to apply the biblical teachings to their own societies (C08 2005) and "not present the gospel in a way that people may think that it is a foreign religion" (C10 2005). One Meru leader notes that his training allows him to see the concept of culture more clearly, "I was thinking my culture is best. . . . All people in the world boast for their culture. Everyone says our culture's good. The other person says that my culture is good. So, there's no good culture or bad culture" (M06 2005). Or as another notes, "But after training, I've seen with people, I don't go to condemn. . . . I would seek to know, 'Why are you Kisii's kind of sacrificing to your ancestors?'. . . That helped me to reach and work within my culture" (N04 2005). A youth minister states, "I can say that I can understand what my culture is, and then I can make corrections, trying to base my view on the Bible. So it has helped me to understand my culture, that is one, and how we can correct my culture as we use the Bible" (N11 2005).

A couple of interviewees suggest that more African teachers would improve the training in making application "because of the experience we have as Africans will help fellow Africans" (N07 2005). Most feel that the long-term American missionary teachers understood their cultures significantly well enough to make valid and useful cultural applications but still see a greater need of fuller African participation. The level of self-contextualization and self-theologizing will be explored more fully in chapter six where interviewees' identify the various ways they make application of the gospel message and how they approach cultural problems.

Here, the interviewees identify four areas that they feel were not and currently are not adequately addressed in their theological training. The four areas described and explored below are: Education Level, Support, Vocational Training, and Socio-Cultural Concerns.

Education Level

Three-fourths of the interviewees identify the need for some kind of addition to the theological education currently being offered in Churches of Christ training centers. Suggestions are divided into two groups. First, some see the need for continuing education seminars for those who have already received a certificate or diploma. Second, others desire more advanced degree programs be made available to people. A number of the interviewees mention a need for both types of continuing education.

Making courses available on an ongoing basis in the form of seminars for active ministers is considered to be very needed to assist in improving and maintaining the ministers' effectiveness (C02 2005). "Refresher courses" for people, particularly for those who have graduated is proposed (M08 2005). As one young minister states, "At least . . . some people like us are willing to do the ministry . . . and we are willing to have some more education in the ministry" (C07 2005). Another notes the need for "continuing education" so he "can give more" because "things keep changing." He points to the need for other courses which can provide areas of improvement in his ministry (N04 2005).

Generally, the ministers see the need for more advanced education opportunities. The majority of the interviewees envision NGCS and the training centers as offering higher degree programs, with this as the ideal as well as necessary to better prepare ministers to meet the changing needs of the church and Kenya.

> It is our prayer and need that the school should climb higher to be able to be offering Bachelor's and Master's degrees. To allow these extension centers to come up to the diploma level. Because these are the children of NGCS, and the child cannot go ahead of the father. So we want NGCS to climb the ladder to the level of BA, or even Master's. (W03 2005)

Interviewees frequently note the improving education level of Kenya and the need for reaching all sections of society. The more educated minister is seen as more desirable to draw people to the church (C02 2005; W04 2005; N07 2005). Higher education for ministers is seen as needed because of "strict competition of education in Kenya" (M01 2005) which is raising the education level of the congregations, and ministers "not well equipped" will not "minister adequately to the congregation" (C04 2005). Along with this is the desire of most people to be taught in their community by "more educated people" and the more educated "the more they are accepted by their community" (N10 2005). As one older minister states,

> The level of education is going up. Now, it seems it is also going up as opposed to when it was you could get a Standard 7 or Standard 8, and it's fine, and you come to Form 4 and that was very good, that was good enough education. But now, since it's going up, even the teachers, the primary teachers are being upgraded to, they are upgrading to diploma, so that there is no lower teaching certificate and so on. So with this kind of thing it means that even within the church, within our education system, it will be hard for a diploma person to reach out to his people who are high in society. (C01 2005)

The interviewees are cognizant of the changing environment of Kenya, particularly in the area of education. They feel it puts pressure on both ministers and the churches to have not only better trained leaders but degreed ministers as a mark of educational respectability in their communities. There is an overall perception that a higher educational level seen by the community will open more doors for the churches' ministries.

Related to this area are two other areas that ministers evaluate as lacking in their theological education, the financial support of ministers and vocational training. Education has been seen as the primary means to achieve financial support both secularly and ecclesiastically in Kenya, and this has been the case in Churches of Christ. However, because the bulk of the American mission teams held a view that mission churches should be self-supporting, the issue of how ministers would be supported was always under discussion.

Financial Support of Ministers

Although no specific initial interview questions are asked concerning the topic of financial support of ministers, eighty-five percent of the interviewees raise the topic on their own as a continuing problem in the churches. They perceive it as a theological issue and one that they strongly feel has not been adequately addressed in the theological process. A leader from a western province feels his theological education did not prepare him well in the "area of support, especially in a situation whereby preachers are not financially able" (W01 2005). After the topic of support is raised by the interviewee, he or she was asked, "Did your theological training teach you in any way to help to solve the problem of support?" the notable answer was "No" (W06 2005). Respondents feel that they need more training not only in how to help congregations to improve their giving to support their ministers but also for ministers to find ways to support themselves better. As one minister states,

> Okay, they taught me good principles, I use them, I'm using today, but then I don't know how I'm going to earn my living because the church does not guarantee support. . . . So I think, maybe in the future, the schools can try to find means on how, okay, provide the spiritual, and even look at the physical also. (C03 2005)

The mission theory under which many of the American mission teams operated from the late 1970s onward was the "three-selves" of which "self-supporting" was understood as needed for a truly indigenous and independent culturally appropriate church. The Sotik team represents the thinking that most teams adopted when they state, "Unless the young church learns to be self-propagating, self-supporting, and self-governing, maturity will be slow, if not impossible" (Allison 1980, 78). Combining this with the primarily rural church planting ministries that the teams were involved in, ministers were often seen as emerging as bi-vocational lay leaders who farmed for a living and preached for little or no remuneration. As the mission teams phased out few of the hundreds of ministers were receiving support from non-national sources and few had adequate support from a local church. Therefore, the issue continues to be revisited by the Kenyans and missionaries alike in a search for answers.

Beyond teaching churches to give better in order to do a better job of supporting their ministers, the interviewees desire a place for theological education to provide training that will assist in generating support through "income generating projects," "tent-making," "vocational," or "secular" training. This type of training is mentioned primarily in response to questions related to three areas: effectiveness of their training, what is lacking in the theological education process which the interviewees experienced, and what should be added to the curriculums.

Vocational Training

There is not a cacophony of calls for outside support of preachers but instead a desire to see theological education provide vocational training alongside the theological training so that employment opportunities are provided beyond farming. A minister states, "I suggest that maybe it should involve some, like, industrial courses, so that after you finish there then you can come and do other things that can help you support yourself as you work for the Lord" (C10 2005). Another suggests a "money-generating project" where the school doing the training and the church of the minister being trained can organize a means of "giving them something to support their preachers or any people who are serving in the church" (N05 2005). No particular "money-generating projects" are in any of the curriculums observed in this research; however, *ad hoc* projects do arise.

An example of this occurred while the author was working with Maasai church leaders in the Meru area the summer of 2006. A group of active ministers of churches among the Maasai on the border of the Liakipia and Meru regions proposed a project by which each church family contributed a goat or a sheep for a "common herd" for their group of churches. In the meeting with this group of Maasai church leaders, they proposed this "income generating project" as a means of providing support for the local minister and churches. Funds from missionaries were used to purchase five goats to match the first five goats given by families of the churches in that area to start the herd.

In fact, the call for more vocational training alongside the theological training is noteworthy as about ninety percent of the interviewees bring up the need for more vocational training. One minister reflects that the training centers "really depend" on outside support from the U.S. and that this could change if governments change, as when the Kenya and Uganda governments were at odds, which could give rise to the "majority support" being lost. He suggests that the training in "projects," like computers and tailoring, will not only help ministers to survive financially but provide income to the training centers (C08 2005). Most of the interviewees suggest vocational courses such as tailoring, carpentry, and computer training which are currently available at a number of extension centers. Others mentioned less frequently are health courses, welding, auto mechanics, driver training, nursing, small business, and opening elementary schools.

"Secular training" is seen primarily as a means of providing support for the ministers and their families (C01 2005; M02 2005). Without "tent-making," it is "very difficult" for ministers to support themselves (M06 2005). As one Meru leader states,

> If you want money, you have to tell the church, "Oh, my brothers," and the people who you are asking, they have a lot of problems. You see? Now it could be very helpful if I was equipped on how to, either to do my other jobs, as well as, as a Christian. . . . But if my daughter comes here [Kambakia Training Center], I want to prepare to be a missionary and while being a missionary she can shear clothes for tailoring, helping even the needy people. (M01 2005)

Not only is the vocational training seen as providing support to the minister, but it also provides him or her with skills to contribute to the community in which the church is established. This also lends status to the minister in his community as not being poor but as being a source of help to the community.

> The theological schools . . . could go on teaching the Bible subjects because that is the most important thing. But like what we are doing now, they could put some courses that earn somebody a trade, so that when they go out, hoping that they will never leave the church. Somebody could teach the church, as well as employing himself, or being employed somewhere. And that could help the church because even the community around, if they see somebody who have nothing, maybe his education was poor but now he had education. . . . Now they would like to follow that person. Because there's nothing that our community hates so much, like somebody who has nothing. (M03 2005)

Or relating to the aspect of status and vocational skills, another states,

> Tent-making, like trades, technical skills, something that you can do and run as you minister to the community . . . can help us in this program. . . . What kills the spirit of ministers . . . is the moment that service comes to an end. . . . It's like some has wasted his time serving a congregation, and then later, when his service comes to an end its, now he's not effective. He goes back either to sell *sukuma wiki* [greens; it is a metaphor for being very poor] or something like that. And obviously you know people in the community will talk about such a person. They say "Look. This was our pastor, this was our minister, this was our evangelist." (N03 2005)

The vocational training is viewed as contributing to the needs of the community while at the same time assisting the church in identifying with the local community in which it is ministering and even providing skills training in their community (N02 2005). As a Nairobi minister verbalizes,

> We need to start training people even [in] vocational skills. So much that when they go to their communities, they not only equip themselves with the gospel, but they also have a trade of some sort that will be useful there. ... He goes there ... and trains other people to that skill, so he becomes useful to the community in that way. Also spiritually he's useful to the community. That is one way that I am really thinking that we should be looking into in our training here. It's not included yet, but I do think if we do, probably it would impact the communities. (N01 2005)

Simply focusing on theological training is seen as very important but too narrow, given the need for ministers' support and community involvement. "We need to diversify our trainings, not only to reach out to the theological curriculum, but also we need to have Christians being trained to other areas in our lives. Because in that way we will be able to reach out into each and every sector of the community" (W02 2005).

Other interviewees view vocational training courses as not only helpful for ministers' self-support abilities but also for church members as a whole. Such courses make it possible to improve their livelihood (W03 2005). One minister states,

> The church becomes a church because of its members and the ability of the members. Let's say materially, or financially, determines the strength of the church also. If they are not strong financially, also the church will be weak. So, for the members to be strong, they have to get also how to operate their income whereby through training ... they could be employed in other sectors. Out of that they ... would be able to contribute or donate to church projects. (W02 2005)

The vast majority of the ministers interviewed are wrestling with the support issue. Since most of the American missionaries have disengaged leaving the Kenyans without a system of support from outside sources, church leaders continue to struggle with the means of building a source of support. Teaching the churches to give to a level where they can support their ministers is considered important, which was the emphasis of the American missionaries while they were on the field, but in many areas the low income of most church members is recognized as an impediment to adequate support of the ministers. From the above comments one gets the impression that "adequate support" for ministers means they generally should have incomes above the average in order to have status in the community and to be able to assist in the community both spiritually and financially.

Though American missionaries, for the most part, did not leave an outside source of support for ministers, the training center system is primarily sustained by outside financial sources. Financial assistance is also given to some students to do their schooling through indirect support from outside sources. Most of the extension centers and NGCS provide support to students or subsidize the training programs. One interviewee wondered at the logic of supporting students to go for theological training only to receive no support when he returns to his ministry position (M03 2005).

Ministers are making the best use of the programs as they are currently offered. They perceive the programs as being highly beneficial but also believe that the vocational education dimension could contribute more fully to solving the problem of support for ministers. They are also attempting to make the best use of the resources available to them.

Socio-Cultural Concerns

Two socio-cultural concerns surfaced during the interview process that are identified as not receiving adequate attention in the theological education process. Most frequently mentioned is the problem of "poverty." Second, the problem of AIDS is referred to, though less frequently.

Poverty. The topic of poverty is raised mainly in response to questions related to problems confronted by ministers in their daily ministries. A number of leaders raise the issue of poverty in the context of their theological education. As one states, "If we want to better our theological training in Kenya with the Churches of Christ, first we have to address the problem of poverty and incorporate something like community development in our theological training in Kenya" (N04 2005). Another notes the heavy emphasis in his education and in ministry on the "spiritual side" while neglecting the "physical side" of peoples' needs.

> There has to be a balance. First if that person I want to minister unto has a physical need, then I have to tend to that physical need first. Then I impact the spiritual need. You see, many preachers, what I think, is have failed in their work, simply because they just want to concentrate too much on the spiritual side.... (C09 2005)

Another minister in Nairobi "from a slum background" notes that people are "lacking housing," money to pay rent, food, and clothing. In response to the question as to whether his theological education helped him to deal with poverty, he states, "That one, it didn't" (N07 2005).

Other interviewees verbalize the lack of emphasis on ministry to widows and orphans. "I would even pray God to put more pressure in those areas, especially when you come to orphans, widows, you know. There seems as though we neglect them sometimes" (C05 2005). Or as a Meru minister notes, "I've witnessed in our churches, since our missionaries left this place, a lot of widows, and widowers, who have been left just like that, and there is no ministry in the church, not about these people" (M01 2005).

Church ministers note a significant lack of training associated with addressing the problems revolving around poverty, ranging from the economic struggles of local Christians to caring for the widows and orphans. Other ministers indicate that little specific training is provided, but they feel the overall training gives them some tools to work with (N04 2005). As one puts it, "I did not learn this [dealing with poverty] from Nairobi Great Commission School. But I have been opened minded about using the nature [Christian principles] that we have to develop it" (N05 2005). Poverty is also associated with the problem of support as noted above. The lack of support and economic resources available to ministers is identified as a major obstacle to the ministers and makes their ministries among the poor more difficult. Poverty as a ministry challenge, how ministers have attempted to address the problem, and problems associated with it will be explored in the next chapter.

AIDS. The second social problem area identified by interviewees where they feel their theological education is not adequately preparing them was in dealing with AIDS. However, less than fifteen percent of the interviewees bring up AIDS in their responses to the interview questions. No direct questions were asked about AIDS in the interview questions except follow-up questions once the topic had been broached. Most bring up the subject under ministry problems they face.

Although a seminar on AIDS was being taught outside of the normal curriculum at NGCS while interviews for this research were going on, ministers note that for the most part they are not taught on handling the problem of AIDS. "We didn't receive a lot of education training, I mean, in NGCS, as far as morality or AIDS and circumcisions are concerned" (W03 2005). "We were not really sharpened towards that" [AIDS] and our classes did not address it even when that was "a problem in our country." The interviewee goes on to suggest a change in the theological education through the incorporation of a "full course on HIV/AIDS" (N04 2005).

Several ministers note problems with the "cultural" responses of people to AIDS. They note problems with suppressing the discussion about the presence of AIDS because of the stigma of "immorality" and the problem with its contraction during circumcision ceremonies (N04 2005; W03 2005). Others point to the problem of sexual immorality and the need for teaching on abstaining from sex and the "need to associate with our wives" (W06 2005; W03 2005).

AIDS is not highlighted by many as an area that the ministers feel is significantly lacking but of the few who did note it, none felt it is adequately addressed as part of the curriculum. However, this does not necessarily imply that the ministers feel they lack the tools for dealing with this problem on a spiritual dimension. In fact a couple of the ministers explain that their training assists them in teaching on the subject and addressing it in the community (W03 2005; C02 2005).

The foregoing evaluation of the Kenyan ministers' theological education provides their perception of its value in preparing them for ministry. It also indicates their critical evaluation of both the effectiveness and inadequate areas of the theological education process. The following chapters discuss the efficacy of the theological education and its level of effectiveness in helping ministers self-contextualize in order to move toward self-theologizing in their ministries and in their theological reflection.

> For Christians, theology is necessary because it enables them to think and live Christianly so that they can love God fully, with heart, mind, soul, and strength.
>
> *Tite Tiénou 2006*

CHAPTER 6
Struggles in the Search for the Fourth Self

Active church ministers were asked to evaluate the level of contextualization and applicability of their theological education towards improving their effectiveness within the various cultural contexts of their ministries. The interview protocol elicits the ministry struggles faced by the church leaders within their cultural contexts. Follow-up questions were asked to allow for further discussion on how their theological education may or may not have assisted them in developing their talents and gifts in effectively wrestling with the problems they face as well as how effectively self-theologizing is practiced. Through their identification of specific challenges they face and discussing the ministers' approaches to dealing with them, a number of ministry challenges are identified that serve as significant examples of their struggles in doing theology. Before discussing these identified challenges to their ministries, it is relevant to note their perceptions of the influence of Western theological bias.

Perceptions of Western Theological Bias

The interviewees were asked about areas of their theological education that help them make application to their culture and areas where it does not help them. One follow-up question was asked directly about the effects of Western teachers and concepts that were used in their theological education. It was asked if the Western teachers and their teaching hindered their ability to make application to their own cultures.

Most verbalize the realization that there was a "western worldview" and a Western missionary's, or teacher's perspective that was present. However, no one seems to consider it to be a significant hindrance to making meaningful application to their own cultural context or to the cultural context to which they are ministering (M03 2005; M07 2005). "They were teaching and then we applied them in our African [way]" (C02 2005). One minister states, "I've been able to look into the perspective that I need to know what is this that is cultural in the Bible, and also the messenger, in this case the missionary, and his influence or his input and be able to bring the gospel out of the two and find out which is actually the gospel and not a Western packaging" (W02 2005).

Instead, the interviewees express their view of how they internalized the teaching from a more critical standpoint with obvious understanding of the Western perspective that was present in the theological education. As one minister states, "I only took the principles that were shared" (C01 2005). Another notes the need to modify what he was taught. "I can't give it to the African people in the way it was given unto me. At least I have to do some modification that this is applicable here" (C09 2005). One interviewee sees the sharing of the gospel as a "bridge." "The Americans make a bridge, a very strong bridge . . . so, joining this side and this side. So the teachings are not from the Westerners. They are from God. True teachings are from God" (C08 2005). Another notes,

> So we received it in class and some of the teachings and things we just left it also in class. . . . And we didn't hate our teachers by saying that, but we understood their Western mind. So we understood and we appreciated their presentation, but we are saying, "Ah! This is not applicable at home. (W03 2005)

One interviewee perceives Kenyans as sometimes "suppressing" their real feelings because of the presence of Western missionaries. He states,

I think for the most part, like the Church of Christ as long as the missionaries are around, they don't want to offend the missionaries. They try to be what the missionary from the West would expect them to be. But inwardly, they are suppressing some of their strong feelings and then the missionaries leave, their real self seems to come out. (W01 2005)

Initially the majority of the providers of theological education were Westerners; more often-than-not, they were long-term missionaries. The interviewees see a distinction between teachers who knew the "African" culture and visiting ones who were less versed in cultural distinctions. "Well, with us, we had an advantage because these brothers [American missionaries] came here and lived among us, and they became almost like us. So, we didn't see much of that Western in them. It didn't prove to be [a problem]" (C04 2005). Others observe a difference between the various long-term missionaries, those that they perceive as understanding the "African" culture well and those who seem to be less in tune with the "African" cultural context (C05 2005; W01 2005). The interviewees note that teachers did teach on cultural distinctives (C02 2005). As one states,

Because you know, these brothers . . . who were teaching us, they would say, you know, "In the West we see things this way, it doesn't always have to be that way, because that's a Western worldview." . . . Most of the time, nearly all of them, they had worked in Africa for several years and maybe different parts of Africa. . . . And we were helped because of the diversity of those brothers and we helped those who had been . . . much Western. (W01 2005)

A number of examples are given by the interviewees that highlight in their minds cultural differences from the West that were represented by their Western teachers (C8 2005). A number pointed to the difference in worship style with the "Westerners worship" far differently "from the way Africans like worship."

Westerners, the way I saw in school is that they worship by, maybe, can I say mentally. But for Africans, we have moved by feelings, we move by emotion, so that we, our worship should be emotional. We need feelings in our deep down in our belly, that at least we are worshipping God. So that when it comes to singing and you clap your hands and move slightly, that is an African way of expressing worship to God. But from the West, some influence that we see is that you need to be people of the songbook, all of the written singing and no twisting, no gesturing, and all this. (W03 2005)

Another minister notes the teaching of counseling was done in the "Western way" which he feels makes it less effective. "When you come home, trying to apply such a thing, it is very difficult." He gives a further example when he asserts,

> Take for example in counseling, when somebody dies. In counseling, according to the Western way, you must make a person to cry who is not crying, let him or her cry so that the feeling can help. But in our community you leave those who are not crying and then you console [those] who are crying. . . . So if you start going around looking for those who are not crying, and then you, you just tell her some things so that they can cry, that is an opposite way. So it is very difficult to apply in our culture. (W04 2005)

The above discussion indicates the ministers' high awareness of the Western influences that were in one degree or another present in their theological education. They feel it did not hinder their application of biblical principles as they perceive them. One believes there was a tendency to show deference to Western missionaries while they were present. Since most American missionaries have phased-out of the work in Kenya, the presence of missionaries is less of an issue.[1] However, most of the interviewees were trained under the theological education system developed and established primarily by long-term American missionaries who used a modified but primarily Western model. Many also received most of their theological training from Western teachers, though this has been changing in the last few years with a decreasing number of missionaries available to teach courses.

The sections below will discuss the perceived ability of the ministers to make relevant cultural application of their theological education. Their perceptions of how applicable they found their theological education to be in dealing with ministry issues provide insights into the level of contextualization and self-theologizing being practiced by those Kenyan ministers interviewed.

Theological Education and Contextualization

A number of interview questions were asked to elicit discussion as to how helpful their theological education is in assisting them in making the gospel message applicable to their various cultural contexts. In chapter 5, it was noted that the teaching on culture and contextualization received by the interviewees is ranked highly as being "most helpful" to them. This section will elucidate more fully their perception of the contributions their theological education makes in their abilities to make meaningful application of the gospel in their cultural contexts which is foundational in moving ministers toward greater contextualization of the message to realize the fourth self.

Interviewees identify a number of areas in which they feel their theological education assists them in making application of the gospel in their cultural contexts. The table below lists the most often mentioned ones and will be discussed in that order.

Table 8.--Theological education's contributions to contextualizing the gospel

Theological Education and Contextualization
Ability to cope with a changing culture
Better understanding of their own culture
Increased understanding of other cultures
Improved understanding of the biblical culture
Making better application of the gospel to the culture
Effective cross-cultural communication

Ability to Cope with a Changing Culture

Ministers in Kenya see their ministry taking place in the midst of rapid cultural changes from primarily rural contexts to situations that are greatly influenced by urbanization and globalization. They recognize that the "old way of life" is changing as are the traditional tribal lines (W02 2005). "We are changing from the way we used to be. . . . In times past we could just serve our own ethnic tribes. But now we're moving from, most people are moving from, rural to urban" (N10 2005). A number of ministers perceive challenges in ministering to more traditional cultures from their less traditional perspective (N08 2005). An example of this is the difference between the Kikuyu or Meru tribes and the Giriama tribe which is seen as having stronger traditional beliefs (C05 2005).

Others note the changing culture in which they are called to minister from the traditional to the "modern" (C09 2005; M08 2005). One interviewee summarizes well what others verbalized concerning the helpfulness of their theological education and its application to culture.

> Today I can understand them [cultures] and, at least, tolerate them and find a way of just twisting them a little bit to fit what the scripture requires. That is also something that is very important when you learn of communication and culture. We learn what a culture requires and where it is not fitting with scripture. Yeah, we are taught that every piece of culture we filter it through the scriptures. And then we use that culture but in a Christian way. (N06 2005)

The effects of the "modern" world and "globalization" are mentioned in seeing people imitating the way of life of others but not necessarily accepting Christianity as a part of their lives (W02 2005).

Better Understanding of Their Own Culture

Some respondents note that the theological education helps them to understand their culture better or, as one says, to see his culture "quite differently" (M07 2005). Others say they are already aware of their own cultural norms and teachings, but that making the transition from the biblical culture to their own is what is most beneficial to them. One states,

> Well, it has helped me to understand my people better. It has helped me to be able to prepare myself to minister to them in their own cultural way of life, as opposed to the previous time, when I could not understand my people well. Yeah. Previously, what I could do probably is just to force the teaching upon the people. But, today, I understand my people, I understand their culture. I've been better equipped to be able to deal with that situation. (C04 2005)

Being able to identify cultural customs in order to understand them in the light of scriptures is noted by a number of respondents (M06 2005). As one minister on the coast states, "This has helped me to identify these customs in our culture which are not favorable [and] which God would like" (C08 2005). Another declares,

I was thinking my culture is the best culture in the whole world. Because of the training, learning about culture and communication, I found . . . all people in the whole world boast for their culture. Everyone says "our culture's good." The other person says "my culture is good." So, there's no good culture or bad culture. Culture is culture. (M06 2005)

Increased Understanding of Other Cultures

A number of people note the training they received in learning about other cultures gives them a wider perspective not only through the teaching received but through the interaction with different professors and students from "different parts of the country or other parts of the world" (W02 2005). The education assists them in evaluating aspects of other cultures. One comments, "I'm now able to identify the other cultures which are good for God and which are not for God. So now I understand that these ones I can continue practicing them. These ones . . . I dare to practice" (C08 2005). One minister summarizes it well when he states,

> [I am able] to know the dynamics of a Christian life, which varies from culture to culture, from one age to another. And also the principles that stand all through, within the gospel. So, in that way it has helped me not only to work, to be able to serve within my local cultural understanding, but also it has given me wider perspective into the lives of others who are outside my culture. (W02 2005)

Improved Understanding of the Biblical Culture

The church leaders also mention having received a better understanding of the "biblical culture" (N06 2005). As another succinctly states it: "After being enlightened of the background of the Bible, the culture of the Bible, it didn't come into just a blank kind of situation as the gospel itself" (W02 2005). This knowledge is seen as assisting them in realizing the gospel is couched in its own cultural situation from which they can draw principles on which to teach in their own culture. As one older evangelist states, "I was much able to understand the biblical culture and because I knew the Meru culture I was able to teach the people. . . . Yes, I was able now to teach well, because I understood my culture, and now I've understood what the Bible teaches better" (M03 2005). Biblical teachings, or "Bible culture" as the term is used here, is seen as a filter by which to understand one's own culture and evaluate the practices. As one young minister states,

> There is the culture of the Bible. And the Bible culture can be transferred, not to fit to the native culture, but can be compared and then it can [be] like a sieve. You are going to sieve the native culture; . . . if it can qualify to rhyme with the Bible culture, now you can use it. . . . Now, it has helped me, when I see anything that is not right in the church, any cultural thing that is not right in the church, I know from the scripture that this thing is not right. But if it is right I maintain it. I tell them "Go home. It is your culture, but it is not a sin." (N09 2005)

This last quote indicates the respondents perceive their ability to contextualize their biblical knowledge to their own cultures or a third culture.

Making Better Application of the Gospel to the Culture

One interviewee from the coast notes, "It's helped me to apply, interpret the word of God, and to apply in our culture so it can also help our people" (C02 2005). He points to being better able to deal with sexual purity before marriage and AIDS. Another gives the example of his theological education providing him the ability to recognize "differences on how people worship." Church leaders indicate that their theological education allows them to work in varied and diverse cultural contexts and apply scripture appropriate to the context (C03 2005).

One minister points to the help his theological education gives him in identifying customs and wrestling with applying the gospel in light of his context. He reflects,

> In our culture, we have some customs, many customs, okay? And this ones, they are some who are good to the Lord and there are some who are not. . . . This [theological education] has helped me to identify . . . and group them. . . . So I could say, this is not applicable; we can't apply them in our ministries in the churches. You have to get rid of them . . . [while] this ones are good. (C08 2005)

He gives the example of pouring out "wine" as calling on *"nkoma"* (spirits) among the Giriama people as a cultural practice he feels is incompatible with Christian teaching as this is like praying to the ancestors. However, many Giriama songs that are sung at weddings "give thanks to God" asking his blessings "so these songs we can accept." He concludes by noting that "we want believers to understand the difference. Otherwise, before, they didn't know" (C08 2005).

Two of the interviewees make an interesting comparison of their contextualization of the gospel, a Meru and a Luo. Both look at their own culture and compare it with the Bible. The Meru minister see many connections between parts of the Old Testament and Meru culture while the Luo minister notes a lot of differences between the Bible and Luo culture. The minister from Meru states,

> Well, there are so many things in the Bible that I learned through this training that are actually similar to the African way. And I was very encouraged when I learnt some of the Jewish practices. Even they were comparing with Meru. And because I was brought up in the tradition, I know very many of the Meru [traditions] that are important and that are not important. So, I even went up to think and start working hard my mind, to see, with actually we are together with these people. (M05 2005)

The Meru culture does have many similarities they can point to which have some correlation with Jewish biblical history. They had a deliverer prophet who performed signs and rescued them from captivity among the people of the "red clothes" and took them across a body of water miraculously. For a scholarly treatment of this tradition by a Meru refer to Alfred M. M'Imanyara's book *The Restatement of Bantu Origin and Meru History* (1992).

They were traditionally ruled by a council of elders (*Njuri Ncheke*) and one or more prophet/priest kings who were called *"Mugwe"* or *"Agwe"* in the plural. Refer to the seminal work on this by B. Bernardi, *The Mugwe, A Failing Prophet: A Study of a Religious and Public Dignitary of the Meru of Kenya* (1959). They had a sacrificial system of pure animals to be sacrificed at sacred high places on nearby hills. They had ethical laws that were strongly enforced. When the author arrived in Meru in 1984 the sacrifices were still going on, particularly related to significant events like calling on God to end a drought. The local council of elders still functioned in *Igembe* (now Northern Location) and *Tigania* areas which were more traditional. The ethical system and enforcement by the elders has largely been displaced by the national government structures.

The operation of the central *Njuri Ncheke* is still a closely guarded secret and in fact may not be discoverable as most, if not all, who last served on it are now dead. This writer's Meru "*baaba*" ("my father," as this writer referred to the man whose compound functioned as his wife's and his home their first three months in Meru, was a member of that council) would never discuss the workings of the *Njuri Ncheke*; even his son knew nothing about its inner workings. *Baaba* explained to this writer that he was bound by an oath to never disclose its workings. *Baaba* died in 2000 keeping his oath.

Similarly, the minister from among the Luo sees his training as helping him to compare scripture with his Luo culture but focuses more on the "areas of weakness." He says,

> The training has helped me to compare to see the weakness of my culture, areas of weakness. Because every culture has those areas of weakness and also there's the strength. We Luos, we have a lot of weakness, which the Bible is against. So, I can interpret when my culture, the weakness, and when I can see areas that the Bible is teaching, and how our people can change. How our people can change from that culture belief to the Christian belief. (N11 2005)

Effective Cross-Cultural Communication

Beyond learning to make the gospel applicable to their own cultures, interviewees also note that their training allows for improved cross-cultural communication in their ministries. "Cross-cultural communication . . . helped me [in] such a way that, to handle different kinds of cultures, to respect every kind of culture. . . . So for my training, I have learnt to respect each one's culture as we transform them to Christian culture" (N07 2005). One minister notes that the strength of people's adherence to their cultural norms calls for "gradually" implementing changes (W05 2005). Or as another notes, "It took them years to have those thing [idols] with them. So to change all of a sudden becomes a problem to them" (C06 2005).

A minister of twenty years observes, the teachings of the gospel "transcend all the cultures" and his theological education assists him in knowing what is "somebody's culture" and what is the gospel. He further states,

And there are those cultural norms and principles that were used in the time of Christ, or even before, to be able to pass the knowledge of God, the way God reaches out to people. And I've also been able to use my cultural norms and understanding to be able to share and bring all the better perspective to those whom I share with, or even my own personal understanding. (W02 2005)

Despite weak areas, they specifically perceive their ability to make valid contextual applications to their own culture and cross-culturally in a positive light. The next section will explore the contextualization process in areas where ministers identify frequent problems, which gives a sense of the "self-theologizing" process as portrayed by the interviewees.

Contextualization and Ministry Problems

Measuring the level of "self-theologizing" or the "fourth self" as it is defined by Paul Hiebert, where church leaders have the right "to study the scripture for themselves and to develop their own theologies" in light of their cultural contexts, is not exact. The following pages will bring to bear the comments of the ministers interviewed as to their perceptions of their theological training in allowing them and encouraging them to develop their theologies in dealing with their cultural contexts. Chapter seven will explore the criteria for evaluating the level of "self-theologizing" and whether the theological education under consideration here is encouraging it.

A series of questions were asked concerning the problems facing the interviewees' ministries, within their churches, their communities and their cultural contexts. They were then asked how they address these problems and to give examples of how they attend to the problems. These questions were designed to elicit discussion that will illustrate the extent to which they are contextualizing the gospel.

The respondents in this research do not indicate that they feel dominated or are not free to interpret scripture openly and develop their own understanding of how scripture should be applied to their ministry contexts. They do indicate areas in which they are faced with ministry problems and their means for addressing the problems. They also discuss areas where American missionaries had held a position on an issue, but they were questioning the validity of that perspective.

Because most areas do not have any fulltime, on-the-field missionaries, missionaries are not looking over the African ministers' shoulders. However, financial support from the U.S. to the training centers with the involvement of off-the-field missionaries may have a continuing influence. As a possible example of this pressure, this author was asked by two groups of leaders at two different locations to discuss an issue with which the leaders were wrestling. In both cases they referred back to the teaching of the missionaries on the subject and were considering moving away from that teaching as a doctrinal issue. They asked this writer to meet with them to get his perception of the issue. It appeared that they saw their decision on this issue as being a break with the past teachings and possibly causing friction in a continuing relationship with off-the-field missionaries and supporters. In one visit to a church in the Kipsigis area the issue in this discussion was already being practiced.

Many ministry problems faced by these active ministers are mentioned, but six problem areas are identified more frequently than others. These ministry problems are listed in the table below.

Table 9.--Most frequently identified ministry problems

Frequently Identified Ministry Problems
Traditional cultural practices
Poverty
Support for ministers
Expectations
Leadership
Spiritual maturity

In chapter 5, two of these ministry problems are identified as areas in which the interviewees felt their theological education is not effective, i.e. poverty and support for ministers. However, theological education related to the area of "traditional cultural practices" as it relates to "culture and contextualization" is perceived as being effectively taught.

These respondents also identified their training in "leadership and ministry" as being effective and valuable. However, in this section, we will note various aspects of leadership in the local churches are seen as problem areas. Two other areas, spiritual maturity and expectations, were not addressed in earlier discussions but will be discussed below. The following six sections will explore particular ways self-theologizing is practiced by those interviewed in dealing with these identified ministry problems.

Traditional Cultural Practices

When the respondents were asked to discuss some of the problems they face in their ministries, they listed cultural problems more frequently than any others. The higher percentage of discussion in this area may stem from the intent of this study to explore the level of "self-theologizing." Follow-up questions were used to explore the extent of the problems, the ministers' approaches to dealing with them, and the contextualization process. Problems cited relate to various traditional practices that vary between tribes. Some are highly people group specific while other problems are prevalent among a number of people groups.

Relating the gospel message to traditional beliefs is seen as a continuing challenge for the ministers. An older leader notes that the ministers have "problems" with people not "synchronizing the gospel" with "traditional beliefs." "They want to intermingle and work both ways but you need to have a clear cut of things in between the gospel and the original religion" (W02 2005). An evangelist sees problems with "traditions" because "each tribe has a culture to pull it and they have traditions. People don't just shirk off the culture immediately. They try to hang with the culture for some time and if they are not careful at one time they go back and do what the culture demands from them" (N02 2005).

"Elders" who exert pressure to retain traditional teachings are still prevalent (C08 2005). As one young evangelist notes, the challenges posed by traditional beliefs is still upheld by many elders.

> We are saying there's a belief that people, our culture, are praying *Asis*. That is the sun God. . . . They were believing that the sun is doing everything. But when they were praying, there was this kind of sacrifice. They were slaughtering cows and [putting] fire into [it] . . . believing the ash should go up so that means the prayer is answered. (W05 2005)

The examples of traditional practices below are provided by the interviewees as cultural practices with which they struggle and out of which they continue to learn to make application of the gospel in more constructive ways. Three categories of traditional practices are identified as challenges from the examples given: circumcision rites, spiritual realm beliefs, and traditional sexual mores.

Circumcision Rite. Both male and female rites of circumcision are mentioned frequently as presenting challenges for the church leaders in their ministries (W04 2005; W06 2005). It was mentioned solely by those in the Meru and Kalenjin areas but arose in numerous discussions. The lack of mention of circumcision among other interviewees is mainly because they work in areas where circumcision is not practiced as a rite of passage to adulthood or is no longer practiced in the traditional way as occurs in the rural areas. Male circumcision as it is practiced traditionally is less controversial by western standards, yet it is seen as a major problem among Christian leaders on par with female circumcision, although it is noted by the ministers that female circumcision was not practiced according to any Old Testament teaching (M03 2005).

Beyond the biblical teachings, the issues revolving around circumcision have to do with the type and level of Christian and local community involvement as it relates to the traditional practices. Everyone referenced some form of conflict between Christian teachings and various traditional practices (M05 2005; W03 2005). Ancestral spirits and witchcraft are seen as involved in circumcision ceremonies, especially in the "traditional culture" of the "forefathers" among the Kalenjin (W01 2005; W08 2005).

> Here in Kipsigis we have things like circumcision rituals and a Christian, a faithful Christian family, might find themselves in a dilemma when one of their children, a boy or girl, would want to undergo traditional circumcision rights. It can cause a lot of problem to a Christian family because if they allow their child to get involved in traditional circumcision ceremonies, which most are demonic, the Christians would backslide and it causes problems in the church. (W01 2005)

The Meru see their problem with male circumcision related to the giving of the "*kioro*" (ritual teaching) to those involved in the circumcision. This "*kioro*" would involve teachings on pleasing the ancestral spirits and the use of beer (M04 2005; M06 2005). Traditional teaching on the role of the ancestral spirits and drinking to the point of drunkenness is highlighted as the main problem in Meru (M07 2005). In a culture study on male circumcision conducted in 1984, one of the missionaries to Meru suggested specifically the need to use "Christian *Agwati*." *Agwati* is plural for *Mugwati* who is a man chosen by the family to care for and teach those in seclusion at the time of circumcision. The Christian *Mugwati* would provide Christian teaching in place of the traditional teaching usually provided to the boys in seclusion (Granberg *et al.* 1984). Seclusion is the set time period the circumcision group remains separated from the community while going through the circumcision rituals.

It is more prevalent now for churches and Christians to utilize a Christian *Mugwati* to provide teaching "about Christ" to the initiates during their seclusion in place of the traditional circumcision ceremonies and teachings about ancestral spirits (M07 2005). However, the mix of community involvement in the ceremonies raises issues for church ministers. The brewing of beer is a problem because "you have to make a kind of beer. . . . It is just like porridge, but it can make you be a drunkard. They drink that because everybody has cooked. Your friends have that one. Your in-laws have made it, every friend of yours, even from far away, they bring" (M03 2005).

A Kipsigis minister sees his theological education as preparing him in handling "spiritual warfare" matters which to him relates to the male circumcision ceremonies to which he was referring. He sees the Christian using "things like prayer, things like faith in God and using the word; it's the sword of the Spirit, it gives courage to the Christians so that they don't go and be involved in demonic activities" (W01 2005). He elaborates on how he handles the male circumcision issue in his family.

> We started the Christian circumcision, like my son I circumcised. I brought a doctor into my home and he circumcised the boys, and I took care of them and taught them the word of God while they were healing. I had Christians come, and we would have prayers and worship God and teach them the word of God. And when they were healed and they would come out and they're whole. (W01 2005)

Among the Meru the emphasis on home-brewed beer drinking and the extent of community involvement in the celebration aspects is an issue to the church ministers (M03 2005; M06 2005). One minister reflects on his efforts for handling the excessive beer drinking associated with circumcision in his area. "So that, what I was teaching myself, especially this year, that if you move beer and other things, put *chai* [tea with milk], and rice or another type of food [to replace the beer], you want the conflict to finish" (M06 2005). Another leader notes his efforts in dealing with the challenges of local Christians' involvement with the community circumcision activities and the wasteful use of food. He desires to find ways to integrate the church in changing the direction of some of these activities through teaching good stewardship.

> I talked with them and told them that even the Jews has some of these things and you remember God, the things they are eating, because at that time they eat things until they waste them. I showed them how they were wasting things like porridge and food and I could use that one as a way to teach to them. . . . God has given us all these things and . . . with the Bible I'm going to pray God. So before you put these things, first of all, we go to the church because God has given us this. (M03 2005)

Female circumcision is approached differently from male circumcision by the respondents. When I lived in Meru, the rite of passage for females from childhood to adulthood was still highly practiced. In fact as late as July of 2006 this author was still being approached by some Meru Christians to assist with the cost of a daughter's circumcision. It had been outlawed by the British colonial powers before independence and later by President Moi. However, enforcement of the law was never practically applied. This was apparent from a culture study done by the Meru Mission Team on female circumcision in the 1980s indicating it was commonly practiced. However, it also notes that the influence of the Methodist church, particularly in the Imenti area, was influencing younger mothers not to circumcise their daughters (Granberg *et al.* 1984). More negative pressure may have come from other Protestant religious groups. In fact, in a trip in 2012, this author's wife learned of a number of cases where there is a second generation of girls now not being circumcised.

One of the arguments this writer heard from Western missionaries is that female circumcision was mutilation on par with what was condemned in the Old Testament. Our mission team rejected this argument as invalid because mutilation in the Old Testament was associated with idol worship, which is not the case in Meru. The Meru Mission Team actually took a neutral position theologically on the matter; it was neither condoned nor condemned, and no doctrinal teaching on it was given. The mission team left it to the wisdom of the local church leaders to grapple with it.

As with the male circumcision mentioned by some Kipsigis respondents, female circumcision is viewed as being involved with "demonic" spiritual forces. However, unlike male circumcision, these respondents are not attempting to provide a Christian female circumcision alternative. Instead, they are teaching that female circumcision should not be practiced. "We are teaching them that the Bible is not allowing the girls to be circumcised." This teaching is reinforced by referring to the example of Abraham and the fact that the circumcision in the Bible was only for males so "you see God did not allow girls to be circumcised" (W06 2005). This teaching on female circumcision was said to have been taught by the Western missionaries (W06 2005).

When a Christian girl is being pressured to undergo circumcision church leaders step in to give Christian guidance in dealing with its practice. The following lengthy quote gives an example of how female circumcision is addressed among the Kalenjin church leaders.

> So, maybe some of the girls are being treated, maybe somebody countered them, said "I want to marry you and because you are a girl you have to be circumcised." Then, if she is not having full faith she might be overcome by that person who is not a Christian. . . . I can solve this through prayer. First, you have to ask God to help you so that you may be able to do it, because we are not willing to do with my own wish but through God's will, I hope everything will be possible. . . . Secondly, I may call the church elders and we all discuss what shall we do and we unite. We call her to come and have the counsel. What we shall do [and] is what to say, the times you go back from the church that is the time you have ruined your life. . . . And we, first thing we have to show those that have gone successfully to the way of light, because there are some who have gone to successful, simply because they go well in their education and after education maybe they have completed the course . . . and maybe she has gotten married to the right person. At the same time, maybe that person maybe is a Christian. We have a good life and we show them the rest that they have been married to the local people. They are still having a hard time, no time to rest, you know, in the evening, not having . . . the clothes used to tie a child. You know most of our people who have not worked hard they don't have even the cloth to tie their child. So we show that if you go that way, you'll be having poverty. (W07 2005)

One Kipsigis interviewee indicates that since the "government has come" the "problem has lessened." Yet, he notes that the church leaders are developing "a Christian rite of passage" for girls not involving circumcision (W01 2005).

The Meru ministers note that they teach against female circumcision and also point to scripture as indicating circumcision is only for boys (M06 2005; M07 2005; M02 2005). One minister argues that female circumcision is a "mixing" of Christianity and traditional culture and going back is "crucifying Jesus Christ again" (M07 2005). One minister states, "So what I could do is to tell them to ask them where they have seen in the Bible a woman being circumcised? I tell them I've never seen anywhere." He goes on to note the popular presence of its practice, but that he cannot say much because the "women can shame you so much." So he notes that the wise direction to go is to use his wife or "some of the women who have understood and they have some education" (M03 2005).

Despite the position against female circumcision verbalized by Meru respondents, they note its ongoing practice and have developed various approaches to its challenges. One approach used by ministers is to call the newly circumcised girls on "the day of celebration in the center of the church." So "we may cook, clap for them, make them happy, feel that they have some something, really, a passage, and the right way" (M02 2005). Another points to the use of regular teaching of young girls in the church before they arrive at circumcision age so that they will already have the Christian teaching on how to live and act as a Meru Christian women. "So we encourage them to be starting it when they are young, as a girl is growing to be knowing that class [movement from childhood to adulthood]. And that is what it is right now, because even in school they are being taught that" (M06 2005).

The various approaches used by Kenyan ministers to face the cultural challenges of both male and female circumcision indicate their contextualization process in dealing with the various dynamics of circumcision in their cultural contexts. Although some see reasons for discontinuing female circumcision on the basis it was not practiced in the Old Testament, most appear to be adopting a functional substitute where the "non-Christian" elements are replaced by Christian teaching.

The interviewees note challenges of traditional culture in areas beyond traditional circumcision ceremonies. One of those areas that is particularly challenging for them is in addressing a range of spiritual realm beliefs and practices.

Spiritual Realm Beliefs. Ministers referred to the challenges of young Christians' and non-Christians' involvement with spirits, particularly ancestral spirits. One example given of such involvement is the *"mahanga"* which is a "party" in which people are "mostly believing the ancestors rather than God. They forget God." They are celebrating another person's passing to the ancestors. "So it is normally difficult to understand the Bible because they feel if they join the church, they feel something, some of the things like those they have to leave them. Because, they do rituals because of slaughtering goats and cows on the grave . . . to please the dead" (C07 2005).

Another minister from the Giriama people relates a practice which he considers contrary to Christian beliefs. He points to a traditional practice in weddings and the involvement of the *"nkoma."* He states,

> In a wedding you have a bottle of wine and the bridegroom will sit in front. Then he will talk some words and he'll say, "Okay, get this," and maybe pour out a little bit on the ground as an acceptance [to the *nkoma*, ancestral spirit]. . . . And even if it's a tradition, for a Christian to pour a little wine just says [we] are giving to the ancestors first. . . . It is like a prayer to the ancestors . . . [asking] blessing on the wedding. (C08 2005)

This interviewee points to another wedding practice that is perfectly acceptable. In this case the wedding party sings songs which "give thanks to God" and mentions how God takes care of them. "These songs we can accept. We can accept as Christians" (C08 2005).

A Kipsigis minister points to some Christians tending to go back to "their old way of life, thinking that maybe it was better for some of the beliefs in the spirits amongst our people" (W02 2005). Or in another case, a person suffering from misfortunes consults "a local witchdoctor" which

> creates problems in the lives of those Christians and even in the church. . . . Usually, like here in Kipsigis, witchdoctors . . . tell you things that have happened in the past, in your family, and suggest that you takes some charms for protection or perform a certain ritual to appease the spirits and that would open the door for demons to come in, or evil spirits to come into the life of that Christian who is involved in, who has been involved in things of a witchdoctor. (W01 2005)

Another Kipsigis minister perceives the problem of "spirits" (ancestral spirits) as a lack of belief in the Christian afterlife. He states,

> We are believing about life after death in the spirits. We are saying, we, the Africans are saying that, if somebody dies, he will come back to life. When a child is born, the spirit of that person is in that child. So, I have seen the problem . . . they cannot understand immediately about this life after death. (W06 2005)

This minister felt that the problems of the works and powers of ancestral spirits need to be approached by providing better teaching about the afterlife.[2] However, other ministers who mentioned the problem of the "spirits" approach the issue of dealing with traditional beliefs in the spirit's power by emphasizing the greater power of God and Christ.

One minister explains the reverting of Christians back to reliance on the "spirits" as the result of "not being reached properly to show the supremacy of God within their spiritual context" (W02 2005). Another from a different people group notes that the problem in dealing with "*nkoma*" is convincing people that God "can have full provision in their life in any way" (C07 2005). A Kikuyu minister working on the coast among the Giriama observes people returning to their "foreign gods" because of the lack of teaching "to rely on God" which for them traditionally "God is very far" away (C05 2005). He understands both the use of witchdoctors who consult the spirits and the belief in a distant God as a power issue, with people thinking that the "witchdoctor is more powerful than God" (C05 2005). It is exactly on this point that the ministers place the emphasis in their teaching. One minister explains,

> I usually try to explain to them that these pieces of wood are like nothing, because if you erect a piece of wood, that is just something that was created by someone, and we should be thinking about the One that created even that thing that we're erecting there. Explaining to them that is, there must be someone who is more powerful, who is more able, who created everything. But, this piece of wood cannot be our god, or our mediator. That there is a mediator with, you know they believe that the shrines are like mediators, because God is too holy that you cannot approach him directly, but you should use the *nkomas* to approach him. But I tell them that since Christ is our mediator, we don't have to go through these *nkomas* [spirits] but Jesus Christ is there and he's our mediator and he's God. (C10 2005)

A minister from Nairobi takes a similar approach in his awareness of sacrifices offered to ancestral spirits that he is familiar with among the Kisii. He does not simply say, "Hey, you are going to hell." His approach has changed because of his theological education. He now describes his approach as a "soft way." He gives the example, "I would seek to know 'Why are you Kisiis kind of sacrificing to your ancestors?' They would say, 'You know. "But that is a good reason, but then allow me to say something about what the blood of Christ can do. Would you allow me?' . . . That has really helped me to reach and work within my culture" (N04 2005).

In the above examples ministers describe their engagement with traditional beliefs from a Christian perspective. They note the challenges they face, the reasons for the need of engagement, and approaches they take in sharing the biblical perspective. In discussing various traditional sexual mores, church ministers follow a similar line of thinking.

Traditional Sexual Mores. Respondents discussed traditional practices revolving around sexual mores which they feel their ministries need to address. Those specifically addressed are polygamy, a "woman marrying a woman," "wife inheritance," "age-set sex," and "traditional festivals." Although polygamy is present in all the people groups interviewed, in this research the other practices are limited to a particular people group to which the respondents minister.

Polygamy continues to be practiced but generally perceived as declining overall (W03 2005; W05 2005). However, it continues to be an issue for ministers in their churches and in their communities. Communities vary as to the prevalence of the practice. One Meru leader notes its presence among the "*wazees* of Igembe," i.e. tribal elders of northern Meru (M01 2005). Another minister comments that "you may find an area is having many polygamists" (N05 2005). Polygamy is seen by the respondents as both a problem in evangelizing and within the church. One Giriama minister summarizes the challenge in his area when it comes to evangelizing.

> This idea of marrying many wives is according to the Giriama culture. They strongly believe, you see, if one marries a wife and she is barren, according to the culture, for that wife to stop being barren, the husband has to marry another wife, a second wife. Then this second wife will make the first wife give birth. That is how the culture is. So, maybe there are some people who, alright, want to become Christians. But you say no, you see, my problem is, I have, alright, I have a barren wife here and I want to marry another wife so as to make my first wife give birth. (C09 2005)

Another respondent points to the "cultural pull" on Christians to take another wife. He states,

> When you talk about that [polygamy], you are talking what a chief is doing, what an old *mzee* [old man] or your father is doing. It becomes a difficult thing. Though it's not Christian, but you see they have to force it to Christianity. And this has been a challenge even to some of our preachers. You see someone who has been trained as a preacher, he is inside the pulpit, and all of a sudden it happens that the culture pulls him very much and then he has another wife. (M01 2005)

An example of just such a situation occurred while the author was living in Meru in the mid 1990s. The Meru mission team learned about a case of a preacher taking a second wife when it was being discussed between church leaders while riding in one of the missionary's vehicles. The leaders were discussing a hyena that kept going back to the river and drinking water until he burst open. When asked what they were talking about, the leaders explained that one of the preachers got a woman pregnant and then told everyone he had to take her as a second wife because she was pregnant. The missionaries were not involved in the problem solving process, but the church leaders in that area asked the minister to repent and not take a second wife. This has continued to be the approach taken by church leaders in Meru when dealing with Christians taking a second wife.

However, in Meru people who become Christians and are already in polygamist situations are handled differently than Christians who take another wife. The missionaries in Meru approached the challenge of polygamy for new converts by baptizing any who became believers. The goal was not to sever family ties and marriages but to teach the next generation Christ's ideal for marriage. The missionaries left the decision to the churches as to which church ministry roles the converted polygamists could participate. Almost all churches limited the role of the man in that he could not serve as an "elder" of the church. In a few churches this did not preclude him from preaching.

Ministers note the need to approach the challenge of polygamy in a sensitive way (W05 2005). Ministers are aware of the various solutions on how to handle the polygamy situations, but it continues to be an area of discussion and debate. One older minister from Nairobi with deep roots in his rural home community notes that the American missionaries he was involved with gave him "several ideas" from taking only one wife and then "disregarding the rest" to living with them all. In the end he said he had to come up with his own position. He summarizes his thinking in this way:

> Some have suggested that when you find a man and several wives, you can advise him to just leave with one wife and discard the others or disregard the others. And that would seem to be the solution. Because, these are people we have lived with many, many years. How is he going to just leave them all of a sudden. It's really a problem. What I teach is that they can stay as they are but the man cannot participate in the leadership of any kind in the church. He cannot be a church elder, he cannot be anything in the church. But he still can be a member of the Lord's church. (N10 2005)

All of those who raised polygamy as a cultural challenge in their ministry would accept polygamists for baptism. However, his role as a leader would be limited, but this limitation varied among the respondents.

An area that is related to the polygamy situation is what is described by the Kipsigis as a "woman who marries another woman" (W03 2005; W05 2005). This "traditional" practice is used to counteract barrenness. One informant describes the practice as follows.

> In our tradition, she [the barren woman] is allowed to marry another woman. Yeah, the husband has married another wife, which is okay. But this one, the woman also, because she is barren, she wants her own children and therefore she marries another young lady. . . . This old woman brings her young lady as her wife. And now when this young lady comes in, the older lady looks for a young man within her family-hood. Close relatives, maybe clan members, or just some relatives so long as they're within. [She] takes a close young man to father the children for her through this young lady. So, the children that are going to be growed up from her belong to this old woman. (W03 2005)

Ministers in the areas where this is practiced note its decline in prevalence but that it still is a challenge to their ministries (W05 2005). In discussing this problem, a minister of fifteen years observed that discussions such as this "didn't surface in the school," but he continues to work on dealing with the issue. He notes that he has not solved it to "a satisfying end." He further elaborates,

But I've just discussed with the concerned people, especially the lady which is asked to stay at home and bear children. I've talked with her, and the only solution that I asked her to do is, the Bible says "obey your parents, because this is the first command, in everything that pertains to the Lordship of God." But when it comes to "how can I now bear children, I want to bear children for my family," Then I say "just to pray for that and God knows the rest." (W03 2005)

Other respondents, whose ministries are among the Luo and Maasai peoples, brought up the problems of wife inheritance, traditional festival, age-set sex, and women delegates. Among the Luo, wife inheritance occurs when a husband dies and his brother inherits his wife. They also have a harvest festival which is "connected so much with sex. . . . Because they say that, when the time of harvest, there is a feast. And in this feast they say they conclude that feast, or they end the feast with sex" (N11 2005).

The Maasai practices of "age-set sex" and "women delegates" were mentioned by Maasai respondents. Each of these is associated with "blessings." "Blessings" generally refers to becoming pregnant and giving birth. "Age-set sex" is a practice that consists of men of the same age-set sharing their wives when they visit each other's home, i.e. the host offers his wife to his age-mate. One respondent describes the practice this way.

We have that problem of culture because culture there is very tough, because men maybe we have this thing called "age-set." According to age-set, me myself, maybe I'll go to your house and sleep with your wife and that thing is very difficult. To tell a man that way or a woman that way, because they believe that when an age-set man sleeps in the house or with your wife, he will leave blessings. When you refuse him to sleep with your wife, it will be a curse. (N08 2005)

The problem of women delegates is seen as a significant challenge to the Maasai ministers involving their communities because of the sexual activity involved. It particularly puts a lot of pressure on the women. The following lengthy quote gives a sense of the community pressure placed on Christians and Christian women in particular.

We have these delegates, women delegates; sometimes they say we have that delegate and they force other women to go. Sometimes they will, that delegate will say, "This delegate is for the church women." And they'll force them! They come and tell, "Oh, mother John, I want, we want you to go, don't refuse unless we curse you." That delegate of women is every woman will come out of their villages, because they want blessings. They smear that fat, then go around. They come to you and "You are the one to bless women." So they go around, collecting cows and sheep, to bring to you because you are the one to bless. So they set a day of the month, they go around collecting those cows until that day. They bring, then you, they give you, then you bless them, so that they can get children. (N08 2005)

Ministers dealing with traditional sexual practices perceive the conflicts the practices bring with Christian teaching. They also note the social problem revolving around the spread of AIDS as well. The traditional practice of "wife inheritance" is seen to correlate with the similar Jewish practice of the levirate marriage. A Luo minister points to the difference between the practice under Judaism and New Testament teaching which can be used "to correct my culture." He also notes that AIDS is much more likely to be transmitted because they "haven't gone to a check-up."

Similarly, regarding the traditional "festivals" the minister points to scriptures dealing with sex, that it "is for procreation, and it is only for the wife and the husband, people who have made an agreement to live together." He notes that besides the spiritual problems, it also facilitates social problems. "Because many people are using sex in the wrong way, which has led to the spread of AIDS, which has led to abortion . . . so many people have died" (N11 2005).

For the Maasai minister discussing the "age-set sex" and the "women delegates" problems, the conflict to Christian living is not questioned, but the difficulty comes on how best to overcome the cultural practice with the least amount of cultural affront. One minister describes his approach to handling the problem of showing proper hospitality to an age-set member.

> If you have a visitor, we don't tell them "don't have visitors," because a visitor is something automatic. It's automatic, it must come. So, if you have the houses you have this, it is a multi-purpose house. You live there, you cook there, you sleep there, you sit there, and you do everything there. So, if the visitor comes, we encourage them to, me myself if I get a visitor, and we have two beds . . . the woman's bed and the man's bed, I sleep with the visitor in my bed [meaning non-sexual], I sleep with him. Then, having no problem there, because I'll not leave him to sleep with my wife on that day. I'll sleep with the visitor. The wife will sleep with the children. (N08 2005)

The "women delegates" problem is a community wide celebration and places pressure on church members to participate. Refusal to participate may result in that person being "cursed." One evangelist points to providing a separate activity for the church women to attend at the time the activities will take place. The women will also receive teaching on how to deal with the activities. He states,

> According to our place, we teach instead of bringing that habit of saying "we'll join a delegate, we'll do this." We'll tell church women to go for a seminar, we arrange for a seminar. And we encourage these women, these church women to stand firm and depend on God because, if anybody comes and tells you "I'll curse you!" How can he curse you when he's not God? How can he curse you and . . . did not go and steal his cow, you did not go and force him to do something. He is coming to force you something. If anybody force you something, that will not affect you, because we do teach them. We are in for a seminar, they go for a seminar. We teach them on how to deal with them. (N08 2005)

The above traditional practices point to the diversity of cultural practices that local church ministers are facing. In meeting the challenges of the various practices the ministers are actively engaging in interpreting scripture and applying it to the given situation. They are also finding ways to engage the practices they perceive to be non-Christian in a way that allows Christians to not participate but also allows personal relationships to be maintained or to avoid unnecessary conflict within their community by providing alternative activities.

Poverty

Though various problems coming from traditional practices are more frequently mentioned as challenging the Kenyan ministers, the problem of "poverty" is the second most frequently mentioned problem. Poverty, the poor economic conditions, of many people in the churches and churches' communities is considered one of the largest problems facing ministers. As one minister reflects on ministry problems in his community, "I would say the greatest we face is poverty" (N04 2005). Or as another puts it, "The biggest problem that I've encountered is to do with the economy" (C09 2005). Poverty is seen as the source of many of the problems people have in their communities, such as idleness, drunkenness, drug use, psychological problems, family problems, stealing, fighting, lack of education, and diseases (C05 2005; N05 2005; W01 2005).

In the previous chapter it was noted that church ministers feel that their theological education is lacking in preparing them to engage effectively with the poverty issues. Some indicate that they did receive "tools" by which they can better address the poverty problem (N04 2005). However, most still see it as one of the primary issues that is most difficult for them to address.

The challenge of presenting the gospel in the midst of people dealing with poverty and economic problems is of concern to the ministers. "There is the problem of . . . poverty. Where you find people, a church, there are so many people, but then three quarters of them are not employed" (C01 2005). As another minister states,

> I mean there is the poverty problem. I mean, we are not preaching the gospel of health and wealth. But at the same time, we have to be concerned about people who are not getting their provision. I mean, in this country, people give under one dollar a day. And this is how the people [live] that we have to give the gospel, that God cares. That's a challenge. (N01 2005)

The ministry of the church is seen as needing to assist in meeting the needs of the people in the midst of poverty situations but as limited as to what it can provide (N07 2005). The church is also viewed as a possible source of help to those in need but cannot meet the expectations of some of those looking to the church for help (N04 2005).

A number focus on how their ministry is hindered by poverty as it obstructs people from being taught "because someone can think that how can I go to church when I don't have food? See, so it becomes difficult to help such a person" (C07 2005). Others note this same idea by saying people in need of food are so consumed with "finding employment" that they are not receptive to spiritual matters or attending church if they are already Christians (C09 2005; W04 2005). As one minister puts it,

> But due to problems at home, scarcity of resources, in terms of food, clothing, shelter, a farm to plant maize, or to keep some animals. Because of that one [the problems], this one now is going to struggle with the gospel, and . . . this person is not going to

grow spiritually. Eventually this man is going to, or this lady is going to leave the church. You follow him and he keeps on repeating his words, "I am coming to church. I am with you, I am part of the church. We are together." But it has been difficult for them to come back to church. Though some do come, but some keep away and they stay just at home like that. (W03 2005)

Another minister argues that the church is not meeting the "felt needs" of the people. He states, "The biggest problem . . . is we don't meet their felt needs" such as "housing," "house rent," food and clothing (N07 2005). One leader notes that the Churches of Christ are "very dormant on the side of development" and though his theological education opened his mind, it did not help him much in dealing with solving poverty issues especially in the area of development. He points to churches in his area, such as the Anglican Church of Kenya, the Catholic Church and some African Independent Churches, that "come up with different kinds of development" (N05 2005).

Ministers, when asked about dealing with the issues of poverty, point to three approaches in dealing with the poverty problem. First, they teach that Christians should ultimately seek dependence and trust in God and that being poor is not a sign of God's displeasure or lack of love. Second, they should be helping themselves to seek out various means of improving their lives. Third, the use of "development" should be encouraged so that people can provide for themselves.

Ministers teach that ultimately people need to be dependent on God as the source of their strength in dealing with poverty. "What I can help him is just to console him that only God [is] the one who will provide for you" (C07 2005). One minister states,

Some preachers, not most, some preachers especially in town, they try to emphasize health and wealth. It's just like they're giving people empty promises. If you come to Jesus, all the problems will go. And I was telling my church, no, we can be poor, but if we have Jesus, we have nothing less than he who has Jesus and everything else that the world can offer. (W01 2005)

An evangelist from the coast points to preaching that emphasizes the eternal versus the physical and the temporary suffering leading to the eternal "rest." He gives an example of his approach.

I usually use that example as a solution to such a problem.... What I'm giving you is something that will help you eternally. Then just the physical needs that you need, which is just for but a short time. So, we are trying to strive, although we suffer here on earth. But, at long last we shall rest. The Israelites, when they were leaving Egypt, they suffered a lot. But at least they were aiming at a place where they would come to a rest. We are on a journey now, which is full of, the road is full of thorns, full of so many discouraging things, but at long last, we shall rest. (C09 2005)

Another minister notes the need to continually give assurance on a "regular basis" of the loving concern of God for people in the midst of their poverty. He explains,

On the gospel, I mean, does God really care? Is God really there? If he's there, why? Why is this happening to me? That is a continuous challenge that I get every day that I have to confirm to people that, you know, God still loves you. You know, despite what is happening in your life that don't remove God from loving you. Giving assurance on a regular basis, almost daily, to people who are hurting because so many people are hurting today. (N01 2005)

A number of ministers interviewed encourage Christians to be seeking means for self-improvement through their own labors. "I've been able to teach, make people to be able to realize their ability, and that they're able also to depend on themselves, to do something they can help themselves" (C04 2005). Some ministers lead the way in encouraging developing means of reducing poverty either by improving current business strategies or by using resources in new ways.

One minister gives an example of this approach and a success story in training Christians to buy and sell seed at better market prices. He describes his effort in this way:

I'm trying to advise people on how to come up with their own solutions toward their own problems, not to depend on gifts from people. Like, this is what I'm doing, and the Bible is clear that each man should work so that he can have something to give to his neighbor. Now this is what I want us to do [with] our church member, just like in the village, especially those who are members to our church.... We want to contribute and buy quality seeds for each of our members. And, you know, we want to bring some money together, like what we did last planting season.... We brought some money together, some would give higher than others. Some would not give at all. They'll go and pick some would give higher than others. Some would not give at all. They'll go and pick some seeds from their store which is not yet treated seed, or rather highbred that you could take from the *shamba* [garden]. . . . Now, we brought some money together, we bought seeds at a cheap price. Not really cheap because, the bigger you buy it, it is almost cheap, rather than buying it small, small, kind of packages. So we bought that big, we gave small seeds to our members. And I tell you the truth that one of our guys, each time he used to cry "I do not have food!" Now he's very comfortable, because of this approach of day's work – go to the *shamba*, don't go to the road. Go to the *shamba*, work! (N04 2005)

When asked about how he works in his community to solve the problem of poverty, another minister points to being able to organize people in using local resources to produce a product.

Now in my area I've introduced something like we are using banana fibers. And we've sat down and sew that, we can use what people neglect to be useless. We can make it be useful. Especially banana fibers, now people are using banana fibers to make something. For now we are making table mats, from banana fibers. We are making serviette rings, and briefcases. (N05 2005)

The poverty issue is related to two other areas that are identified by respondents as significant problems. The first is the area of support and the second is the area of expectations.

Support for Ministers

The issue of support for ministers was briefly discussed in chapter 5 where respondents verbalize a significant lack of training towards helping to deal with support and the call for more vocational training. There it was noted that the overall emphasis among Churches of Christ missionaries from the church growth perspective was for ministers to be self-supporting, or for self-supporting churches to provide the support for their ministers, or a combination of both.

The problem of how to support ministers is a major area of concern throughout mission circles, and this research was not designed to explore this issue among Churches of Christ in Kenya. However, judging from the responses in the interviews, such a study on this issue would be most helpful. This section will elaborate the ministers' perceptions of the support problem and their attempts to address the problem.

The ministers verbalize a number of elements that they feel are involved in the "support" problem. First, churches are, for the most part, not supporting their preachers. Second, there is a need for more teaching in the churches on giving. Third, the lack of support for preachers is hindering the effectiveness of ministers. Fourth, church leaders are not being provided with enough opportunities to develop the skills to make a living. Fifth, the theological education process should address more directly the support issue.

The interviewees are concerned about the support problem but do not affix blame in pointing at Western missionaries as hindering support, not giving support in order to dominate the churches, or in order to control church leaders. Nor is there a wide call for outside support from missionaries and western churches. One person calls for more partnership between national churches and "donors," but even this is within the context of providing "good projects" to help with support (C02 2005). Another calls for continued support from outside sources beyond the theological education to support the ministry of the graduating student (N08 2005). However, most verbalize the need for churches to be independent and to support their own preachers. A number note that churches are not doing enough to support their own preachers and need to be taught more fully on giving and providing for their own ministers. A number of ministers put it succinctly. "Basically in our churches here, giving is very, very poor and these ministers . . . they need to be supported" (C02 2005). "The other problem is we need to teach our church to support our preachers" (W06 2005). "So our church . . . needs to be encouraged to be in a position to be able to reach out and help their leaders. So leadership support from the churches is also not strong" (W02 2005). "Another problem is . . . preachers right now, not many of our churches pay their preachers. . . . The church needs to be aware that it has to pay their preachers" (N10 2005). ". . . It is high time that we should teach our people how to support our people, how to support our churches, by ourselves. Because we need that a church should be taught how to give so that we may support our pastors, for them to work more effectively" (N06 2005).

The lack of financial support to ministers is seen as having negative consequences for effective ministry. The interviewees note that ministers who graduate from the programs do not have plans for how they will "earn a living as well as serve God." "They taught me good principles, I use them, I'm using today, but then I don't know how I'm going to earn my living" (C03 2005). A Meru leader states, "And when they finish [school] . . . there's no support. They are unable, they don't know what to do. Although I know the original intent was for them to be able to learn and they take the education to the churches" (M03 2005).

The interviewees identify a number of negative effects such as ministers dropping out of ministry because "they don't have any earning" and because of having to "cope" with providing for their families (N07 2005).

> I'm well equipped, in fact, but I'll not be a full minister in the church because of poverty. . . . You'll go somewhere else and you'll get support somewhere, and then you can, you can proceed with your ministry. So some . . . people may be equipped here and go back home and go and forget . . . because of their poverty, because they don't have any other support to support them. (N08 2005)

As another minister states, "After training, we are dumped to the rural areas without support. It will force me to go to work for my family to get the daily bread. So I will not concentrate too much on ministering. I will concentrate too much on how my family will be" (N05 2005). Ministers most frequently mention the negative effect on their time for ministry because of the amount of time they must spend searching for a means of support (M02 2005; M06 2005; N04 2005).

> I have a great knowledge from here [NGCS]. And then I go home and then I go, I am a business man, I go buy cattle, maybe maize, I do that and that. When I come back home, I don't have time to read even the Bible. I don't have time even to see what I learned from the school or those things. Then, the only place that we meet with members is on Sunday, then maybe it is a rush hour. . . . Then . . . other members got problems. Maybe others died, something like that. Nobody to follow them. . . . But, the problem only is, is the time to be with the members. (N09 2005)

Other identified problems are associated with lack of support. The ability to help meet others' physical needs is limited because of ministers' personal precarious financial limitations (C09 2005; N04 2005). Mismanagement of church funds by ministers is seen as more prevalent because of the lack of support of ministers (C03 2005). The lack of support also leads some ministers to move to other religious groups for financial reasons (N08 2005).

In solving the problem of support, ministers mention their struggles in returning to their home churches from their education experiences, only to find no or very little support for ministering fulltime. Most ministers describe situations of searching for employment or returning to work on their farms (N08 2005; N09 2005; W04 2005; M06 2005).

> Like the problems I've faced myself after NGCS is that my church had no place for the future for the people like us . . . who went to college. So, after there, I came home and there was no plan, and so it was actually hard for me to adapt to that and start working, maybe organizing myself again and starting . . . [to] think on how you're going to earn your living as well as serve God. (C03 2005)

A few spoke about launching out in faith with no sure support for fulltime ministry (C05 2005). "Since the church needed somebody who will be . . . [a] fulltime minister, I had to do that and it was difficult decision to make for my family. . . . So being a minister, it's a total sacrifice and a total sacrifice that we have to make" (N07 2005).

As discussed in chapter 5, most of the respondents see some form of "vocational," "tent-making," or "money generating projects" training as the most helpful in solving the support issue. They believe this can best be done through the extension training system and NGCS. As one respondent summarizes it,

> So we need to introduce some other ministries so that they can help them to have their living, to support them. . . . I know without these courses the ministers will go on to finish their education, let's say in Nairobi Great Commission School, or Siriat Bible School and will be done. . . . Nothing he or she will do at their churches because you know our churches are not supporting us. So we need to work, like Paul was a tent-maker. So we need to work in other ways to get something for our families and continue with the work of God. (W06 2005)

Most of the problems expressed by those interviewed in this research concerned poverty, the lack of giving by churches, and ministers' struggles for making a living while serving in the churches were common themes when American missionaries were on the field and after leaving the mission field. This author has been involved in this issue in Meru for over twenty-five years now, and it has been discussed each year even after he left fulltime ministry in Meru. Each year the problem of the support of ministers is revisited and ways are discussed in which local churches can improve their support for preachers and evangelists. After a number of years of the Meru leaders experimenting with various formulations of encouraging churches to support their own ministers, multi-church cooperation in providing support along with indirect assistance from American missionaries, the summer of 2006 unveiled a plan led by Meru leaders that has begun to show signs of a practical means of support for ministers.

Church leaders from multiple congregations have organized cooperating churches into a cluster of churches working closely together to share teaching from the leaders of each church, discussing and dealing with problems that may occur in those churches, evangelizing together, and providing support for the local ministers for that group. For example, the "AKIKA" group consists of the Andula, Kirindine, Antuamouo, and Kibilaku Churches of Christ. They describe their purpose as a group in their "covenant conditions." They state that this group's purpose is:

> (a) To build a faithful society by teaching people to obey God's commands in order to prepare them for eternal life. (b) To peacefully gain converts from all walks of life to participate in this ministry of the gospel of Christ. (c) To organize periodic Maketha in aid of preachers and their families while they are in their preaching mission. This assistance will be done by local churches of AKIKA and in case of a major problem the team can ask missionary brothers to assist. (AKIKA 2005, 4)

This group and two others in Meru began forming after a leaders' meeting in August of 2005 where I spent hours in discussion with some one hundred church leaders on the topic of support of local ministers. It was at that meeting the first practical ideas emerged concerning ways to increase local congregations' support of their ministers. Church leaders were asking that more vocational training be made available for church leaders and members for a more long-term solution of providing income for leaders and church members. They also asked for some form of assistance from missionaries or churches in the U.S. to supplement churches' support. However, there was no system to identify any amount of support being given to local ministers from the churches to supplement. This led to a discussion of a practical means of encouraging local congregations in contributing specifically to supporting their ministries. Monthly assistance in each congregation was not seen as practical or sustainable on an individual congregation level. However, ideas began to surface about churches grouping together and holding a *"maketha"* (literally means "harvest" but refers to a special time of giving), which traditionally was a means of people pooling resources to assist others or to accomplish large projects in villages.

The former missionaries along with this writer had discussed this problem in a meeting in Dallas a year earlier and had decided that direct support of church ministers was still very risky and the potential for jealousy was extremely high as not all of the leaders could or should be supported. The missionaries did recognize that most of the leaders had continued in their ministries despite the lack of financial support, the dwindling size of farm lands available, and the poor economic conditions that continue to plague Kenya. A form of partnership and indirect support beyond the continued implementation of vocational training was seen as viable because of the maturity of a number of church leaders. However, the missionaries did not have a clear perception of a method for providing indirect support.

The *"maketha"* proposal at the August 2005 leaders' meeting was considered to be worth attempting and a number of leaders said they would try it. This author was asked if the expatriate missionaries would consider participating in contributing to this. This author proposed that the missionaries would contribute to *"maketha"* when they received a bank report from the church leaders indicating the amount the group of churches contributed to the support of the ministers. Beginning in September of 2005, leaders from the congregations encouraged their members to implement this method of ministerial support.

In July of 2006 this writer met with the church leaders from some forty congregations in Meru. Three groups of churches submitted reports of contributions received at their monthly or bi-monthly *maketha*. Former missionaries added their contributions to the *makethas*.

The response of the participating church leaders has been very positive thus far. They report good participation of church members and the church leaders verbalize being pleased with the system. Other churches are beginning to form cluster groups similar to the three initial ones. It is interesting to note that the three groups of churches that formed were in the most traditional areas of Meru, the Igembe and Maasai areas, where clan and family lines are strongest. The *maketha* approach does not demand a certain amount from outside sources, but missionaries and churches freely participate with free-will offerings. As of 2012 a number of congregations continue to utilize this approach.

The problems of "poverty" and "support" are connected to a theme that surfaced during the interview process. The theme of "expectations," particularly of ministers and their roles as leaders in the church and in their communities, are tied to both the poverty and support issues.

Expectations

"The poor do not lead" one minister quotes from a local Kenyan politician. He points to this quote indicating that the expectations of people is that church leaders have resources and financial support to assist them. He further explains what this means, "And what he meant by that is you put somebody who doesn't have any wealth, who doesn't have any social income in leadership and people will not follow him. So one of the challenges we face as ministers is our income" (N03 2005).

Christians and communities where ministers serve are perceived to have expectations of the ministers as having access to financial and other physical resources beyond fulfilling the spiritual needs (C04 2005; C10 2005; N10 2005). As a minister in South Nyanza notes, "In the community where we plant the church, and even the one we planted recently in May, the community or the people who come in expect us to be the ones donating money to pay that church" (N02 2005). One minister listed two expectations from his area of ministry but emphasized the second above the first. He states,

> Problem number one: people look at you for all the solutions, for all answers. . . . They think once you've gone to a training like the Great Commission School you know everything from the Bible which is a lie. Number two: they think they can gain from you. They think since you've gone to school, maybe, you'll be paid. (N04 2005)

Sociological expectation of leaders' status as being more financially secure or at least having access to greater resources is highlighted by some. One minister gives an example when he says,

> Maybe we are meeting in a maize field, weeding maize. Then they come and say, "When we're with our Pastor weeding maize." You see . . . they will not take you very much

important. We are like, we are alike. You know sometimes as a minister you need to separate maybe to have a certain dignity, they expect that. (N09 2005)

A minister among the Kalenjin notes the expectation of the communities in which churches are located is to have notable leadership positions. "The community, when we try to preach to them, so they have been asking us, 'Who's your Bishop?,' 'Who's your Reverend?,' 'Who's your Pastor of your church?' They are looking for position" (W06 2005). Position in church leadership and resources are perceived to be intertwined so that the ministers feel the pressure from church members and their community to have access to resources others lack. One evangelist verbalizes this when he states,

Okay, the general problem that occurs is that the communities generally may have, majority of them have wrong perspectives of what Christianity is all about, or who is a Christian. . . . When you go out and preach unto them and try, and you teach them, show them the love of Christ, some may take advantage of wanting to squeeze out whatever they have from you, because they feel like your heart is generous, he can give you anything, or you can help in any way. . . . So that is one of the things that they do. For example, what I'm doing here at the center, they expect that the center will be started, or a training school will be started, should be equipped with everything. It's a news of traveling around, whenever that you need for use here, food or whatever, they look to it as a place where you can take a cup for help. If they need food, they need money for transport; they want that kind of things. So, they just want to come and say, "Okay, this is what I would like you to help me with, I'm suffering from this and that." Just like, if you explain to them, or tell them that this is not here with me, I don't have this and I don't have that, they will not believe you. They will say, "Okay, you are not a good person, you are mean," and such like things. (W02 2005)

The "expectation" pressures from people in the communities and from church members on the local ministers may be due to the situation that ministers are receiving their training from resources primarily instituted and provided by the missionaries and overseas churches. One leader notes that people in his area and even his parents expected him to be employed after graduating from the NGCS. They look for that support to come and be helpful to them and when it doesn't materialize he is pressured to ask for support (C10 2005).

Expectations placed upon church leaders from within the church and from their communities is an ongoing struggle for church ministers. Having resources or access to resources increases their prestige as a minister according to those interviewed. This, among other challenges, surfaces various leadership issues.

Leadership

In chapter 5 it was noted that ministers see their theological education as being effective in preparing them as leaders. However, despite the interviewees rating their theological education as helpful in improving their leadership abilities in a number of areas, they point to several leadership problems that concern them.

Over two-thirds of the church ministers interviewed express some type of leadership problem that they perceive to be present in the Churches of Christ in Kenya. Their leadership concerns can be categorized into three areas which do overlap to one degree or another. These areas are: (1) the lack of trained leaders in the churches; (2) tension between trained leaders and "lay-leaders"; and (3) the "bwana kubwa" complex.

Lack of Trained Leaders. Many of the interviewees identify the lack of competent trained leaders as a major problem in the churches of Christ as a whole (C01 2005; M01 2005). There is a "lack of leadership because the people who you get to work with you, they have not been prepared well to take the responsibilities which are there" (N02 2005). As another leader comments, "They need leadership training. Ministers are leaders . . . how they lead people is very, very important" (N11 2005). A number of church leaders see the lack of trained leaders as hindering the church's stability, growth, spiritual development, and vision (W05 2005). "The problem is we are not stable, the leaders in our churches, in Churches of Christ. That's why we are not so much growing; we are not stable in the church" (N09 2005). Another evangelist comments,

> But I feel that the elders of the church should be trained so that every vision, or any development, spiritual development may come from the whole leadership, not just one person. You know, when only one person is trained, now sometimes it's very hard to share that vision with the others, or to share those teachings with the others. (C10 2005)

The availability of trained leaders is seen as crucial to the growth and spiritual maturity of the church (W08 2005). Others point out the need for the training not to just be a generic type of leadership training like in preaching but rather training that takes into consideration the gifts a person has. "There is this thing I think can work a bit. When we train the leaders, we train them according to their ability. . . . Not to train them generally but according to [their] talent. If we can identify those talents" (M01 2005). Another minister states, "I think we mess up in the sense that everyone can lead and all of us, we are priests, and then we mess up everything." He sees the "mess up" as the lack of identifying specific areas of ministry for leaders. He argues,

> Like our teaching in the Church of Christ, we know that each of us, we are servants. But then, you realize that we do not have specification after training that "you are gifted in evangelism. Why can't we allow you a hand on matters pertaining to evangelism? And Brother, we think that you make a good teacher.". . . And then get to other point and say that "Brother, we see that God has given you a gift of administration. Why can't we allow you to have that gift, or I mean that place or rather responsibility in the church?" (N04 2005)

The general sense of interviewees' responses points to an overall desire for more trained leaders with a vision for spiritual maturity, church growth, and centered on their gifts. As one minister summarizes, "Leadership is a problem right now in Kenya. Even in churches which are not attached to Church of Christ, they are finding it difficult to have the right elders, the right ministers, the right deacons" (N02 2005).

Tension between Trained Leaders and Lay-Leaders. Beyond just the lack of trained leaders the most frequently mentioned problem in leadership is the tension and conflict between school-trained leaders and "lay-leaders" who frequently are the initial leaders and have little formal or non-formal theological education. "So, there's a very big gap" (W04 2005).

Most ministers feel their training prepares them well for their leadership roles, particularly in being "servant leaders," assists them in specific ministry skills such as teaching or preaching, nurturing and counseling. However, one minister notes that they were not well prepared for dealing with the leadership problems related to tension and conflict between them as "trained leaders" and older lay-leaders. "When it comes to leadership in the church, we were taught theoretically, but practically it's proved to be slightly hard to show leadership in the church" (W03 2005). One minister from the coast expresses his frustration when he states,

> There was a problem in my church there at the time I was graduated from Nairobi Great Commission School, and which is leadership. So, we were many ministers in the church. So there was that kind of confrontations. We are there, everybody wants to be recognized, to preach. So, sometimes you are not given time to say anything. I could finish three months, you go in the church service, you don't even speak. . . . Because I am from college, I feel that I could speak help but no opportunities. (C03 2005)

The gap between trained leaders and lay-leaders is recognized to some extent as a conflict from a cultural perspective in an area where more traditional leadership roles prevail over theological training.

> The culture it is only the old men should be the opinion leaders. And most of them, those who think they can make opinion leaders, they have that view of culture inside them. . . . [Therefore] they can't give you the time for somebody who has knowledge inside them. They have to give opinions. (M02 2005)

Trained leaders, especially younger ones, feel that the older, untrained leaders view them as a threat to their leadership. As one thirty-four year old evangelist states,

> Because here you come with your diploma certificate, and now you're trying to teach. And here is an old man, who has been in the church for ten, fifteen, twenty years, but he's leading unchristian way of life. You try to prove him wrong, and he says "No, you are just very new. I've been in the church fifteen years; you know nothing. You still are a young man or a young lady." (W03 2005)

Even older church ministers that receive training note this tension between leaders when a trained leader returns with a diploma. As one middle-aged minister observes,

> What I see as if they are avoiding so much is for them to be in the same church. Because there are so many others who have no education and they're preaching. . . . They don't care whether you preach well, they don't care whether they have a diploma or not. But

they look nice; that means that those who have the diplomas and advanced certificate, they can go on and do the work they were trained to do [i.e. church planting and evangelism], but not to continue for preaching positions all the time at the same church. (M03 2005)

A number of interviewees point to means by which they are trying to resolve this conflict or, at least, reduce its negative effects. Beyond just encouraging trained leaders not to "run away from this responsibility" but continue to find ways to work where such conflicts exist, other leaders are involved in various ways of bridging the gap between the trained and untrained church ministers (C09 2005).

Others identify this conflict as the trained ministers not showing respect and listening to "lay-leaders" who are preaching in the churches. One minister summarizes his approach when he states,

First thing is the connection between me and other leaders, because I am not the only leader there. There are other leaders, there are other lay-leaders. More I can say, and there are elders also who are above. And then, it has helped me to go and humble myself before the elders. And then, when I humble myself, they give me their ears, then, I can tell them what we can do together with them, with the leaders, and with the other lay-leaders. Now, it has helped me that we have formed unity between elders, me, and then the other lay-leaders, that we can work together. . . . And then, it has helped us to divide the work. (N09 2005)

Other interviewees note that finding ways of cooperating with lay-leaders and sharing the training they received provides a foundation for sharing leadership roles. In one area, annual leadership clinics for both trained and non-trained leaders are held to study the Bible together and jointly determine "how we can apply it today so that we can fit in God's message of their times and in our times and in our situation, in our own language" (N04 2005). Such leadership meetings are used by some to resolve conflicts while providing a "friendly atmosphere" in which to clarify teachings that have been seen as contradicting one another and thus "will look like we are fighting and that would be very dangerous for the church" (W01 2005). Providing a venue for open and friendly discussions and study between church leaders is seen as very beneficial in overcoming the tension between church leaders and is already being practiced by a number of ministers.

Related to the problem of tension between trained leaders and lay-leaders, a number of interviewees see the problem of the *"bwana kubwa"* (big boss) church leader as significant. Approximately thirty percent of those interviewed pointed to this problem as being detrimental to their ministry.

The Bwana Kubwa Complex. Despite the emphasis interviewees placed on their theological training providing them an understanding of church leadership as "servant leadership," the problem of the *bwana kubwa* (big chief) in the church was identified as an area of concern.[3] "There are those who want to be the bosses, I mean, of the church. . . . So there are some of those who want to be in those positions . . . that they may use . . . in the church, and misuse that position, also, for mistreating members, or using it for his own personal interest." It even gives rise to competition between ministers in the church (W02 2005). Or as one minister says, "One leader sees himself as better than the other" and does not want to be a servant but a "big man" (N10 2005). This is viewed as bringing about conflict within Churches of Christ as multiple ministers and a body of elders and deacons make up the leadership of a local congregation. Conflict because of the *"bwana kubwa"* attitude is seen as a prideful nature in leaders. "Some people, it's like, they fight for position" (C06 2005). As one minister reflects on the "African" church leaders, they "try to make themselves high priests" (M08 2005). Another notes the tendency of "going for the big posts in the church" (M02 2005).

Others see a leader's desire for being the "boss" as propelled by the fact that "so many other churches are doing like this" (C10 2005). As one minister notes, "We have been having some problems with some of the leaders we put in the church. Sometimes they are going astray from the teachings of the Church of Christ; they have been influenced. Sometimes they see what others are doing and they may try to do what people are doing" (C03 2005).

Whatever the source of the *"bwana kubwa"* problem is, leaders seem to be approaching the problem in the same way. They are holding leadership seminars with churches' ministers. One minister describes his method in dealing with a dominating church leader through the use of special courses to prepare qualified leaders to replace a *bwana kubwa* leader.

> [If] somebody in the leadership had a bad spirit and he was sort of wanting to dominate everything, he was almost a dictator. So, what I did was to develop what would be a group of people who would be leaders in the event that this person and his team were

removed. So, we had some training. Then we began to talk to that person but apparently he did not want to, because he was the one in charge. So everyone who will approach him will be saying the same. But, we did it for almost a year, just trying to approach him. But since this group had been mandated by that leader and the others to be ministry coordinators, coordinating various ministries, they eventually came up and told this leader, "No, today you've got to step down." (C01 2005)

Spiritual Maturity

Identified less frequently than leadership problems was the general problem of the lack of spiritual maturity among church members. "The biggest problem we face in the church is to bring them up to maturity; maturing the congregation, or maturing the Christians to obey and live a Christian life" (N07 2005). This lack of maturity manifests itself in the church in various ways. One leader notes, "People cannot tell truth. That is the biggest problem. Nobody's willing to tell the truth. Yeah, and all these are Christians. It does not matter, Christians, non-Christians, they are the same" (M03 2005). Another minister points out the "two-faced life" that Christians are living (N04 2005). "People, by what they are doing are showing they are not mature," says a leader from the West. "The problem now is people, many people; there is some not understanding the word of God. So that is the thing that the church wants to teach them, to be matured in the word of God" (W08 2005).

Ministers recognize the long-term maturing process that comes with increasing spiritual maturity. As one interviewee notes, "If you are with Christianity you can't grow overnight. You have to grow slowly, slowly, slowly.... It's going to work, and God is the one who helps a person to grow" (M06 2005).

In providing a positive environment for encouraging spiritual growth, ministers identify the need to provide good examples themselves. As one leader states, "To stay faithful, I think what we should do is to show the good work to them, to be humble to the other people, not to be harsh. To be humble as Christ came to the earth, humbled himself, and even [to] the poor people [and] the sinner people" (W07 2005).

Other ministers point to their use of personal visits, teaching, and organizing midweek courses and seminars apart from Sunday. One explains his approach to the problem.

Since we don't have matured people, or mature Christians, one of them escapes and goes and has some drinks. . . . Then they will come and tell me, "Pastor, I have seen so and so doing this." Then what I would normally do, I call him privately. . . . I try to teach him, you know, if you are a Christian, you are supposed to go on this life. . . . Otherwise, if not, when you disown the church, you are making the church not be recognized by outsiders. They might start asking questions, "Hey, what church is that doing this and this?" So, I keep on explaining, explaining. (M07 2005)

Movement toward "Self-Theologizing?"

The above data indicates that Kenyan ministers interviewed perceive their theological training as contributing to their ability to contextualize the gospel to their ministry contexts. Their descriptions of traditional cultural challenges and their processes for bringing the gospel to bear on those processes show not only theological acumen but also practical approaches to remain sensitive to the cultural implications. They are not just bringing to bear simplistic answers but continue to struggle with the issues and the best response for the particular problem in its given context.

They are also able to identify other problems beyond traditional culture conflicts. The problem areas of poverty, support of ministers, expectations, leadership conflict, and the lack of spiritual maturity of Christians are seen as significant areas of concern. The problems of poverty, support of ministers and expectations of ministers are all intertwined in the discussion of how to resolve the support of ministers in the midst of economic limitations or "poverty" in order to meet the expectations of Christians and the communities of the churches.

The leaders interviewed feel confident in dealing with the problems of culture and spiritual maturity and see themselves as well prepared for this in their theological education. However, poverty, support and expectations were identified as issues which they are finding more difficult to address and for which their theological education did not adequately prepare them. In recognizing the problem in these areas, they continue to struggle with them in various ways as surveyed above. It is particularly in these areas that these ministers, in one form or another, see the need for improvements related to their theological education.

The very fact that they identify strengths and weaknesses in their theological education and ministries indicates that self-theologizing is taking place. Their ability to critically evaluate their ministry situations with both strengths and weaknesses also indicates that they are perceiving their ministries as directed by God and requiring their gifts to be used by God for their ministry tasks.

It is possible to discern from the foregoing perceptions of the interviewees a certain level of self-theologizing by observing the examples of the working out of theology within the cultural contexts guided by the gospel and applied to their life situations. There is a sense of a fuller realization that it is God at work in them and guiding them. There is the realization that the local church must bring scripture to bear on its life situations. There is the recognition that the original heralds of the gospel message are not the message or the authorities of the authorized interpretation but fellow pilgrims in God's kingdom. They do identify a need for a fuller exploration of the scripture by the church leaders and members in relation to the culture in which the church exists and works. They do perceive that God uses scripture and the various challenges of cultures to increase people's theological reflections.

The interviewees articulate that they are contextualizing the message well. It is possible to see from the preceding data that they see God working in them and that they, in the context of their local churches, are bringing the gospel to bear on their life situations. Western missionaries are considered a resource but are not seen as the authority or providing the authorized interpretation of scripture to their context. Also, the interviews show that the ministers are continuing to explore scripture to make better application to their cultural context. Their cultural challenges are giving rise to theological reflection that goes beyond simple preaching and teaching. They are bringing scripture to bear on the daily struggles that impact the minister and those to whom they minister.

The level to which the theological education in the Kenya Churches of Christ is facilitating the search for the fourth self will be explored in chapter 7. The data of this research points to the theological education being more effective in some areas than others in facilitating the search for the fourth self.

> The fourth self, self-theologizing, recognizes that Christians need to develop theologies that make the gospel clear in their different cultures.
> *Hiebert 1985*

CHAPTER 7
Discovering the Fourth Self: Implications for Theological Education

Kenyan ministers evaluated their theological education in facilitating self-theologizing based on its assistance in improving their ability to contextualize the message effectively and solve ministry challenges within their various ministry contexts. Their evaluations provide a number of insights into the level of self-theologizing being practiced by these ministers in various dimensions of self-theologizing. This chapter will first discuss the various dimensions of self-theologizing that have been identified and utilized in missiological writings and how they apply to this research. Second, the findings from this research will delineate six dimensions that assist in measuring the level of self-theologizing being practiced by the church leaders and how well the theological education process appraised in this research is facilitating the practice of the fourth self in each of the dimensions. Third, the chapter will discuss a number of implications of the six identified dimensions as they relate to the level of self-theologizing, i.e. cognitive, affective, evaluative, ministerial, missiological and structural.

Dimensions of Self-Theologizing

Arriving at a means for measuring the level of self-theologizing requires establishing some categories by which to measure the level of contextualization that the theological education process has attempted to facilitate. The data provided by active ministers in this research surfaced a number of dimensions of contextualization which correlate well with a number of dimensions of contextualization that have been identified by missiologists.

Hiebert's critical contextualization provides three categories in which he proposes the need to "translate the biblical message into the cognitive, affective, and evaluative dimensions of another culture" (1994, 89-91). The TEF Third Mandate identifies four areas of contextualization that need to be addressed for "renewal and reform of theological education:" "missiological," "structural," "pedagogical," and "theological" (Lienemann-Perrin 1981, 174-175). Kinsler identifies "key issues" in facilitating contextualization: the nature of ministry; the model of theological education; the relationship between theological education and the ministers; personal, ecclesial and social transformation from the community of believers; and structurally rooted in the realities of the context of the ministries (1999, 11-15). African theology identifies key elements which interact to contextualize the message from an emic perspective that are represented in the six dimensions, i.e. biblical context, African traditional context, current socio-cultural African contexts, the church and the western Christian intellectual and cultural heritage.

Taking into consideration the above elements for the purpose of analysis in this research, six dimensions will be proposed by which to evaluate the level to which the Kenya Churches of Christ theological education process is perceived by ministers to be providing the tools for facilitating self-theologizing. The dimensions of self-theologizing identified are Hiebert's three categories (1985, 30-33), two categories from the TEF Third Mandate (TEF Staff 1972, 31), and one category from Berquist, who elaborated on the categories suggested by the TEF Third Mandate (1973, 246-250). The six dimensions are cognitive, affective, evaluative, missiological, structural, and ministerial.

The cognitive dimension refers to the ability to conceptualize biblical knowledge from the educational process, from personal study, and from experience in their African context, often with a mix of Western Christian intellectual and cultural heritage. The affective dimension involves the feelings the ministers have toward their theological education experiences, both positive and negative. Evaluative refers to the ability to interact with one's own cultural heritage, the current socio-cultural context, and the church context to apply the biblical message to make decisions in determining right and wrong within a ministry context (Hiebert 1985, 32-33). This correlates with TEF's "theological" category (TEF Staff 1972, 31). The missiological dimension focuses on developing training that addresses renewal and reform issues in the church dealing with human development and justice in its particular context. The structural category refers to the administrative and infrastructure of the church and its various institutions for carrying on ministry and providing training sensitive to the socio-economic and political contexts (TEF Staff 1972, 31). The ministerial dimension carries the idea that the ministers and other church leaders see themselves as developing in their ministry skills and personally experiencing a dynamic relationship with God in their churches and communities. This dimension, suggested by Berquist's "patterns of ministry" crises, is closely aligned with TEF's "pedagogical" category (1973, 247; TEF Staff 1972, 31).

Summary of the Six Dimensions of Self-Theologizing

The general perception of the Kenyan ministers who were trained in the theological institutions of the Kenya Churches of Christ, overall, rate their theological education as being very beneficial in their ministries. However, when their evaluation of their education is divided into the six dimensions both strengths and weaknesses are more readily identifiable. The sections below will summarize the findings gathered from the abovementioned data by utilizing these six dimensions of self-theologizing. The data indicates that the cognitive, affective, evaluative, and ministerial dimensions are perceived overall as being adequately addressed by the theological education process in providing effective ministry tools and processes. However, the ministerial dimension is perceived to be adversely effected by the two weakest dimensions, the missiological and structural. The church leaders did not consider the missiological and structural dimensions to have been adequately addressed in their theological education process. These two dimensions will be discussed later. First, the four positively perceived dimensions will be discussed.

Affective Dimension

The affective dimension as used here reflects the ministers' feelings as to the value and level of satisfaction with their theological education. The ministers were highly positive toward the value they found in receiving their theological education but with some caveats of areas of improvements that would expand their academic experience. As they reviewed their non-formal and formal education opportunities, they indicate that both were beneficial and provided various levels and broader opportunities for leaders to participate in some type of leadership training. Localized courses, TEE style courses, and local training centers were seen as contributing to a wide variety of educational possibilities, thus allowing a broader spectrum of Christians and leaders to take advantage of learning experiences because of proximity to churches and less expense in attending. They concluded that all the types of training are valuable but that the more formal is preferred and provides a "higher" level of training for the contemporary Kenyan context. All the leaders saw the local training centers as highly important for the future theological education in Kenya Churches of Christ. They suggested increasing the level of theological education above what is currently being offered at both the extension centers and NGCS.

The interviewees indicate a high satisfaction level related to the affective dimension of self-theologizing. However, they did not hesitate to verbalize areas of limitations and where they perceived improvements are needed in other dimensions.

Cognitive Dimension

Ministers identified a number of reasons for pursuing their theological education at the training centers or NGCS. The top reasons for pursuing theological education correlated with three of the top five areas that were identified as areas in which their theological education strengthened their ministries. These were evangelism and church planting, ministry skills and biblical knowledge.

The most frequently given reason for ministers pursuing their theological education was for greater biblical knowledge. This was also evaluated as being an area in which they felt their theological education helped them the most. The increased knowledge was perceived as improving their ministry skills, assisting them in making better application of the gospel to the ministry contexts, and enhancing their ability to communicate the gospel to people of higher educational levels. Ministers perceived this improved biblical knowledge as assisting them to meet the challenges of the changing culture with its more educated sections of society as opposed to ministering with a "bush" preacher's level of knowledge.

Ministers voiced no criticisms related to the level of biblical knowledge they received. They did note that there was a Western influence in the teaching they received from Western teachers. They divided the Western teaching into two categories: teaching from long-term American missionaries to Kenya and teaching from Westerners with little experience in Africa. They note that they were able to recognize teaching that was from a "Western worldview" and yet they felt they could remove the Western coating, identify the "principles" being taught, and make "modifications" for their own contexts. They observed that the long-term missionaries who lived among them and "became almost like" them were perceived as being less Western in their teaching because they understood "African" culture.

The data in this research indicates that the cognitive dimension was rated the highest of all the dimensions. The increased biblical knowledge was seen as important in improving ministry elements associated with the other dimensions. Despite the high praise given for the biblical knowledge they received, they were very open to discussing areas that they thought were lacking or need improvement, particularly in socio-cultural needs, whether it was more training in counseling, or better teaching related to the problems of AIDS and poverty.

Evaluative Dimension

The active ministers in this study also identified their theological education process as significantly assisting them in the evaluative dimension. The data indicates a high degree of agreement that trained ministers perceive an increase in their abilities to contextualize the message effectively in a variety of contexts. The increased ability to contextualize the biblical message was mentioned by the ministers as an important aspect of their training which they felt was highly effective.

The ministers perceive that they are better prepared through their theological education in the following ways: (1) cope with a changing culture, (2) have a clearer understanding of their own cultures, (3) better understand other cultures, (4) better understand the biblical culture, (5) make better application of the gospel to the cultural context in which they minister, and (6) improve their cross-cultural communication.

This research indicates that the ministers are engaging the challenges of their ministries' cultural contexts in a more informed manner. They are integrating the biblical context, their cultural context, the church, and the Western Christian intellectual and cultural heritage in the interpretation process and in making application to their ministry challenges. The data related to ministers' approaches to dealing with cultural challenges indicates a dynamic interaction in their ministries.

There is a recognition that biblical teaching must bear on the lifestyle and cultural practices of people. One is struck by how ministers referred to going back to scripture to decide how they might approach particular cultural practices. Examples of valid and questionable hermeneutics are noticeable in their contextualization processes. In the example of cultural practices involving sexual activities beyond one's spouse, ministers are engaging the challenges with biblical teaching and recognition that God's power is greater than any "curse" that might be received for refusing to participate. They not only address the biblical issue of holiness, but they then address the practical problem of how to reduce the cultural pressure brought by friends and neighbors. They address this by providing either functional substitutes or other venues of activities during the time of the events.

Ministers are able to identify points of contrasts as well as connections between the biblical teaching and the ministry contexts in which they engage in contextualizing the gospel. A number of problem areas were identified which the ministers found challenging in the self-theologizing process. The ministers proffered several traditional practices that they thought raised issues of "synchronizing the gospel" with "traditional beliefs." These areas were circumcision rites, traditional sexual mores, and spiritual realm beliefs. The discussion on how they met the challenges these practices presented gives insight into the level of self-theologizing in which they are engaging.

Circumcision. The hermeneutical approach of some may indicate areas of improvement for fuller self-theologizing. The discussions related to circumcision of both males and females surfaces an example where the hermeneutical process needs further development. The rationale given by most of the respondents for stopping the practice of female circumcision is that the practice is not mentioned in the Bible while male circumcision is. Not a single respondent dealt with the original purpose of biblical circumcision in discussing its relationship to the purpose of traditional circumcision practices. They propose keeping male circumcision with a functional substitute of Christian teachings for the traditional teachings associated with ancestral spirits, "demonic" aspects, and drunkenness. Female circumcision is seen as having the same problems as male circumcision, but some ministers are proposing that it be replaced entirely while others are providing some type of functional substitute. Female circumcision is seen by some as "mixing" of traditional culture and Christianity, but this is based simply on the fact that it does not appear in scripture as a practice. The fact that ministers were not engaging the biblical meaning of circumcision and the traditional function of female circumcision particularly in the cultural contexts indicates a greater need for better exegesis of both the cultural contexts and biblical teaching for a clearer hermeneutical approach.

Traditional Sexual Mores. The ministers express concern over syncretism and generally look to biblical precedents to address issues related to cultural practices which fall into the area of "sexual mores." In the case of levirate style marriages, "traditional festivals" and "age-set sex" the ministers are practicing a significant level of self-theologizing. For example, there is recognition that in the levirate style marriage one needs to distinguish between what was appropriate to the Old Testament system as opposed to what is in accord with New Testament principles.

The traditional festivals and age-set sex used for procuring "blessings" or pregnancy are identified as cultural practices contrary to biblical teaching. The emphasis ministers give to keeping sex within the marriage bonds is heavily stressed in their teaching. It is also possible to conclude from this data that they are meeting these challenges by providing teaching that addresses the fear of a "curse" through emphasizing the power of Christ. They are also providing alternatives to the non-Christian aspects of traditional practices while still upholding important and biblical elements of the culture such as hospitality that is involved in the age-set sex situation or care of family members in the case of levirate-style marriages. They are also making available alternate activities to relieve cultural pressures as in the case of the traditional festivals.

In dealing with the problem of a "woman marrying a woman" one minister condones allowing the practice, based on the teaching that the girl selected to be the child-bearing person should be obedient to her parents as put forward in the Bible. The value of this command is seen to supersede the marriage bond teachings. Although syncretism is considered by the ministers as something to avoid, this may serve as an example that biblical teaching may at times be interpreted to allow a practice based on one biblical teaching while ignoring the implication that it supports a practice contrary to other biblical teachings. The strong value of family cohesiveness in Kenyan society is supported by scripture but the biblical teaching on holiness and the sanctity of marriage may call for deeper hermeneutical discussions in order to wrestle with this dichotomy.

This research indicates that ministers have generally come to a consensus when dealing with polygamy. They accept polygamists for baptism and as capable of being Christians, though the missionaries themselves were divided on the issue. They do believe the goal of the church related to this issue is to teach the next generation to adhere to Christ's ideal of marriage. There is still some debate over the role a polygamist can take in the church. What does seem clear is that ministers are involved in self-theologizing in this area.

Ministers are also using the problem of the spread of AIDS to combat some traditional sexual mores. They look to scripture for their direction in deciding whether a cultural practice is right but may at times argue against it based more on social concerns rather than on making the spiritual point the center of the concern.

Spiritual Realm Beliefs. Overall the ministers identify a significant amount of wrestling with the place of spirits and the spirit world in traditional beliefs. Certain practices are seen as involvement with "*nkoma*" (spirits) and giving precedence to ancestral spirits rather than to Christ or God. In evaluating these practices, the ministers identify four areas of teaching that need to be emphasized to bring a more Christian perspective to the beliefs regarding the spiritual realm. First, they note the need for improved teaching on the biblical perspective of the afterlife. Second, they recognize there is a power issue because people are "not being reached properly to show the supremacy of God within their spiritual context." Third, they see a need to emphasize the imminence of God and the role of Christ as mediator in contrast to the idea that

"God is very far" from people and only approachable through *nkoma*. Fourth, they see the sacrifice of Christ as a connecting point and substitute to traditional sacrificial practices.

The data of this research does indicate that the evaluative dimension is showing a strong tendency toward self-theologizing. Ministers are interacting with their own cultural heritages, current socio-cultural contexts, and the biblical text. They do not see themselves as just repeating missionary teaching of the past but as engaging their various ministry contexts with the biblical message to meet their ministry challenges. The teaching they received from the American missionaries is considered a "bridge" rather than an obstacle in facilitating their theological reflections, although weaknesses in various hermeneutical approaches are present which raises areas of discussion for improving the theological education process.

Ministerial Dimension

The ministerial dimension generally is recognized as an area where ministers receive good theological training in developing ministerial skills and assisting in the spiritual formation process. In fact ministry skills was the third most mentioned area in which ministers felt their theological education was most helpful. However, the "ministerial" category is negatively impacted by problems stemming from both the missiological and structural dimensions. Ministry skills in the areas of evangelism and church planting, church organization and administration, spiritual growth, and leadership were identified most frequently as those that the ministers rated significantly helpful and gave very positive evaluations.

Evangelism and Church Planting. Improving their evangelism and church planting skills was the third highest reason students gave to pursue further theological education. The data indicates that the ministers were unanimous in indicating that their theological education prepared them well in the areas of evangelism and church planting. They note that their training helped them to have a greater vision for evangelism and given the ministerial skills to effectively plant churches and competently evangelize in their home communities and in other cultural contexts.

Church Organization and Administration. Ministerial skills related to the "administration" and "organizing" of the local church were generally identified by the ministers as contributing positively to their ability to lead. Skills dealing with such things as division of labor and organizing church services and church functions contributed to their ministry abilities. However, the issue of "autonomy" was considered to be a concept that was causing congregational problems, but this will be discussed below under the structural dimension.

Spiritual Growth. Improved spiritual formation was identified as one of the areas in which the ministers' theological education helped them the most. Ministers in this research saw their theological education as contributing to their spiritual growth not only in their ministry but also in their personal lives. They pointed to greater spiritual formation with improved Christian lifestyles.

Leadership. Ministers listed leadership as one of the reasons for pursuing further theological education. It was one of the ministry skills they found most helpful. The data indicates that for the most part they perceive the education they received on leadership positively. They particularly identified the concept of "servant leadership" as enhancing their abilities to develop the proper attitude of a leader as opposed to the "*bwana kubwa*" (big chief) mindset. They identified positive leadership skills particularly in teaching and preaching, nurturing of Christians, and counseling.

Their evaluation of leadership did surface several problems for which they felt their theological education did not adequately prepare them. First, they felt that though the counseling course they received was good, they could use more training in that area and that at times the Western nature of it made it less applicable. Second, they were not prepared to deal "practically" with the tension between trained leaders and "lay-leaders." Third, they perceived the problem of the "*bwana kubwa*" or "high priest" attitude of leaders in the churches as not being well addressed, especially in how to handle this attitude.

In each of the three problem areas the data indicates that the ministers were still doing self-theologizing even when they felt that they were not adequately trained in those areas. In counseling they point out that some of the counseling concepts were not accepted as valid for their cultural context, so they felt free to change them. In the leadership area the ministers felt that they received good "theoretical" teaching on leadership conflict. On the practical side they did not perceive their theological training as providing useful application in resolving the tension between lay-leaders and trained ministers. However, they are showing that they are self-theologizing in this area by recognizing some cultural differences between elder leaders and younger ones, showing respect and listening to lay-leaders, finding ways of cooperating, and planning meeting in a "friendly atmosphere" to discuss teachings that may conflict with each other. In dealing with church leaders who are acting as a *"Bwana Kubwa,"* they have developed various means for approaching the issue to correct or remove those falling into this mindset.

Missiological Dimension

The missiological dimension is identified most frequently as being the least effective dimension of self-theologizing. They perceive their theological education process as not assisting them in addressing the ministry challenges brought about by poverty and economic concerns. Here too, the curriculum is seen to be lacking courses that address these issues and other related issues. Poverty was the primary problem they felt was not addressed.

Most of the ministers are serving in churches or planting churches in poorer areas, whether urban or rural; therefore, poverty is an ever-present reality. It is the second most frequently mentioned area of ministry problems, after traditional cultural practices. However, unlike their more positive evaluation of their ability to deal with traditional practices they feel they were not prepared well for addressing the poverty issue. They note that they received little theological training in how to develop their ministries to address socio-economic concerns related to poverty. The implication is that the theological education process addresses traditional cultural issues and even current morality issues but provides little guidance in the missiological dimension in addressing socioeconomic problems. The ministers see their roles and the ministries of the church as needing to address the issue of poverty. They identify poverty issues such as the scarcity of resources, diminishing size of farmland plots, the lack of food, and the difficulty of finding employment. They indicate that these issues raise many problems for them in their ministries and are as detrimental as non-biblical traditional teachings and morality issues.

Although they note the need to continue teaching people to depend on God and to help themselves to improve their lives, there was a broad consensus that the church can do more to promote "development" or small-business projects. Courses in these areas are substantially absent from most of the curriculums. These types of projects are seen as something that churches can offer to their members and communities to raise the standard of living and provide alternative income beyond the current limited means.

The lack of emphasis on dealing with poverty issues may be due to the American missionaries' own training and cultural heritage which was primarily white middle class. Poverty is not generally considered a theological issue in the universities related to the Churches of Christ in the U.S. This lack of training received by the missionaries may be reflected in the curricula instituted at the training centers.

The poverty issues impact a couple of structural problems. Ministerial support and expectations should not be considered as completely separate issues. The lack of resources available raises issues as to the level and means of support for ministers and the social expectations of the churches' communities.

Structural Dimension

Various structural problems dealing with the administrative and infrastructure of the Kenya Churches of Christ and its various institutions for carrying on ministry in their socio-cultural contexts are identified. This makes the structural dimension the second weakest dimension, primarily because of the problems revolving around the support of ministers, social expectations for ministers, and the challenges raised with the autonomy concept.

Ministerial Support and Expectations of Congregations and Their Communities. With eighty-five percent of the interviewees mentioning the problem of support of ministers without a single question in the interview protocol directly addressing this issue, the support problem is a major concern in the structural category. Related to support are the expectations the communities place on churches and their ministers which also sheds light on how ministers understand the support issue.

The "self-supporting" of the three-selfs strategy was fundamentally adhered to by the American missionaries in Kenya and set the early tone for the support of ministers. The missionaries generally worked on the assumption that leaders would arise from among the Christians in the local congregations and become bi-vocational ministers with each local church maturing to the point of providing the needed support for its minister. Church ministers point out that this is not happening and admit that churches need to be taught to give more. The ministers feel that the church ministries are hindered by the lack of financial support which makes it hard for the minister of the church to meet the expectations of the church and its community.

The church, instead of the government, is often seen as the source of direct help for church members and the congregation's community. There is an expectation that ministers and churches have access to financial and other resources. A political slogan quoted earlier by a minister sums up well the expectation of people as it relates to ministers and the local congregation: "The poor do not lead" (N03 2005). The implication is that the church and ministers are structurally perceived as a source not only of meeting spiritual needs but of providing resources and guidance in meeting physical needs.

The theological education process is effective in preparing Christians for evangelism and church planting. Yet in the practical matter of support of ministers and their resources it is still proving to be an issue that has not been addressed to the satisfaction of ministers and to many Western missionaries who are stakeholders in the work in Kenya. This author knows from many conversations with missionaries to Kenya on and off the field that the "problem of support" continues to be an area of concern and debate. While doing this research, one on-the-field veteran missionary with more than twenty-five years of experience asked this author if his research would help with the "support issue". The implications are that ministers perceive themselves as hindered in not being able to effectively fulfill leadership roles in their churches nor fulfill their community responsibilities. Part of the problem of addressing the support issue may stem from organizational issues since Churches of Christ emphasize congregational autonomy.

Congregational Autonomy Concept. Also related to the structural dimension is the concept of congregational autonomy. Ministers perceive the concept of congregational autonomy as negatively influencing Churches of Christ. The problem of autonomy was first raised by a Kenyan minister in 1992 at the first Africans Claiming Africa Conference held in Embu, Kenya. One Kenyan minister questioned whether it was a hindrance to churches working together. He states,

> Now, the third point I want to bring up that I believe is a hindrance to growth at least to churches that I know of in Kenya here is the question of wholesome autonomy. We have been sold the idea of autonomy – we have been given the whole thing. Everything that accompanies the autonomy was sold to us and we took it. I would like to suggest that forums for bringing Christians together should be encouraged. They should be encouraged so that several churches in an area should work together. (Akumu 1992, 4.12)

He goes further in suggesting a means of collecting funds, developing a structure of churches working together and argues that the concept of autonomy should be "killed." "We should come out of this place with a new concept of autonomy. This has been a problem" (Akumu 1992, 4.12). Another leader at the conference voiced his concern for an understanding of autonomy that is too strict when he says,

> I think of this atomity [*sic.*] and I become a little afraid at one point. Say you go to a little village, establish a church, sometimes even without a preacher. You get 5, 6, 7 people around, very immature, and you leave them to fend for themselves. You say, 'Ah, brothers, you know – atomity [*sic.*]. Brothers, this won't help us. (Boateng 1992, 4.26)

He, too, called for the pooling of resources together for a "common cause or goal" (Boateng 1992, 4.24). The Kenya delegation at the conference submitted their "Kenya Strategy" in which they concluded that they were resolved to remove the word "autonomy" from their vocabulary and "replace it with the word INTERDEPENDENCE. Each congregation can be self managing, at the same time leaning on one another for the benefit of strengthening the whole body with one head in the name of Jesus Christ" (Okoth 1992, 7.3). However, a church leader from Nigeria at the conference pointed out that the pooling together of funds and setting up a body to administer it was "unscriptural" (Ekanem 1992, 4.20). Another said autonomy only applies to mature churches with elders and deacons while new churches would have less autonomy (Boateng 1992, 4.24).

Despite this declaration for "interdependence" the autonomy concept continues to be a problem and has negative implications for ministry. First, ministers believe it allows a leader to become a "dictator" with no accountability. Second, some church leaders use it as an excuse for not cooperating with other local churches or leaders. Third, it limits the means by which churches can fund ministries and projects.

The last two issues identified in this data where ministers particularly recognized limitations in their theological education process were in the lack of vocational training and the need for an increased level of education. Both of these are related to the poverty and support problems.

Vocational Training. The ministers were unanimous in pointing to the weakness of their theological education in not providing them a means of support in their ministries. One of the answers they put forward is to provide significant training in a vocational trade which could be practiced while they are involved in ministry. They call for increasing the vocational side of the training centers' educational programs.

Vocational training was not prominent in the training centers when the first ones were begun in the 1990s. The 1992 Africans Claiming Africa Conference took place during the rise of the first training centers in Kenya. The Kenya delegation mentions in their "Kenya Strategy" the need to encourage "evangelists to have small-scale businesses" (Okoth 1992, 7.2). Other than a couple of mentions of the need for "development projects" to address needs in Kenyan communities, there is no mention of the need for vocational training (Akumu 1992, 4.12).

In the past ten years vocational training has been added to a number of training centers' educational offerings. Of the five training centers visited during this research, all have at least one form of vocational training. However, ministers see the need for increased vocational training. They also indicate that the regional training centers are very important for both vocational and theological training. The importance is that these centers are closer to large groupings of churches, more readily available to church communities and Christians, more affordable, and available to older leaders who have responsibilities in their communities or have limited opportunities for education elsewhere.

The reasons surfaced for increased vocational training revolve around providing assistance to relieve poverty, helping church members to find employment, offering training to the community that will financially assist people and the community, providing a means of support for ministers, and fulfilling expectations of the communities where churches are ministering. A related area is the need to offer a higher level of education and continuing education.

Continuing and Higher Education Needs. There is a perceived need to provide continuing education to those who have already gone through some form of the certificate or diploma programs as well as a need for offering higher degree programs. This is based on what church ministers perceive as an essential need for the leadership so they are able to be more effective in the changing, contemporary Kenya environment. Nor can it be disconnected from the poverty and support issues which it is perceived to address as well.

Providing seminars and continuing education courses is seen as assisting ministers in improving and maintaining their ministry skills and knowledge. Seminars are seen as useful to bring leaders together to study in order to better meet the changes that are constantly confronting ministers. Seminars to discuss ministerial matters are also seen as providing good communication opportunities between ministers who do not see each other frequently.

Those already receiving training have a desire for more advanced education opportunities being offered at NGCS and the training centers. They identify this need on a number of criteria. First, a higher education level for church leaders is necessary to meet the changing needs of the church and the country. Second, the educational level as a whole is improving in Kenya. Third, greater education is needed for improving ministry overall. Fourth, leaders with higher education receive greater respect in their communities and can offer greater resources to the community in which they minister.

There is an overall vision for NGCS and the training centers to grow and be able to offer more advanced education opportunities. This would entail offering a BA and Masters level degrees at NGCS and offering Advanced Certificates and above at training centers.

Implications

Ministers in this research highlight a number of problems related to the structural and missiological dimensions of self-theologizing which have an impact on the ministerial dimension. The recognition that their theological education is limited in these areas or did not prepare them well indicates that the three dimensions of self-theologizing, the cognitive, the evaluative, and to a lesser degree the affective, are showing a high level of self-theologizing. The missiological and structural dimensions appear to pose the greatest problems with ministerial implications. The theological education process is not yet adequately addressing the issues in these two dimensions to the level that the local ministers believe it should.

These six dimensions intersect to a degree in that the deficiencies in one impacts another and the strengths in one carries over into another. The ministers are able to identify areas where their theological education process is effective and also areas of weaknesses which allow this research to make a general assessment of the perceived effectiveness of their theological education in facilitating self-theologizing. Illustration 1 below gives a visual overview of the level of effectiveness in the six dimensions.[1]

Illustration 1.--A summary of the level of self-theologizing by dimension

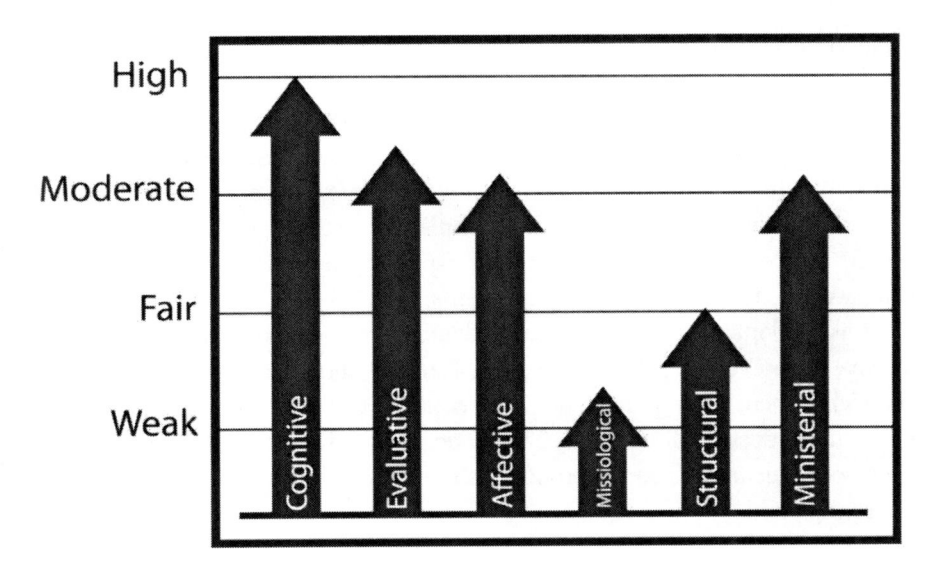

As illustration 1 above indicates, of the six dimensions identified, four could be rated on the high side toward effective self-theologizing and two on the low side. This points to a number of implications related to the theological education process of Kenya Churches of Christ. First, ministers perceive their theological education as particularly strong and effective in the cognitive and evaluative dimensions as related to their ministries, and the level of training in these areas should be maintained. The affective dimension also is rated high but to a lesser degree than the others. In fact, when asked to rate their satisfaction level with their theological education, they often rated it "very good." However, given their overall evaluation of the theological education they received, their satisfaction level is tempered by the problems and limitations in the two weaker areas, missiological and structural. The ministerial dimension is still recognized as having contributed significantly to the leaders' ministry and leadership skills, but the limitations in the missiological and structural dimensions are perceived to hinder the ministerial dimension.

Second, the areas identified as weak in facilitating self-theologizing are not related to contextualizing the gospel or addressing traditional cultural teachings, though they frequently create challenges. Third, the areas that were identified as particularly problematic are related to current socio-economic challenges and church structural problems.

Five significant areas are identified that have implications for improving the level of self-theologizing in both the missiological and structural dimensions which in turn would assist in improving the ministerial dimension. These areas are: (1) poverty issues, (2) ministerial support and expectations of the churches and communities, (3) the concept of autonomy, (4) vocational training, and (5) continuing and higher education needs. These five issues are intertwined with each other and, though treated separately above, they in fact all impact one another in various related ways. For example, the autonomy issue impacts the support problems and vocational training while higher education issues address poverty challenges and the support problems.

It is important that these identified areas of weakness be addressed to improve the level of self-theologizing. Kenyan church leaders are certainly identifying them as important areas of concern that need to be explored for further and deeper discussion. The concluding chapter will discuss these perceived weaknesses and propose some possible recommendations for addressing them.

> There is neither Jew nor Greek, there is neither slave nor free man, there is neither male nor female; for you are all one in Christ Jesus. And if you belong to Christ, then you are Abraham's descendants, heirs according to promise.
>
> *Gal. 3:28-29*

CHAPTER 8
"Solidarity Partnership": the Next Step in the Search for the Fourth Self?

The fourth self in conjunction with the three-selfs has been historically linked to the idea in missions of "handing-over the mission" or "ministry transfer." The idea is that missionaries from the West would eventually phase out of the mission effort and the mission church would stand on its own by being self-supporting, self-governing, self-propagating and self-theologizing and, as such, would be able to continue the ministry without outside support. Steven Estes provides a good literature review of various perspectives on ministry transfer among evangelical writers. He defines "ministry transfer" as "a change in leadership and financial support" of a mission that "was run by foreign personnel and financially supported by foreign funds" (2012, 175). He notes the tension between total ministry transfer, partial ministry transfer versus "partnership and interdependence" as preferable to transfer (2012, 185). However, whether ministry and leadership transfer take place or partnership and interdependence are practiced, the financial involvement and power wielded by those who have the financial resources continues to be an issue.

The mission efforts that spawned the theological education program evaluated in this research had in mind from the outset a ministry transfer goal based on the three-selfs and later adding the fourth self. It was believed that the best things the mission efforts could do was plant churches and develop effective leaders so that all leadership responsibilities for churches and institutions established would be continued by the Kenyans. However, subsidizing of various works continues and the great majority of the theological institutions continue to be highly subsidized. This raises issues of the ongoing relationship between the Kenyan Churches of Christ and the Western churches for the future.

The search for the fourth self has brought evangelicals to the point of engaging the issues in globalizing theology and recognizing the fourth self with the right of equal dialogue between Western and non-Western participants. This partnership of sharing the doing of theology should act as a reminder that it is not simply an academic endeavor but draws participants into partnership in other ways. Regarding this, Kim Marie Lamberty suggests that our mission training recognize the need to move beyond "doing missions," what she calls the "old paradigm", to recognizing the need for missions from a "solidarity partnership" perspective (2012, 186). She recognizes that this will require material assistance and "support for the actions of the poor to release themselves from the death of poverty in all its dimensions" (2012, 184). She notes that this boundary-crossing solidarity in the mission work between churches and other Christian institutions with mission points "can be transformational for all parties in tangible and intangible ways. . . . It can reduce national, cultural, or economic divisions and promote a deepening awareness of our shared identity as children of the One Creator" (2012, 181-182). This shared identity may also contribute to reducing theological hegemony.

As was indicated in the introduction, Kenyan leaders are seeking "a new breed of missionaries" that will enter into partnership with them to tackle "one of their greatest weaknesses", that is "the inability of the African church to address the myriad of complex social problems such as poverty, HIV, corruption, illiteracy and unemployment" (Young 2012, 91). Sarojini Nadar notes this failure of "Western forms of theologizing" to meet critical needs in Africa. He calls for an "epistemological shift" in theological thinking. He states,

> I would argue that this situation has arisen because, while we have become well trained in Western forms of theologizing, when people are dying all around us these theologies which we have inherited and learned so well are epistemologically inadequate to respond critically to the crisis. We know how to be scholars of theology and to apply abstract theoretical principles that sometimes even allow us to be cognizant of our context, but we do not know how to *do* theology, because doing requires that we go beyond being aware *of*, to being committed *to*, our context. It is only when our theologies allow us this commitment that we will be able adequately to respond not just to the HIV and AIDS crisis, but to acts of genocide, racism, sexism and other such evils that dehumanize people created in the image of God. (2007, 239)

He goes on to emphasize that "we are called to understand such an issue in the light of the experience of discrimination, colonialism and poverty, we are also called to understand our theologies in the light of discrimination, colonialism and poverty" (2007, 239). This "inability" to address these issues is highlighted in this research as well. Kenyan leaders participating in the highlighted theological education process note a similar failure of the theological training to effectively assist them in addressing these poverty and social justice related issues. They too see the need for some kind of partnership with their church community in relation to the larger global Christian community in the West. Nadar further notes that the

> Global North may after all not be helpful in our quest for an adequate theology of HIV and AIDS, because not only are they unwilling or unable to take context seriously, but they are also perhaps even reluctant to make the linkage between HIV and AIDS, social injustice and gender injustice. A truly ethical understanding calls us all to make this linkage. (2007, 239)

The evaluation of Christian ministers of Kenya Churches of Christ in this research point to similar weaknesses in their theological education related to such issues of poverty and other socio-economic concerns. This raises the question as to what both the Kenyan and Western stakeholders should consider to be the next step. Is this simply the next stage of Kenyan church leaders moving forward to address these issues strictly from their own resources within their own cultural and sociological contexts or are these global church issues that will require partnership, interdependence and solidarity?

Self-Theologizing and the Next Step

The weaknesses in theological education of not adequately addressing socio-economic and poverty issues raise the question as to where do those involved in providing theological education go from here. Does seeking the fourth self point to not only a shared dialogue in theological reflection but a partnership in theological action or, as Lamberty proposes, a "solidarity partnership"? We already see ongoing partnerships through Western sources providing financial resources for theological education and vocational training at Nairobi Great Commission School (NGCS) and various extension centers. The early vision of a total ministry transfer may not be possible in the near future. Perhaps those who are stakeholders should reconsider the idea of total transfer and move to some form of partnership which shares not only theological reflections but financial and other resources as well. By default we are in a form of partnership while waiting for some future total transfer of ministry. However, there is little concrete vision, long-term plans, or goals as to the direction the theological education system should pursue. Nor is the nature of the partnership defined.

A long-term partnership with defined goals to be reached through combining physical, personnel, spiritual, and financial resources is being suggested by church leaders. A "solidarity partnership" focuses on supporting their perceived needs, setting directions and goals for ministries and dialoguing as equals in doing theology while avoiding the hegemony that is possible by those who provide the funds.

The issues of the current education process in place for Kenya Churches of Christ is based on local training centers with NGCS acting as a central training center from which many local training centers coordinate their curriculums. These centers have become a central part of training for Christians and church leadership alike. They are unanimously perceived as positive institutions in assisting the Churches of Christ in Kenya. For example the Meru School of Theology with which this author has been personally involved since its inception has become the hub for education, communication and interaction among the Churches of Christ in Meru, but it also draws other church leaders not associated with Churches of Christ. This also appears to be the case for the other centers visited in this research.

Among Churches of Christ, the centers provide a common ground that helps the church leaders plan, work, and solve problems at a multi-congregational level. The centers facilitate cooperation and unity between local congregations in a region by providing venues for solving problems and encouraging better inter-congregational relationships.

Realizing that these centers are institutions that the Churches of Christ in Kenya will depend on for the foreseeable future, Kenyan and Western stakeholders need to proactively discuss and plan how the theological education process can better address the missiological and structural issues that have been identified. It is recognized that there are major resource, financial, institutional, and personnel questions involved. Therefore, whatever direction is envisioned for the future of these institutions, both Kenyan and Western resources will be impacted if the missiological and structural challenges are to be met.

Most of the training centers are subsidized by outside funds. The five centers visited in this research are significantly supported by funds from churches and former missionaries in the U.S. This probably accounts for these five centers being the most active in providing various levels of theological training, as well as vocational training. Those involved in providing this funding will be impacted by a number of the recommendations below. Therefore, those who are partnering in providing financial and advisory resources will need to be involved in planning and implementing some of these recommendations.

A long-range plan of partnering between Western stakeholders and their resources and Kenyan personnel and resources is needed in maintaining and further developing the educational infrastructure related to Churches of Christ in Kenya. Recommended areas of exploration based on the Kenyan ministers' evaluations would include curriculum expansion that deals with missiological and structural issues, a yearly system of seminars for continuing education, increasing vocational training and small business development offerings, and developing an educational improvement committee to explore ways to provide higher levels of education.

The economic and socio-cultural situations in which the churches and their leaders minister is continuing to challenge them in dealing with poverty and other socio-economic issues which in turn effects many other areas of ministry. Curriculum expansion is needed in the areas of socio-economic and socio-cultural issues, especially with poverty and related challenges. The goal of this part of the curriculum would encourage theological reflection and practical application in the Kenya context in addressing the missiological and structural issues. This would be intended to surface ideas and practical means to address these issues in their ministry. It should also aim at facilitating changes in the training centers' educational programs so as to better provide resources to prepare students to serve effectively in dealing with poverty challenges and other missiological and structural church issues in their local contexts and in Kenya at large. A course or courses on self-theologizing focusing on these issues might be useful in addressing the above concerns in order for the students to define their pressing socio-economic and cultural challenges while searching for the hermeneutical direction in addressing them.

In response to the ministers' concerns for continuing education as voiced in this research, a yearly system of seminars could be instituted that provides a structured, continuing education program for leaders who have completed various levels of studies. These seminars would not necessarily be limited to ministers who have completed programs but also be a venue for other leaders to be involved in as well. These seminars could be scheduled at multiple training center locations to reduce travel costs.

Some of these seminars could also be designed to function as directed brainstorming sessions on relevant issues of Churches of Christ across Kenya. These seminars would hopefully surface useful, concrete ideas to be pursued by a variety of ministries in the church. The issues particularly related to autonomy and cooperation between churches and the problem of support are certainly areas that are of vital concern to local congregations and the church as a whole. Judging from the data in this research, these areas are in need of much more discussion among all stakeholders, Kenyans and Westerners alike.

The data in this research has shown that ministers perceive a need for greater vocational training and small business opportunities to address socio-economic issues. Since NGCS and the training centers are already providing some vocational training, stakeholders should consider the possibility of expanding those offerings and extend curriculums to address vocational training and small business development. This would require training centers to develop an educational strategy applicable to their particular context as various locations will find a greater need for certain vocational skills and small business ventures than others. The urban and rural contexts may call for varying types of course offerings. One aspect of increasing the vocational side of the educational process that needs to be discussed is the impact a wider variety of training will have on providing quality theological education.

The desire of students for our institutions to provide higher levels of education needs to be addressed. In the U.S. we have multiple levels of training available to church leaders, Christians and non-Christians alike ranging from Graduate Schools, Liberal Arts Universities, Bible Colleges, to Preacher Training Schools. The long-term educational goals related to the Kenya Churches of Christ fellowship need to be explored more fully. Through the training centers and greater educational opportunities nationally in Kenya, Churches of Christ are seeing a larger cadre of leaders moving forward educationally in desiring to pursue higher education degrees. Because of the financial resources associated with such institutions both foreign and African stakeholders involved with the Kenya Churches of Christ need to partner to organize an educational improvement committee to explore directions for more advanced educational opportunities. Partnerships with stateside universities need to continue to be examined.

Conclusion

In searching for the fourth self, the theological education process explored in this research has tried to reflect the perceptions of the Kenyan ministers as to the effectiveness of that process by shedding light on how well the educational process is providing tools for self-theologizing. The evaluation provided by the active ministers involved in the theological education process indicates that the theological education is perceived as contributing significantly to the cognitive, evaluative, affective and, to a lesser degree, the ministerial dimensions of self-theologizing. Critical thinking is taking place among the ministers and is reflected in the use of their education to contextualize the message in their various ministerial contexts. Overall, they see the process as meeting a significant number of their educational needs in enhancing their ability to effectively minister. They particularly note that their theological training has increased their biblical knowledge and enhanced their ability to contextualize the gospel in their own and other cultures. They also indicate they are better prepared to identify and cope with cultural challenges, evangelize and plant churches more effectively and more mature in their personal spiritual lives.

The research also surfaces concerns where ministers identify areas they perceive as weaknesses in the theological education process, particularly related to the missiological and structural dimensions which in turn have a negative impact on the ministerial dimension. These areas where ministers feel less prepared were viewed as hindering their ministries. The identification of these weaknesses in their theological education provides a direction to pursue for those involved in the education process in order to improve the theological education for Kenya Churches of Christ. The preceding recommendations may be a starting point for exploring ways of providing better tools for ministers to develop greater abilities to engage in self-theologizing and finding the fourth self. This search for the fourth self is not just a Kenyan journey. Westerners share in this journey as all concerned are participating in the globalizing of theology and in so doing, hopefully, move all participants toward a "partnership of solidarity" in our Christian pilgrimage that needs to be defined more fully and strengthened for the future.

In the theological education process in sub-Saharan Africa there is more give-and-take and dialogue taking place among many evangelicals as we see a greater globalizing of theology with the southern shift of Christianity. Westerners participating in the theological education process need to fully enter into a dialogue with African Christians and leaders, not only hearing but recognizing the value of their contributions to theology through their self-theologizing. Their participation in this theological dialogue will improve the church locally and universally. Tennent reminds us, "We have much to learn as well as to relearn from Africa, although there is also much that our own heritage, history, and collective Christian memory have to teach Africa" (2007, 106).

This research not only exposed weaknesses in the theological education in which the students participated but their self-theologizing exposed our Western heritage bias and theological training slant that creates our own theological myopia. Our own self-theologizing is improved by others participating in the theological process where both benefit from the search for the fourth self. Andrew Walls may be correct when he notes, "Shared reading of the Scriptures and shared theological reflection will be the benefit of all, but the oxygen-starved Christianity of the West will have the most to gain" (2002, 47). The search for the fourth self should move all involved to recognize some form of a "partnership of solidarity" in both sharing in the theological dialogue and doing theology, i.e. participating in addressing each other's socio-cultural and socio-economic issues. The search for the fourth self in the global scope of Christianity will be an ongoing process of doing theology that involves Westerners and non-Westerners alike participating in a pilgrimage together.

NOTES

Introduction

1. In the Festschrift *Globalizing Theology: Belief and Practice in an Era of World Christianity* in honor of Paul Hiebert, Harold Netland defines "global theology" or "globalizing theology" as "theological reflection rooted in God's self-revelation in Scripture and informed by the historical legacy of Christian community through the ages, the current realities in the world and the diverse perspectives of Christian communities throughout the world, with a view to greater holiness in living and faithfulness in fulfilling God's mission in all the world through the church" (2006, 30).

Chapter 1

1. Although this volume focuses on the Protestant tradition, the Catholic Church has its own history of moving from a replication model emphasis on contextualization, or enculturation, from its early attempts at accommodation among pagans, i.e. the Jesuits' work by Xavier, Robert De Nobili, and Matteo Ricci, to the *Propaganda Fide*.
2. Churches of Christ trace their origin as a religious movement from the restoration call to "apostolic Christianity" at work in the American religious circles at the turn of the nineteenth century as they emerged from various denominations. "Among the Methodists there was James O'Kelley; among the Presbyterians, Barton W. Stone; and in both the Presbyterian and Baptist ranks a little later, there was Alexander Campbell" (West 1964, xi).
3. Gailyn Van Rheenen and his coworkers, Fielden Allison and Richard Chowning, were a significant influence on a number of the mission teams that came to Kenya in the late 1970s and early 1980s. Their methodology of church planting, use of the vernacular language, and ideas on leadership training were influential. Their work among the Kipsigis of Kenya in

1972, and Van Rheenen's subsequent teaching at Harding University as a visiting missionary provided later mission teams with concepts and models by which to initiate other mission efforts. Van Rheenen's critique of the use of the "institutional model" of theological education in a "third-world" setting was influential on a number of mission teams (1983, 32-33).
4. Monte Cox's dissertation gives a summary of the influence of the "three-selves" strategy on a number of the rural mission teams' mission philosophies (1999).
5. This author was one of the original members of the Meru mission team and co-developed what became known as Leadership Training by Extension and Evangelism (LTEE). The addition of the second "E" was to place more emphasis on the practical application aspect of the theological education. Two church growth studies completed in 1987 and 1990 give a history of its purpose, development and evolution as it moved toward an extension center model (Granberg et al. 1987; Granberg et al. 1990).
6. In Mwanza, Tanzania there is the Mwanza Extension Center. The three training centers in Uganda are Busoga Extension Center, Messiah Theological Institute in Mbale (now Livingstone International University), and Fort Portal Extension Center. The twelve centers in Kenya are: Meru School of Theology in Meru; Uzima Training Center outside of Malindi; Mariwa Bible School in Awendo; Siriat Bible School in Sotik; Mombasa Extension Center; Kaule Training Center in Kisumu; Eldoret Extension Center; Mt. Elgon Extension Center; Kitale Extension Center; Ewaso Nyiro in Narok; Winyo Extension Center in Rongo; and Mogesa Bible School in Kisii.
7. A description of the disengagement of several missionary teams and a brief overview of those teams' leadership training vision as influenced by the "three-selves" concept can be found in *"Euthanasia of Mission" or "Partnership"?: An Evaluative Study of the Policy of Disengagement of Church of Christ Missionaries in Rural Kenya.* This study notes the use of the training centers as a departure from the "three-selves" strategy (Cox 1999).

Chapter 2

1. Bergquist lists the "five crises" as "missiological faithfulness," "patterns of ministry," "soundness of pedagogy," "financial dependence," and "theological faithfulness." His "patterns of ministry" expands on the "structural contextualization" proffered in the Third Mandate (1973, 246-250).
2. Bevans first proposed five models in his 1992 volume *Models of Contextual Theology: Faith and Other Cultures*. In this work he added the "countercultural model" as one step further toward the "scripture tradition."
3. Although Gilliland proposes this model from Geertz's discussion, Geertz is not proposing a contextualization model. He is simply stating that a person is a

"symbolizing, conceptualizing, meaning animal" and thus "it seems unnecessary to continue to interpret symbolic activities—religion, art, ideology—as nothing but thinly disguised expressions of something other than what they appear to be"(1973, 140-142).
4. Hiebert defines the cognitive, affective, and evaluative dimensions in a culture in *Anthropological Insights for Missionaries*. The cognitive dimension is the "knowledge shared by members of a group or society" which "provides the conceptual content of a culture" that are organized into categories. The affective dimension involves the "feelings people have–with their attitudes, notions of beauty, tastes in food and dress, likes and dislikes, and ways of enjoying themselves or experiencing sorrow." The evaluative dimension consists of the "values by which it judges human relationships to be moral or immoral" and value judgments on cognitive beliefs, emotional expressions, and determining right and wrong (1985, 30-33).

Chapter 3
1. During the Second Mandate Shoki Coe was one of the associate directors of TEF. He would become director of TEF during the Third Mandate after the death of the first director.
2. Ralph D. Winter's book, *Theological Education by Extension,* contains a number of the early documents produced by those involved in the early implementation of the TEE concept (1969).
3. Wayne Weld documents the number of TEE students and programs functioning at the end of 1972, noting a student population of approximately 14,000. The distribution of those students was 73.3% from Latin America, 8% from North America, 7% from the Caribbean, 6.1% from Africa, and 5.5% from Asia (1973, 41-44). The regional distribution of extension students changed dramatically between 1972 and 1980, especially for Africa. Of the 55,378 students approximated to be on the TEE rolls, Africa had the greatest increase in number of students. The percentage of African extension students rose from 6.1% to 15.3% in 1975. This trend continued with 19.7% of extension students in Africa in 1977, increasing to 38.1% in 1980, surpassing Latin America's 37% (Weld 1980, 4).
4. The Meru mission team developed a LTE program which was entitled Leadership Training by Extension and Evangelism (LTEE). "Extension" pointed to its use in the rural environment and "evangelism" underscored training in practical localized preaching and teaching (Granberg *et al.* 1987, 96).

Chapter 4
1. Besides the Kipsigis mission team, there were other teams working on the western side of Kenya. Work in the Kisumu area among Abaluyia and other groups had begun as early as 1969. The team that began the work among the Kipsigis had originally been in Uganda but

had been forced out after Idi Amin Dada's régime came to power. This team split up with two families beginning the mission effort among the Kipsigis and the other two families began a work among the Luo tribe in South Nyanza. A brief history of these works may be found in *Church Planting, Watering, and Increasing in Kenya* (1980).

2. The Meru team accepted the stages of local church growth used by the Sotik team but defined them for their ministry context.
   1. Preaching Point: The stage of development from the time the evangelist makes a teaching contact in a new area to the time when there are a sufficient number of adult converts to form a <u>viable</u> fellowship
   2. Initial Church: The stage of development from the time when there are a sufficient number of adult converts to form a viable fellowship to the time when the new church is able to <u>functionally</u> carry on its own regular worship.
   3. Established Church: The stage of development from the time the new church is able to functionally carry on its own regular worship to the time it is <u>self-functioning,</u> possessing, without the benefit of experience, the knowledge, the ability, and the personnel to sustain the body, mature the members, and produce other fellowships.
   4. Independent Church: The stage of development from the time the church is self-functioning to the time it has appointed leaders (elders and deacons) and has gained through experience the maturity of knowledge, the ability, and the personnel to sustain the body, mature the members, and produce other fellowships.
   5. Mature Church: The final stage of development where the church has appointed leaders and has the maturity of knowledge, ability, and personnel to sustain the body, mature leaders, and produce other fellowships. (Granberg, McLarty, and Trull 1984, appendix 2)
3. In August of 1987 the Meru team added a third family who would remain on the field until 1995, a year after the original two team families disengaged.
4. The Meru team was aware of the TEE books being produced in Kenya and had copies of them. However, after evaluating them, it was decided that the current educational level at which the books were written was too high for those that were being taught through the LTEE.
5. Besides visits by this author, his co-worker has also visited several times with both finding the same information and coming to similar conclusions.
6. KTC had an oversight board of Meru leaders from Meru which was to be sure that the training center continued to function properly. The last American missionary family moved to Nairobi some five hours away and continued to give indirect oversight. A chicken project was implemented to provide income to KTC, but this was not sustained. During the years 2000 through 2002, KTC became less functional. In 2001, after this author met with the leaders there, a plan was developed to improve the situation. While in Kenya this author discussed the situation with two of the Board of Trustee members in Kenya, one American missionary and one Kenyan, and then returned to the U.S. to meet with two others on the Board of KTC, both Americans. In February of 2002, three of the board members met in Dallas and discussed the situation. It was decided to initiate plans to assist in implementing the suggestions of the church leaders in Meru. The author met with the church leaders in Meru in the summer of 2003 and discussed with them the plans for the future of KTC. There

was a church leader who had been assisting the missionary in running KTC but with no official position and minimal salary. He was a graduate of NGCS with an Advanced Certificate and had proven his effectiveness over the years. With the blessings of the other church leaders, he was officially selected as the Principal of KTC and given a salary commensurate with his job. He currently continues to administer KTC, and this writer communicates with him via email and works with him each summer by holding courses and improving KTC's physical plant, Bible training courses, and vocational courses.

Chapter 5

1. A complete description of the research methodology and interview process is available in this writer's dissertation "An Evaluation of Leadership Training to Facilitate Emic-Theologizing for the Local Church Ministers in Kenya Churches of Christ".
2. The extension centers offer three "degree plans" which students may follow. The "Advanced Extension Certificate" requires students to have an "advanced knowledge" of the English language and to take twenty courses with a minimum of thirty classroom hours per course. "The Basic Extension Certificate courses are open to any approved student who has at most a Kenya Certificate of Primary Education. S/he must be able to read, write and understand English or Kiswahili." To receive the Basic Certificate they must complete twenty courses with a minimum of thirty classroom hours per course. The Audit Extension Certificate opens courses "to church leaders who are interested in formal training" but are not proficient in reading or writing English. They may or may not be able to read and write in their mother tongue.

    NGCS offers three degree plans. The Baccalaureate Degree is provided in conjunction with Daystar University where the student earns his or her Bible hours at NGCS and then completes the remainder with Daystar. The "Advanced Diploma" requires a high proficiency in reading and writing English, a total of 87 semester hours and a two year residency. The "Advanced Certificate" requires proficiency in reading and writing English, 74 semester hours, and a two year residency. This program is designed for those unable to meet the academic qualifications for the Advanced Diploma (2000, 9-10).
3. This leader was interviewed because of years of involvement in the church going back 28 years which makes his involvement in ministry in the Churches of Christ the longest of all those interviewed. It was thought by the Principal of NGCS that his perspective as a student in various capacities over the years and now as an elder and long time minister would add a long-term perspective.
4. For a historical review of issues related to congregational autonomy in Churches of Christ see Richard T. Hughes' *Reviving the Ancient Faith* (1996, 217-253).

Chapter 6

1. By the early 2000s, the primary areas of work started during the second period, the vernacular period, had seen the phase-out of almost all the missionaries involved in evangelism, church planting, and leadership training. By May 2006, two remaining long-term missionaries relocated to Dar es Salaam, leaving one missionary in Nairobi who works with NGCS and one in the Central Province.
2. This view of an ancestral spirit coming back in a newborn child is part of the Kipsigis traditional belief system but is not a part of some of the other groups interviewed. This belief does not strongly exist among the Meru, though they do traditionally see ancestral spirits as highly influential in peoples' lives and so understand the problem with ancestral spirits as a power issue.
3. Starting in 2003 and going through 2005, Churches of Christ in Kenya experienced a power struggle among some of its leaders. Certain leaders perceived other leaders as trying to gain a national leadership position over the churches. This author had many discussions with leaders about the situation during three visits in that time period. This situation caused many problems in churches and between churches throughout Kenya. There continues to be an underlying tension related to these problems. This may have added to why interviewees identified leadership problems as significant in their ministries.

Chapter 7

1. Students were not asked to rate these six dimensions so this diagram is only for a visual display of the general level of self-theologizing as garnered from the overall data. "High" means the data related to that dimension of self-theologizing reflects the interviewees' perception of highly effective training with few identified problems. "Moderate" is meant to convey a substantial level of perceived satisfaction with the effectiveness of that self-theologizing dimension but moderated by a few identified problems. "Fair" represents a dimension that is perceived as functioning but in need of improvement because of a substantial number of identified problems. "Weak" indicates a dimension of self-theologizing that is perceived to be substantially lacking in the theological education process.

Bibliography

AKIKA. "Churches of Christ: AKIKA (Antuamuo, Kiegoi and Kanthiari) Zone." Meru, Kenya: Privately published, 2005.

Akumu, Charles. "Evangelism in Africa." In *Africans Claiming Africa Conference Held in Embu, Kenya, April 1-10, 1992*. Edited by Sam Shewmaker, 4.9-4.13. Nairobi: Kenya Church of Christ, 1992.

Allen, Roland. *Missionary Methods: St. Paul's or Ours?* Grand Rapids: Wm. B. Eerdmans Publishing, 1962.

Allison, Fielden. *Church Growth among the Kipsigis: A Statistical Picture of the Church of Christ among the Kipsigis in South West Kenya.* Vol. 1. Edited by Kipsigis Team. Sotik, Kenya: Privately published, 1977.

_____. "God's Work among the Kipsigis." In *Church Planting, Watering, and Increasing in Kenya: The Study of Church Growth among Churches of Christ in Kenya, 1965- 1979*. Edited by Kenya Mission Team, 75-80. Austin, Texas: Firm Foundation, 1980.

Anderson, Rufus. *Foreign Missions: Their Relations and Claims.* New York: Charles Scribner and Co., 1869.

_____. *The Theory of Missions to the Heathen: A Sermon at the Ordination of Mr. Edward Webb.* Boston: Press of Crocker and Brewster, 1845.

Assensoh, A. B. *African Political Leadership: Jomo Kenyatta, Kwame Nrumah, and Julius K. Nyerere.* Malabar, Florida: Krieger Publishing Co., 1998.

Beaver, R. Pierce. *To Advance the Gospel: Selections from the Writings of Rufus Anderson*. Grand Rapids: Wm. B. Eerdmans Publishing Co., 1967.

Bediako, Kwame. "The African Renaissance and Theological Reconstruction: The Challenge of the Twenty-First Century." *Journal of African Christian Thought* 4 (2001): 29-52.

_____. *Christianity in Africa: The Renewal of a Non-Western Religion*. Maryknoll, N.Y.: Orbis, 1995.

_____. "Facing the Challenge: Africa in World Christianity in the 21st Century: A Vision of the African Christian Future." *Journal of African Christian Thought* 1 (1998): 52-57.

_____. "Gospel and Culture: Some Insights for Our Time from the Experience of the Earliest Church." *Journal of African Christian Thought* 2 (1999): 8-13.

_____. *Theology and Identity: The Impact of Culture upon Christian Thought in the Second Century and in Modern Africa*. Irvine, CA: Regnum Books, 1992.

_____. "'Whose Religion is Christianty?' Reflections on Opportunities and Challenges in Christian Theological Scholarship: The African Dimension." In *Mission in the 21st Century: Exploring the Five Marks of Global Mission*. Edited by Andrew Walls and Cathy Ross, 107-117. Maryknoll, N.Y.: Orbis, 2008.

Bergquist, James A. "The TEF and the Uncertain Future of Third World Theological Education." *Theological Education* 9 (1973): 244-253.

Bernard, H. Russell. *Research Methods in Anthropology: Qualitative and Quantitative Approaches*. 3d ed. Walnut Creek, CA: AltaMira Press, 2002.

Bernardi, B. *The Mugwe, a Failing Prophet: A Religious and Public Dignitary of the Meru of Kenya*. London: Oxford University Press, 1959.

Bevans, Stephen B. *An Introduction to Theology in Global Perspective*. Maryknoll, N.Y.: Orbis, 2009.

_____. *Models of Contextual Theology: Faith and Other Cultures*. Maryknoll, N.Y.: Orbis, 1992.

Blakemore, Kenneth, and Brian Cooksey. *A Sociology of Education for Africa*. London: George Allen & Unwin, 1981.

Boateng, Douglas. "We Can Do It Financially." In *Africans Claiming Africa Conference Held in Embu, Kenya April 1-10, 1992*. Edited by Sam Shewmaker, 4.24-4:26. Nairobi: Kenya Church of Christ, 1992.

Bosch, David J. *Transforming Mission: Paradigm Shifts in Theology of Mission*. Maryknoll, N.Y.: Orbis, 1991.

Campbell, Alexander. "Education." *The Millennial Harbinger*, Second series II (1838): 256.

_____. "Schools and Colleges." *The Millennial Harbinger*, Third series VII (1850): 121-125.

Carey, William. *An Enquiry into the Obligations of Christians, to Use Means for the Conversion of the Heathens in which the Religious State of the Different Nations of the World, the Success of Former Undertakings, and the Practicability of Further Undertakings, are Considered*. Leicester, 1792.

Clark, Sidney J. W. *The Indigenous Church*. London: World Dominion Press, 1928.

Coe, Shoki. "Contextualizing Theology." In *Mission Trends no. 3*. Edited by Gerald H. Anderson and Thomas F. Stransky, 19-24. Grand Rapids: Eerdmans, 1976.

_____. "A Rethinking of Theological Training for Ministry in the Younger Churches Today." *South East Journal of Theology* 4 (1962): 7-34.

_____. "In Search of Renewal in Theological Education." *Theological Education* 9 (1973): 233-243.

Cole, Victor. "Africanising the Faith: Another Look at Contextualization of Theology." In *Issues in African Christian Theology*. Edited by Samuel Ngewa, Mark Shaw, and Tite Tiénou, 12-23. Nairobi: East African Educational Publishers, 1998.

Conference on Missions Held in 1860: At Liverpool. London: James Nisbet & Co., 1860.

Costa, Ruy O. "Inculturation, Indigenization, and Contextualization." In *One Faith, Many Cultures.* Edited by Ruy O. Costa. Maryknoll, N.Y.: Orbis Books, 1988.

Cox, Monte B. "Euthanasia of Mission" or "Partnership"? An Evaluative Study of the Policy of Disengagement of Church of Christ Missionaries in Rural Kenya. Ph.D. diss., Trinity Evangelical Divinity School, 1999.

Curtin, Philip, Steven Feierman, Leonard Thompson, and Jan Vansina. *African History: From Earliest Times to Independence.* 2nd ed. London: Longman, 1995.

Day, Lal Behari. *Recollections of Alexander Duff, D. D., LL. D. and the Mission College which He Founded in Calcutta.* London: T. Nelson and Sons, 1879.

Dickson, Kwesi A. *Theology in Africa.* Maryknoll, N.Y.: Orbis, 1984.

Duff, Alexander. *India and Indian Mission.* Edinburgh: John Johnstone, Hunter Square, 1840.

Dyrness, William A. and Veli-Matti Kärkkäinen, eds. *Global Dictionary of Theology.* Downers Grove, IL: InterVarsity Press, 2008.

____. "Telephones, Bible Studies, and Education in the African Church: Reflections from Abroad." *Missiology: An International Review* 36 (2008): 373-385.

Ecumenical Missionary Conference New York, 1900: Report of the Ecumenical Conference on Foreign Missions, Held in Carnegie Hall and Neighboring Churches, April 21 to May 1. Vol. 2. New York: American Tract Society, 1900.

Eisner, Elliot W. *Educational Imagination: On the Design and Evaluation of School Programs.* New York: Macmillan, 1985.

____. *The Enlightened Eye: Qualitative Inquiry and the Enhancement of Educational Practice.* New York: Macmillan, 1991.

Ekanem, Sunday. "We Can Do It Financially." In *Africans Claiming Africa Conference Held in Embu, Kenya April 1-10, 1992*. Edited by Sam Shewmaker, 4.20-4.22. Nairobi: Kenya Church of Christ, 1992.

Elliston, Edgar. "Designing Leadership Education." *Missiology: An International Review* 16 (1988): 203-215.

____. "Leadership Theory." In *Evangelical Dictionary of World Mission*. Edited by A. Scott Moreau, 567-68. Grand Rapids: Baker Books, 2000.

Emery, James. "The Preparation of Leaders in a Ladino-Indian Church." *Practical Anthropology* 10 (1963): 127-134.

Estes, Steven. "A Review of the Literature on Ministry Transfer." *Missiology: An International Review* 39 (2012): 175-185.

Ferguson, Everett. *The Church of Christ: A Biblical Ecclesiology for Today*. Grand Rapids: Eerdmans, 1996.

Ferris, Robert W. *Renewal in Theological Education: Strategies for Change*. Wheaton, IL: Billy Graham Center, 1996.

Fleming, Bruce C. E. *Contextualization of Theology: An Evangelical Assessment*. Pasadena, Calif.: William Carey Library, 1980.

Frostin, Per. "The Hermeneutics of the Poor: The Epistemological 'Break' in Third World Theologies." *Studia Theologica* 39 (1985): 127-150.

Gaikwad, Roger. "Theological Equipping of Ecclesia: An Asian Reflection on the All Africa TEE Conference." *Ministerial Formation*, 108 (2007): 25-28.

Gall, Meredith D., Walter R. Borg, and Joyce P Gall. *Educational Research: An Introduction*. 6th ed. White Plains, N.Y.: Longman, 1996.

Gatimu, Kiranga. "Viability of Theological Education by Extension in Africa." *Ministerial Formation* 86 (1999): 5-19.

Geertz, Clifford. *The Interpretation of Cultures*. N. Y.: Basic Books, 1973.

Gilliland, Dean S. "Contextual Theology as Incarnational Mission." In *The Word among Us: Contextualizing Theology for Mission Today*. Edited by Dean S. Gilliland, 9-31. Dallas, TX: Word Publishing, 1989.

Goetz, Judith Preissle, and Margaret Diane LeCompte. *Ethnography and Qualitative Design in Educational Research*. San Diego, Calif.: Academic Press, 1984.

Goff, Reda. *The Great Nigeria Mission*. Nashville, Tenn.: Lawrence Avenue Church of Christ: Nigerian Christian Schools Foundation, 1964.

Granberg, Stanley E., Bruce McLarty, and Richard E. Trull, Jr. *Church Growth among the Meru: A Church Growth Study of Churches of Christ in Meru, Kenya, 1984*. Meru, Kenya: Privately published, 1984.

____, Roger K. Pritchett, and Richard E. Trull, Jr. *Church Growth among the Meru: Ministry of the Churches of Christ in Meru, Kenya, 1987*. Meru, Kenya: Privately published, 1987.

____, John Mark Nicholas, Roger K. Pritchett, Richard E. Trull, Jr., and A. Keith Williams. *Church Growth among the Meru: A Ministry of the Churches of Christ in Meru, Kenya, 1990*. Meru, Kenya: Privately published, 1990.

Greenman, Jeffrey P. and Gene L. Green, eds. *Global Theology in Evangelical Perspective: Exploring the Contextual Nature of Theology and Missions*. Downers Grove, IL: InterVarsity Press, 2012.

Gurganus, George, ed. *Guidelines for World Evangelism*. Abilene, TX: Biblical Research Press, 1976.

Haleblian, Krikor. "The Problem of Contextualization." *Missiology* 11 (1983): 95-111.

Hardin, Daniel C. *Mission: A Practical Approach to Church Sponsored Mission Work*. Pasadena, CA: William Carey Library, 1978.

____. "Preparation for Missions." In *Guidelines for World Evangelism*. Edited by George Gurganus, 227-247. Abilene, TX: Biblical Research Press, 1976.

Hesselgrave, David J. *Communicating Christ Cross-Culturally*. Grand Rapids: Zondervan, 1978.

____. *Communicating Christ Cross-Culturally: An Introduction to Missionary Communication*. 2^d ed. Grand Rapids: Zondervan, 1991.

_____. *Planting Churches Cross-Culturally: A Guide for Home and Foreign Missions*. Grand Rapids: Baker, 1980.

_____. *Planting Churches Cross-Culturally: North America and Beyond*. 2nd ed. Grand Rapids: Baker, 2000.

Hiebert, Paul G. *Anthropological Insights for Missionaries*. Grand Rapids: Baker, 1985.

_____. *Anthropological Reflections on Missiological Issues*. Grand Rapids: Baker, 1994.

_____. "Critical Contextualization." *International Bulletin of Missionary Research* 11 (1987): 104-112.

_____. "Metatheology: The Step Beyond Contextualization." In *Reflection and Projection: Missiology at the Threshold of 2001*. Edited by Hans Kasdorf, and Klaus W. Müller. Bad Liebenzell, West Germany: Verlag der Liebenzeller Mission, 1988.

_____. "The Missionary as Mediator of Global Theologizing." In *Globalizing Theology: Belief and Practice in an Era of World Christianity*. Edited by Craig Ott and Harold A. Netland, 288-308. Grand Rapids: Baker, 2006.

Hogarth, Jonathan, Kiranga Gatimu, and David Barrett. *Theological Education in Context: 100 Extension Programmes in Contemporary Africa*. Nairobi, Kenya: Uzima Press, 1983.

Holter, Knut. *Yahweh in Africa: Essays on Africa and the Old Testament*. N.Y.: Peter Lang, 2000.

Huffard, Henry. "Christian Education in Africa." *100 Years of African Missions: Essays in Honor of Wendell Broom*. Edited by Stanley E. Granberg, 215-227. Abilene, TX: A.C.U. Press, 2001.

Hughes, Richard T. *Reviving the Ancient Faith: The Story of Churches of Christ in America*. Grand Rapids: Eerdmans, 1996.

Ilo, Stan Chu. "The Second African Synod and the Challenges of Reconciliation, Justice, and Peace in Africa's Social Context: A Missional Theological Praxis for Transformation." *Missiology* 40 (2012): 195-204.

Johnston, James, ed. *Report of the Centenary Conference on the Protestant Missions of the World Held in Exeter Hall (June 9th – 19th), London, 1888.* London: James Nisbet, 1988.

Kato, Byang H. "The Gospel, Cultural Context and Religious Syncretism." In *Let the Earth Hear His Voice.* Edited by J. D. Douglas, 1216-1223. Minneapolis: World Wide Publications, 1975.

_____. "History Comes Full Circle." *Evangelical Review of Theology* 28 (2004): 130-139.

_____. "Theological Issues in Africa." *Bibliotheca Sacra* 133 (1976): 143-152.

Kenya Mission Team. *Church Planting, Watering, and Increasing in Kenya: The Study of Church Growth among Churches of Christ in Kenya, 1965-1979.* Austin, TX: Firm Foundation Publishing House, 1980.

Kinsler, F. Ross. *Diversified Theological Education: Equipping All of God's People.* Pasadena, CA: William Carey Library, 2008.

_____. "Doing Ministry for a Change? Theological Education for the Twenty-First Century." *Ministerial Formation* 108 (2007): 4-13.

_____. *The Extension Movement in Theological Education: A Call to the Renewal of the Ministry.* Rev. ed. Pasadena, CA: William Carey Library, 1981.

_____. "Theological Education by Extension: Equipping God's People for Ministry." In *Ministry by the People: Theological Education by Extension.* Edited by F. Ross Kinsler, 1-29. Maryknoll, N.Y.: Orbis, 1983.

_____. "The Viability of Theological Education by Extension Today." *Ministerial Formation* 85 (1999): 5-18.

Kitale Team. "The Kitale Area Report: January 1987." In *Advancing the Kingdom: Church Growth through Leadership Development.* Papers from the 1987 workshop of the Churches of Christ, at Limuru, Kenya, 22-24 January. Edited by the Kenya Mission Team, 20-24. Meru, Kenya: Privately published, 1987.

Kombo, James Owino. "The African Renaissance as a New Context for African Evangelical Theology." *Africa Journal of Evangelical Theology* 19 (2000): 3-24.

Kraft, Charles H. *Christianity in Culture: A Study in Dynamic Biblical Theologizing in Cross-Cultural Perspective.* Maryknoll, N.Y.: Orbis, 1979.

Kuhn, Thomas S. *The Structure of Scientific Revolutions.* Chicago: Chicago University Press, 1962.

Kwan, Simon Shui-man. "From Indigenization to Contextualization: A Change in Discursive Practice Rather than a Shift in Paradigm." *Studies in World Christianity* 11 (2005): 236-250.

Lamberty, Kim Marie. "Toward a Spirituality of Accompaniment in Solidarity Partnership." *Missiology: An International Review* 40 (2012): 181-193.

Lienemann-Perrin, Christine. *Training for a Relevant Ministry: A Study of the Contribution of the Theological Education Fund.* Madras: The Christian Literature Society, 1981.

Makhulu, Walter Khotso. "Theological Education in Africa: *Quo Vadimus?*" In *Theological Education in Africa: Quo vadimus?* Edited by J. S. Pobee and J. N. Kudadjie, 18-31. Geneva, Switzerland: WCC, 1990.

Makulu, H. F. *Education, Development and Nation-Building in Independent Africa: A Study of the New Trends and Recent Philosophy of Education.* London: SCM Press, 1971.

Malindi Team. "The Malindi Area Report: January 1987." In *Advancing the Kingdom: Church Growth through Leadership Development.* Papers from the 1987 workshop of the Churches of Christ at Limuru, Kenya, 22-24 January. Edited by the Kenya Mission Team, 6-7. Meru, Kenya: Privately published, 1987.

Manning, Basil. "Theological Education by Extension: A Reflection on the Botswana Theological Training Programme." In *Theological Education in Africa: Quo Vadimus?* Edited by J. S. Pobee and J. N. Kudadjie, 148-161. Geneva, Switzerland: WCC, 1990.

Matthews, Ed. "Leadership Training in Missions." In *Guidelines for World Evangelism.* Edited by George Gurganus, 123-139. Abilene, TX: Biblical Research Press, 1976.

Mbiti, John S. *African Religions and Philosophy*. Garden City, N.Y.: Anchor Books, 1969.

_____. *Bible and Theology in African Christianity*. Nairobi, Kenya: Oxford University Press, 1986.

_____. "Theological Impotence and the Universality of the Church." In *Mission Trends No. 3: Third World Theologies*. Edited by Gerald H. Anderson and Thomas F. Stransky, 6-18. New York: Paulist Press, 1976.

McKinney, Lois. "How Shall We Cooperate Internationally in Theological Education by Extension?" In *Cyprus: TEE Comes of Age*. Edited by Robert L. Youngblood, 27-40. Exeter, Great Britain: The Paternoster Press, 1986.

_____. "Leadership: Key to the Growth of the Church." In *Discipling through Theological Education by Extension: A Fresh Approach to Theological Education in the 1980s*. Edited by Vergil Gerber, 179-191. Chicago: Moody Bible Institute, 1980.

Merritt, Hilton. "Kisumu: A Team Effort." In *Church Planting, Watering, and Increasing in Kenya: The Study of Church Growth among Churches of Christ in Kenya, 1965-1979*. Edited by the Kenya Mission Team, 39-46. Austin, Tex.: Firm Foundation, 1980.

M'Imanyara, Alfred M. *The Restatement of Bantu Origin and Meru History*. Nairobi, Kenya: Longman Kenya, 1994.

Moreau, Scott A. "Comprehensive Contextualization." In *Discovering the Mission of God: Best Missional Practices for the 21st Century*. Edited by Mike Barnett, 406-418. Downers Grove, IL: InterVarsity Press, 2012.

_____. *Contextualization in World Missions: Mapping and Assessing Evangelical Models*. Grand Rapids: Kregal, 2012.

_____. "Contextualization that is Comprehensive." *Missiology: An International Review* 34 (2006): 325-335.

Nadar, Sarojini. "Contextual Theological Education in Africa and the Challenge of Globalization." *The Ecumenical Review* 59 (2007): 235-241.

Netland, Harold A. "Introduction: Globalization and Theology Today." In *Globalizing Theology: Belief and Practice in an Era of World Christianity*.

Edited by Craig Ott and Harold A. Netland, 309-336. Grand Rapids: Baker, 2006.

NGCS. *Nairobi Great Commission School Extension Program Catalogue, 2004-2007.* Nairobi, Kenya: Nairobi Great Commission School, 2003.

Nevius, John L. *The Planting and Development of Missionary Churches.* The Presbyterian and Reformed Publishing Company, 1958.

Nicholls, Bruce J. *Contextualization: A Theology of Gospel and Culture.* Downers Grove, IL: InterVarsity Press, 1979.

North Kalenjin Team. "A Report on the Work among the North Kalenjin." In *Advancing the Kingdom: Church Growth through Leadership Development*. Papers from the 1987 workshop of the Churches of Christ, at Limuru, Kenya, 22- 24 January, ed. the Kenya Mission team, 41-43. Meru, Kenya: Privately published, 1987.

Nthamburi, Zablon John. *A History of the Methodist Church in Kenya.* Nairobi, Kenya: Uzima Press, 1982.

Nyerere, Julius K. "The Arusha Declaration: Ten Years After." Dar Es Salaam, Tanzania: Government Printer, 1977.

Okoth, Dennis. "Summary of the Kenya Strategy Session of the ACA Conference." In *Africans Claiming Africa Conference Held in Embu, Kenya April 1-10, 1992*. Edited by Sam Shewmaker, 7.2-7.3. Nairobi: Kenya Church of Christ, 1992.

Orobator, Agbonkhianmeghe E. "Contextual Theological Methodologies." In *African Theology on the Way*. Edited by Diane B. Stinton, 3-11. London: SPCK, 2010.

_____. *Theology Brewed in an African Pot.* Maryknoll, N.Y.: Orbis, 2008.

Ott, Craig. "Globalizing Theology." In *Globalizing Theology: Belief and Practice in an Era of World Christianity*. Edited by Craig Ott and Harold A. Netland, 309-336. Grand Rapids: Baker, 2006.

_____ and Harold A. Netland, eds. *Globalizing Theology: Belief and Practice in an Era of World Christianity*. Grand Rapids: Baker, 2006.

Plueddemann, James. Course notes handout. Revitalizing Global Theological Education, DME 910. Trinity International University, n.d.

Pobee, John S., and J. N. Kudadjie, eds. *Theological Education in Africa: Quo Vadimus?* Geneva, Switzerland: WCC, 1990.

_____. *Towards an African Theology.* Nashville, Tenn.: Abingdon Press, 1979.

Reese, Robert, and Wimon Walker. "A Survey of Work in South Africa." In *100 Years of African Missions: Essays in Honor of Wendell Broom.* Edited by Stanley E. Granberg, 63-87. Abilene, TX: A.C.U. Press, 2001.

Report of Commission III: Education in Relation to the Christianisation of National Life. Edinburgh: Oliphant, Anderson, and Ferrier, 1910.

Ritchie, John. *Indigenous Church Principles in Theory and Practice.* New York: Fleming H. Ravell Company, 1946.

Rubin, Herbert J., and Irene S. Rubin. *Qualitative Interviewing: The Art of Hearing Data.* Thousand Oaks, CA: SAGE Publications, 1995.

Sanchez, Daniel R. "Contexualization and the Missionary Endeavor." In *Missiology: An Introduction to the Foundations, History and Strategies of World Missions.* Edited by John Mark Terry, Eddie Smith, and Justice Anderson, 318-333. Nashville: Broadman & Holman, 1998.

Sanneh, Lamin. *Abolitionists Abroad.* Cambridge, MA: Harvard University Press, 1999.

_____. *Translating the Message: The Missionary Impact on Culture.* Maryknoll, N.Y.: Orbis, 1989.

_____. *Whose Religion is Christianity? The Gospel Beyond the West.* Grand Rapids: Eerdmans, 2003.

Schreiter, Robert J. *Constructing Local Theologies.* Maryknoll, N.Y.: Orbis Books, 1985.

_____. "Contextualization from a World Perspective." *Theological Education* 30 (1993): 63-86.

_____. *The New Catholicity: Theology Between the Global and the Local.* Maryknoll, N.Y.: Orbis, 1997.

Shaw, R. Daniel. "Beyond Contextualization: Toward a Twenty-First Century Model for Enabling Mission." *International Bulletin of Missionary Research* 34 (2010): 208-214.

Shenk, Wilbert R. *Changing Frontiers of Mission*. Maryknoll, N. Y.: Orbis Books, 1999.

_____. "Contextual Theology: The Last Frontier." In *The Changing Face of Christianity: Africa, the West and the World*. Edited by Lamin Sanneh and Joel A. Carpenter, 191-212. Oxford: Oxford University Press, 2005.

Sifuna, Daniel N. *Development of Education in Africa: The Kenyan Experience*. Nairobi: Initiatives Publishers, 1990.

Smalley, William. "Cultural Implications of an Indigenous Church." *Practical Anthropology* 5 (1958): 51-65.

Smith, Colin. "De-Suburbanizing Theological Education in Nairobi." *Ministerial Formation* 108 (2007): 14-24.

Snook, Stewart G. *Developing Leaders through Theological Education by Extension: Case Studies from Africa*. Wheaton, IL: Billy Graham Center, 1992.

Spanje, T. E. Van. "Contextualization: Hermeneutical Remarks." *Bulletin John Rylands Library* 80 (1998): 197-217.

Stackhouse, Max L. *Apologia: Contextualization, Globalization, and Mission in Theological Education*. Grand Rapids, MI: Eerdmans, 1988.

Stake, Robert E. "The Countenance of Educational Evaluation." *Teachers College Record* 68 (1967): 523-540.

Stanley, Brian. "Christian Missions and the Enlightenment: A Reevaluation." In *Christian Missions and the Enlightenment*, ed. Brian Stanley, 1-21. Grand Rapids: Eerdmans, 2001.

Stephens, Larry. "I Am an Abaluyia Christian." In *Church Planting, Watering, and Increasing in Kenya: The Study of Church Growth among Churches of Christ in Kenya, 1965-1979*. Edited by the Kenya Mission Team, 34-38. Austin, TX: Firm Foundation, 1980.

Strauss, Steven. "Creeds, Confessions, and Global Theologizing." In *Globalizing Theology: Belief and Practice in an Era of World Christianity*. Edited by Craig Ott and Harold A. Netland. Grand Rapids: Baker, 2006.

TEF Staff. *Ministry in Context: The Third Mandate Programme of the Theological Education Fund (1970-77)*. Bromley, England: New Life, 1972.

Tennent, Timothy C. *Theology in the Context of World Christianity*. Grand Rapids: Zondervan, 2007.

_____. *World Missions: A Trinitarian Missiology for the Twenty-First Century*. Grand Rapids: Kregel, 2010.

Tiénou, Tite. "Christian Theology in an Era of World Christianity." In *Globalizing Theology: Belief and Practice in an Era of World Christianity*. Edited by Craig Ott and Harold Netland, 37-51. Grand Rapids: Baker, 2006.

_____. "Forming Indigenous Theologies." In *Toward the 21st Century in Christian Missions*. Edited by James M. Phillips and Robert T. Coote, 245-252. Grand Rapids: Eerdmans, 1993.

_____. "Issues in the Theological Task in Africa Today. *East Africa Journal of Evangelical Theology* 1 (1982): 3-10.

_____. "The Problem of Methodology in African Christian Theologies." Ph.D. diss., Fuller Theological Seminary, 1984.

_____. "The Theological Task of the Church in Africa." In *Issues in African Christian Theology*. Edited by Samuel Ngewa, Mark Shaw, and Tite Tiénou, 2-11. Nairobi: East African Educational Publishers, 1998.

_____. "The Theological Task of the Church in Africa: Where Are We Now and Where Should We Be Going? *East Africa Journal of Evangelical Theology* 6 (1987): 3-11.

Ukpong, Justin S. *African Theologies Now: A Profile*. Eldoret, Kenya: Gaba Publication, 1984.

_____. "Inculturation Hermeneutics: An African Approach to Biblical Interpretation." In *The Bible in a World Context: An Experiment in Contextual Hermeneutics*. Edited by Walter Dietrich and Ulrich Luz, 17-32. Grand Rapids: Eerdmans, 2003.

Vähäkangas, Mika. "Modelling Contextualization in Theology." *Swedish Missiological Themes* 98 (2010): 279-306.

Van Engen, Charles E. "Critical Theologizing: Knowing God in Multiple Global and Local Contexts." In *Evangelical, Ecumenical and Anabaptist Missiologies in Conversation*. Edited by James R. Krabill, Walter Sawatsky, and Charles E. Van Engen, 88-97. Maryknoll, N.Y.: Orbis, 2006.

Van Rheenen, Gailyn. "A Biblical Perspective on Church Growth." In *God's Increase among the Kipsigis*. Edited by Kipsigis Team, 37-69. Sotik, Kenya: Privately published, 1981.

_____. *Biblically Anchored Missions: Perspectives on Church Growth*. Austin, TX: Firm Foundation, 1983a.

_____. "Introducing the Kenya Church Growth Philosophy." In *Church Planting, Watering, and Increasing in Kenya: The Study of Church Growth among Churches of Christ in Kenya, 1965-1979*. Edited by Kenya Mission Team, 5-10. Austin, TX: Firm Foundation, 1980.

_____. "Leadership Training." In *Church Growth among the Kisigis: A Statistical Picture of the Growth of the Church of Christ among the Kipsigis in Southwest Kenya*, vol. 4. Edited by Kipsigis Team, 37-55. Sotik, Kenya: Privately published, 1983b.

_____. "Looking Back." In *Church Growth among the Kipsigis: A Statistical Picture of the Church of Christ among the Kispsigis in South West Kenya*, vol. 5. Edited by Kipsigis Team, 69-89. Sotik, Kenya: Privately published, 1985.

_____. *Missions: Biblical Foundations & Contemporary Strategies*. Grand Rapids: Zondervan, 1996.

Walls, Andrew F. *The Cross-Cultural Process in Christian History*. Maryknoll, N.Y.: Orbis, 2002.

_____. *The Missionary Movement in Church History: Studies in the Transmission of Faith*. Maryknoll, N. Y.: Orbis Books, 1996.

Weld, Wayne C., ed. *The World Directory of Theological Education by Extension*. Pasadena: William Carey Library, 1973.

____, ed. *The World Directory of Theological Education by Extension: 1980 Supplement*. The Committee to Assist Ministry Education Overseas, 1980.

West, Earl Irvin. *The Search for the Ancient Order: A History of the Restoration Movement 1849-1906*. Vol. 1. Nashville: Gospel Advocate Company, 1964.

Winter, Ralph D., ed. *Theological Education by Extension*. Pasadena: William Carey Library, 1969.

Young, F. Lional, III. "'A New Breed of Missionaries': Assessing Attitudes toward Western Missions at the Nairobi Evangelical Graduate School of Theology." *International Bulletin of Missionary Research* 36 (2012): 90-94.

Young, M. Norval. *A History of Colleges Established and Controlled by Members of the Churches of Christ*. Vol. 1. Kansas City, MO: The Old Paths Book Club, 1949.

Youngbood, Robert L., ed. *Cyprus: TEE Comes of Age*. Exeter, Great Britain: The Paternoster Press, 1986.

Zokoué, Isaac. "Educating for Servant Leadership in Africa." *Africa Journal of Evangelical Theology*, 9 (1990): 4-13.

Index of Authors

A

AKIKA: 144

Akumu, C.: 170-171

Allen, R.: 12

Allison, F.: 61, 104

Anderson, R.: 11, 12

Assensoh, A. B.: 43, 48

B

Beaver, R. P.: 11

Bediako, K.: 2, 3, 6, 10, 24, 39

Bergquist, J.: 28, 49, 158-159, 184

Bernard, H. R.: 77

Bernardi, B.: 119

Bevans, S.: 28, 30-32, 34-36, 184-185

Blakemore, K.: 49

Boateng, D.: 170

Borg, W. R.: 77

Bosch, D. J.: 2, 26-27, 31

C

Campbell, A.: 14

Carey, W.: 42

Clark, S.: 12

Coe, S.: 25-26, 49-51, 185

Cole, V.: 28

Conference [1860]: 44

Cooksey, B.: 49

Costa, R. O.: 13

Cox, M. B.: 63-64, 184

Curtin, P.: 48

D

Day, L. B.: 42

Dickson, K.: 38

Duff, A.: 42, 44

Dyrness, W. A.: 43

E

Ecumenical [1900]: 2, 45
Eisner, E. W.: 72
Ekanem, S.: 170
Elliston, E.: 21, 43
Emery, J.: 51
Estes, S.: 175

F

Ferguson, E.: 100
Ferris, R. W.: 47, 50
Fleming, B. C. E.: 29
Frostin, P.: 3, 42

G

Gaikwad, R.: 53
Gall, J. P.: 77
Gall, M. D.: 77
Gatimu, K.: 51, 53, 73
Geertz, C.: 33
Gilliland, D. S.: 31-35, 185
Goetz, J. P.: 77
Goff, R.: 16
Granberg, S.: 18, 57, 64-70, 125-126
Green, G. L.: 27
Gurganus, G.: 55

H

Haleblian, K.: 31
Hardin, D. C.: 56

Hesselgrave, D. J.: 10, 13, 28-29
Hiebert, P. G.: 4, 5, 9, 17, 24-25, 29, 31, 35, 41, 58, 157-159, 183, 185
Hogarth, J.: 51-52
Holter, K.: 3
Huffard, H.: 16
Hughes, R. T.: 188

I

Ilo, S. C.: 40

J

Johnston, J.: 45

K

Kato, B. H.: 39-40
Kenya Mission Team: 56
Kinsler, F. R.: 51-54, 158
Kitale Team: 63
Kombo, J. O.: 2
Kraft, C. H.: 31-32
Kuhn, T. S.: 26
Kwan, S. S.: 26

L

Lamberty, K. M.: 176, 178
LeCompte, M. D.: 77
Lienemann-Perrin, C.: 26, 158

M

M'Imanyara, A. M.: 119

Makhulu, W. K.: 53
Makulu, H. F.: 48
Malindi Team: 63
Manning, B.: 52-53
Mathews, E.: 55
Mbaku, J. M.: 43
Mbiti, J. S.: 23, 37, 41
McKinney, L.: 50, 52, 66-67
Merritt, H.: 60
Moreau, S. A.: 29, 31, 36

N

Nadar, S.: 176-177
Netland, H. A.: 183
Nevius, J. L.: 11-12
Nicholls, B. J.: 10, 29
North Kalenjin Team: 63
Nthamburi, Z. J.: 41, 47
Nyerere, J. K.: 48

O

Okoth, D.: 170-171
Orobator, A. E.: 40
Ott, C.: 40

P

Plueddemann, J.: 21
Pobee, J. S.: 37, 53

R

Reese, R.: 15
Report [1910]: 45-46
Ritchie, J.: 12
Rubin, H. J.: 77
Rubin, I. S.: 77

S

Sanchez, D. R.: 10, 14, 28
Sanneh, L.: 9-11, 24, 42
Schreiter, R. J.: 13, 24, 30-31, 33, 36
Shaw, R. D.: 29, 36
Shenk, W. R.: 7, 10-11, 13, 25
Sifuna, D. N.: 48-49
Smalley, W.: 12
Smith, C.: 53
Snook, S.: 53
Spanje, T. E.: 30-31
Stackhouse, M. L.: 31
Stake, R. E.: 72
Stanley, B.: 42
Stephens, L.: 17, 62
Strauss, S.: 5

T

TEF Staff: 28, 47-50, 158-159
Tennent, T. C.: 3, 25, 30, 182
Tiénou, T.: 2-3, 39, 42

U
Ukpong, J. S.: 38

V
Vähäkangas, M.: 36
Van Engen, C. E.: 29
Van Rheenen, G.: 17, 56, 60-64, 183

W
Walker, W.: 15
Walls, A. F.: 10, 44

Weld, W. C.: 185
West, E.: 15
Winter, R. D.: 185

Y
Young, L.: 4-5, 176
Young, N.: 15

Z
Zokoué, I.: 59

Index of Subjects

A

administration: 86, 89-90, 98-99, 165-166

African theologies: 6-7, 9, 13, 23-24, 28, 37-38, 40-42, 158

AIDS: 108-110, 118, 135, 161, 164, 177

autonomy: 98-100, 166, 168-171, 174, 188

B

biblical knowledge: 82, 84-85, 96-97

C

church planting: 62, 65-66, 81-82, 87-89, 97-98, 104, 160, 165, 169

Churches of Christ: 5-7, 14-21, 54-57, 59-61, 64, 69, 71, 73, 77, 79, 81, 93, 99, 102-103, 108, 138, 140, 144, 148, 152, 155, 183, 187-188

circumcision: 124-128, 162-163

contextual: 9-10, 13, 17-18, 51-54, 57, 59, 61, 65-67, 71

contextual theology: 25, 28, 31, 34-35

contextualization: 3, 10, 13, 14, 19, 22-42, 50-53, 57, 73, 88, 91, 96, 101, 111, 114-115, 119, 121-123, 128, 157-158, 161-162, 183-185

counseling: 96, 114, 149

curriculum: 70, 72

E

education, continuing: 96, 102, 172

education, higher: 77, 83-84, 172, 174, 179, 181

eduactions, informal: 75, 78-79, 81-82

education, institutional: 62

education level: 92, 101-102

education, non-formal: 78-79, 160

education, theological: 2-7, 11, 14-18, 20-21, 23-25, 27, 41-57, 60, 62-64, 67, 69, 71-73, 75-76, 78, 82-

84, 86-89, 91-96, 98, 100, 102-104, 108-116, 118, 120-122, 125, 131, 137-138, 141, 148-149, 154-155, 157-162, 165-167, 169, 171, 173, 176-182

evangelism: 61, 63, 65-66, 68, 81-82, 87-89, 97-98, 160, 165, 169

extension centers: 55-57, 59, 73, 78-80, 91, 102, 105, 108, 187

F

financial support: 103, 122, 141, 145-146, 175

fourth self: 1, 5-7, 17, 20-25, 35-36, 42, 58, 73, 111, 157, 175-176, 178, 181-182

G

global Christianity: 42

global theologizing: 3-5, 13, 25, 27, 41, 176, 182-183

I

identificational: 60, 62

indigenization: 10-11, 13-14, 26-27, 35

indigenous: 11-15, 17-18, 23-25, 27, 39, 45-47, 49, 51, 56-58, 61

K

Kenya Churches of Christ: 158-160, 168, 173, 177-178, 181-182

L

leaders, Christian: 42-43, 45-49, 51-53, 55-57, 61, 65, 67, 69

leadership: 42-43, 45, 47-49, 52, 55-57, 59, 61-62, 64-67, 70, 83, 85, 88-89, 92-93, 122, 148-149, 160, 165-166, 169, 172, 174-176, 178

leadership training: 55-57, 59, 62, 65-68, 70-71, 73, 148-152

Leadership Training by Extension (LTE): 17-20

M

ministry skills: 82, 87, 89-90, 93-94, 96

ministry transfer: 175-176, 178

Missio Dei: 13, 43

Modernity: 43, 48-49

N

Nairobi Great Commission School (NGCS): 14, 18-20, 57, 59, 63-64, 70, 73, 76, 79, 91, 94, 109, 160, 172, 178, 180, 187-188

P

partnership: 175-178, 182

poverty: 108-109, 122, 127, 136-140, 142-143, 146, 154, 161, 167-168, 171-172, 174, 176-179

S

self-theologizing: 1, 5-7, 19-21, 23-25, 27, 35, 42, 60, 71-73, 75, 77, 101, 110-111, 114, 121, 123, 155, 157-167, 172-175, 180-182

sexual mores: 131, 162-164

spiritual formation: 88, 90, 165-166

spiritual maturity: 122-123, 149, 153-154, 165-166

support for ministers: 122, 140, 168-169

T

Theological Education by Extension (TEE): 1, 24, 51-55, 57, 66-67, 185-186

three-selfs: 11-12, 17, 27, 35, 47, 175

V

vocational training: 92, 101, 104, 169, 171, 174, 178-180

W

Western education: 46, 49, 51, 161

Western teachers: 112-114

Western theology: 9-10, 21, 46, 176

world Christianity: 42-43

Bible & Theology in Africa

The twentieth century made sub-Saharan Africa a Christian continent. This formidable church growth is reflected in a wide range of attempts at contextualizing Christian theology and biblical interpretation in Africa. At a grassroots level ordinary Christians express their faith and read the bible in ways reflecting their daily situation; at an academic level, theologians and biblical scholars relate the historical traditions and sources of Christianity to the socio- and religio-cultural context of Africa. In response to this, the Bible and Theology in Africa series aims at making African theology and biblical interpretation its subject as well as object, as the concerns of African theologians and biblical interpreters will be voiced and critically analyzed. Both African and Western authors are encouraged to consider this series.

Inquiries and manuscripts should be directed to:

Professor Knut Holter
MHS School of Mission and Theology
Misjonsmarka 12
N-4024 Stavanger, Norway
knut.holter@mhs.no

To order other books in this series, please contact our Customer Service Department:

(800) 770-LANG (within the U.S.)
(212) 647-7706 (outside the U.S.)
(212) 647-7707 FAX

Or browse online by series:

www.peterlang.com